Andrew Oldham and Tony Calder are responsible for managing and discovering such rock legends as the Rolling Stones, Marianne Faithfull, the Small Faces, Eddy Grant, the Bay City Rollers and Jive Bunny, and use their unique experience of the music industry to give a rare and distinctively individual insight into one of the supreme pop fantasies of our age. Along with another big fan, journalist and broadcaster Colin Irwin, they aim to put Abba in their rightful place among the all-time greats.

ABBA
THE NAME OF THE GAME

Andrew Oldham, Tony Calder
& Colin Irwin

PAN BOOKS

First published 1995 by Sidgwick & Jackson

This edition published 1996 by Pan Books
an imprint of Macmillan Publishers Ltd,
25 Eccleston Place, London SW1W 9NF
Basingstoke and Oxford
Associated companies throughout the world
www.macmillan.co.uk

ISBN 0 330 34688 1

Copyright © Andrew Oldham, Tony Calder & Colin Irwin 1995

The right of Andrew Oldham, Tony Calder and Colin Irwin to be identified
as the authors of this work has been asserted by them in accordance
with the Copyright, Designs and Patents Act 1988.

The copyright details on p viii-ix constitute as extension to this copyright page.

9 8 7 6

A CIP catalogue record for this book is available from
the British Library.

Photoset by Parker Typesetting Service, Leicester
Printed and bound in Great Britain by
Mackays of Chatham plc, Chatham, Kent

CONTENTS

DEDICATED TO THE
NEXT GENERATION
Sean and Max Oldham, Georgina,
Anthony and Harriet Calder,
Kevin and Christy Irwin

ACKNOWLEDGEMENT

In the true traditions of rock 'n' roll, the authors found no shortage of volunteers ready, willing and able to share their thoughts, recollections and entertaining stories about rock in general and Abba in particular. We thank them all and respect their mostly unanimous insistence – again in the great rock tradition – on anonymity. They made us laugh and oh, but could we have printed some of the more extreme anecdotes we encountered on our travels! The one thing they – and we – all agree on is the enduring brilliance of Abba's music.

We'd also like to say a special thanks to Katherine Courtnay, whose encyclopaedic, personal knowledge and extensive library of all things Abba proved invaluable and helped fill in the finer details. Katherine runs the English wing of THE AGNETHA BENNY BJORN FRIDA FAN CLUB, 1 Barrow Hill Road, Shirehampton, Bristol, BS11 9QT.

ACKNOWLEDGEMENT

'One Of Us'
Written by Benny Andersson and Bjorn Ulvaeus
© 1981 Union Songs AB
Lyrics reproduced by kind permission of the publishers
'I Have A Dream'
Written by Benny Andersson and Bjorn Ulvaeus
© 1979 Union Songs AB
Lyrics reproduced by kind permission of the publishers
'Super Trouper'
Written by Benny Andersson and Bjorn Ulvaeus
© 1980 Union Songs AB
Lyrics reproduced by kind permission of the publishers
'Eagle'
Written by Benny Andersson and Bjorn Ulvaeus
© 1977 Union Songs AB
Lyrics reproduced by kind permission of the publishers
'SOS'
Written by Benny Andersson, Bjorn Ulvaeus and Stig Anderson
© 1975 Union Songs AB
Lyrics reproduced by kind permission of the publishers
'Knowing Me, Knowing You'
Written by Benny Andersson, Bjorn Ulvaeus and Stig Anderson
© 1976 Union Songs AB
Lyrics reproduced by kind permission of the publishers
'Money, Money, Money'
Written by Benny Andersson and Bjorn Ulvaeus
© 1976 Union Songs AB
Lyrics reproduced by kind permission of the publishers
'The Winner Takes It All'
Written by Benny Andersson and Bjorn Ulvaeus
© 1980 Union Songs AB
Lyrics reproduced by kind permission of the publishers
'Mamma Mia'
Written by Benny Andersson, Bjorn Ulvaeus and Stig Anderson
© 1975 Union Songs AB
Lyrics reproduced by kind permission of the publishers

1

BRIGHTON ROCKS

'Though we never thought we could lose, there's no regret
If I had to do the same again, I would my friend'

'Fernando'

It was to be some time before it was officially decreed by salivating journalists that she had the finest bottom on God's earth, but when Agnetha strutted provocatively through the lobby of the plush Grand Hotel in Brighton that night it was still a heart attack job for the more elderly clientele.

Hers was a smouldering sexuality – she looked like a virgin who'd escaped from a convent and just enjoyed her delicious deflowering. Long blonde hair flowed behind her like a trophy and she looked exotic, if totally alien to these surroundings. This was the type of woman for whom cabinet ministers might happily destroy their careers and reputations in exchange for one night of passion. A model? A tennis coach? A motor racing groupie? You could almost sense the questions spinning in the minds of the men whose eyes leapt from their sockets to follow her progress, with their tongues in hot pursuit.

But if Agnetha looked arrogant she certainly didn't feel it. She'd been a singer for years, even a major star back home in Sweden. But the rest of Europe thought Sweden was a joke and this was the rest of Europe. In Sweden the sun never shone, they couldn't play football, and they kept their hands down whenever there was a war. Worse, this was England and England had never even heard of Sweden.

There was one other thing making her feel uneasy. She could barely walk. That was the pants. She'd been sewn into the pants in the hotel suite and looked in horror at herself in the mirror: a Napoleonic pant suit clearly designed by a lunatic. Whatever she and the rest of the band did for the rest of their careers nobody would ever take her seriously again if she set foot on stage in that absurd pant suit.

Her misgivings were laughed aside. This was 1974. This was the age of glam and glitter and cartoon pop stars. Odd characters like Marc Bolan and David Bowie and Gary Glitter and Alvin Stardust and Mud and Slade and Suzi Quatro and, God help us, the Bay City Rollers ruled the roost in 1974 with ever more ludicrous wardrobes. Pop fashion had gone bonkers.

So maybe Agnetha's bottom-busting pant suit didn't seem as nonsensical to everybody else as it did to her. The four of them had already tacitly agreed that this was the big one. They'd do whatever it took. They'd perform triple somersaults in see-through leotards if it would help. They'd sing folk songs outside No. 10 Downing Street for the newly-elected British prime minister Harold Wilson if necessary. They'd have a photo-call in a sauna with a party of Brighton hookers if need be. This was the year Abba were going to win the Eurovision Song Contest and nothing was gonna stop 'em.

Agnetha looked anxiously at Bjorn and her husband smiled encouragingly back at her. He thought she looked sexy. Besides, he had his own skin-tight, jackbooted, ruffle-shirted monstrosity to contend with. They laughed at each other and fretted over baby Linda, one year old and a seasoned traveller already. Not your average young Swedish family trying to make ends meet, that's for sure. They were happy. For the time being.

There was more tension in the red corner, where Benny and Anni-Frid completed the love quartet. Anni-Frid's tension was self-evident. All their tensions were self-evident. Stig Anderson, manager, producer, human dynamo and would-be Svengali, was running around like a cat on a hot tin roof telling them they were going to win, but they didn't dare believe him. The jokes got hollower. The mood began to blacken. The odd temper started to fray. Mostly they just retreated into their own private thoughts and neuroses. An ominous silence descended over Abba.

To all intents and purposes they had the perfect scenario. Two young couples, helplessly in love, close friends all, with even a baby on board and a talent of sorts too, on the precipice of a success people scarcely even dream about. Glamour, security and family bliss. Mr and Mrs Ideal and their best mates the Groovies, all heading for a glorious adventure. Benny, Bjorn, Agnetha and Anni-Frid weren't to guess that strange, magical, bewildering, fateful night in Brighton the riches that lay before them – and the jealousies, greed, bitterness, egotism and excesses that would also come as part of the package to destroy them.

The prospect of failure at Brighton haunted them all. The Eurovision Song Contest was dismissed as a fatuous irrelevance by any self-respecting rock student – and would subsequently be laughed off the map partly as a result of their enduring influence on it – but in 1974 at

3

least the public at large still had a mini-obsession with the contest that was guaranteed to rocket the winning song instantly to the top of the charts all round Europe and turn the victorious artists into overnight stars. Nobody lusting after fame and fortune would turn their noses up at that kind of passport to international success. Certainly not if they were Swedish. A silly frock is a small price to pay for such rewards.

Stig Anderson had long seen Eurovision as the key to Abba's elusive international breakthrough. They'd had high hopes of making it the previous year with their song 'Ring Ring' and there was a national outcry at home when it only made third place in the Swedish Song For Europe contest and something called Lena Anderson was selected to represent the nation instead. Such was the stink that followed that the rules were changed to allow the public to vote on the country's entry rather than let a faceless committee decide. So when it came to the '74 vote it was virtually a no-contest, Abba getting in with 'Waterloo' and a landslide.

Summit meetings had been held on how to come up with the right song to take them to Eurovision in '74. The goalposts had been moved to accommodate them so they had better make sure that this time they found the back of the net. 'Ring Ring' had been a successful record for them in many territories but let's be honest: it was a donkey of a song which had caused as much excitement as a team of morris dancers in a brothel when it had been released in Britain, and had ultimately failed them.

Benny, Bjorn and Stig Anderson spent many hours devising the perfect Eurovision song. Stig reckoned that first and foremost they had to come up with a good snappy title and build the rest of the song around it.

Something simple. Something that would mean something to the whole of Europe. Something jolly and uncontentious. Something like . . . 'Ring Ring' . . . oh no, they'd tried that one. Thinking international and obviously inspired by the Neil Sedaka school of banality, Stig came up with 'Honey Pie'. It had its merits. Not that we can think of any now, but they thought so. They lived with it for a while, formed the basis of a bright, positive tune for it and then, on an inspired whim, Stig kicked it into touch and changed it to 'Waterloo'. Yeah, a song about a London railway station, why not? Luckily they remembered there had also been some sort of battle of Waterloo, and Bjorn, Benny and Stig came up with a suitably positive number cleverly linking the climax of the classic battle to the finale of a love affair. There were a few last-minute jitters about its suitability as they produced other tunes and different titles. They wouldn't get any points from the French for a start, would they? Bringing up Napoleon's worst defeat for the rest of Europe to sing along with like a triumphal victory march wouldn't go down at all well with the judges in Paris. But in the end they said, 'Sod it,' and decided to go with their initial hunch.

The reaction in the home leg was ecstatic. The Swedes *adored* it. They danced like dervishes, sang it from the rooftops and wanted to have its babies. When they heard Abba perform it at the qualifying contest, the other competitors rolled over on their backs, kicked their legs in the air and waved the white flag. The government had all but passed a law saying that Abba were to represent Sweden at the Eurovision Song Contest and Abba won by not so much a landslide as their own personal snowstorm.

And now the nation expected. 'Waterloo' dutifully topped the charts all over Scandinavia, was whistled by bankers and fishermen alike, and the press went over-board hyping up the challenge. Stig went about his appointed task of delivering their coveted prize with painstaking precision, systematically trying to convert the rest of Europe to the idea of the unthinkable – a serious Swedish bid for international glory.

It wasn't just Anni-Frid, Agnetha, Bjorn and Benny he was doing it for now. The whole nation, for Godsake, was watching him now, wanting, urging, anticipating. Swed-ish national pride felt it was owed. Hell, Luxembourg – bloody *Luxembourg* – had won for the past two years with a couple of cute but bland solo ballad singers, Vicky Leandros and Anne Marie David, and Denmark had got it a decade earlier with something called Grethe and Jorgen Ingmann, so what was wrong with Sweden anyway? Two fabulous-looking women, a couple of earnest musos behind them, outlandish image, love interest. And a bright, thumping song with an international theme. Sweden for Eurovision? Why the hell not?

And such was Anderson's preparation for the event that people did start taking Abba seriously. Tapes of the track were sent to anyone and everyone likely to sway public opinion on the matter, snaps of the loving foursome appeared all over the place, and 'Waterloo' stickers even started mysteriously appearing in remote corners of Brighton. For the first time the dreaded possibility began to dawn on the organizers that Sweden might actually win the bloody thing. The rules stated clearly that the contest should be won on a rota system by the UK, France, Italy and Monaco, with Luxembourg suddenly being allotted their belated share in return for an agreement to stop playing Bay City Rollers records on Radio Luxembourg. No mention of Sweden. But here they were, being installed as one of the bookies' favourites along with sexpot Olivia Newton-John, all figure-hugging frock and winsome smiles, representing the UK; and the already semi-famous Mouth & McNeal, singing for Holland. They, of course, lost it with the beard. Abba's Benny had a beard, but his was subtle and studious – the curiously named Mr Mouth looked like Rasputin on a bad night. One look at him on stage at Brighton and the judges fled.

Anderson had been carefully scrutinizing the opposition at the rehearsals. Observe the technicians. If they stopped lugging leads around and chatting loudly among themselves it must obviously mean a half-decent song had escaped into the proceedings. Either that or there was a woman on stage, which unless you were Yugoslavia (who inexplicably fielded a five-person group, all male) or Israel (six men with beards!), then that was virtually everyone. Worse, the Israeli group were called Poogy. Six strapping guys, beards and Poogy. Israel didn't seem to be taking this seriously. They looked like refugees from a kibbutz, which is what they might very well have been.

Monaco didn't want to win either. They were fielding a 33-year-old circus acrobat called Romuald in a flamboyant costume that made Abba look like old maids. He was singing something with the preposterous title 'He Who Remains And He Who Lives', which sounded more like a university thesis in Chinese philosophy than a finger-popping, toe-tapping, popperoonee hit for Europe. No, Monaco definitely didn't want to win. Severine had won it for them in 1971 with 'Un Banc, Un Arbre, Une Rue'. Tradition decreed that whoever reigned triumphant in Eurovision had to pay a fearsome penalty – they had to stage the wretched thing the following year.

The nightmares it had caused them when the world had descended on them for the return bout expecting the mother of all parties had been an experience they didn't wish to repeat in a hurry. Monaco was yachts and million-aires and roulette tables and Grand Prix and diamonds and Princess Grace and oodles of money. It wasn't scruffy journalists and endless camera crews and excitable Latins and sausages on sticks and, bless her, Katie Boyle, the dame of Britain, now firmly installed as permanent presenter of Eurovision, mainly due to her supreme mastery of numbers one to ten in thirty-eight languages.

Poor old Luxembourg. They'd won it two years running, but after Anne Marie David had come up trumps in '73 with the instantly forgettable 'Tu Te Reconnaîtras', the grand duchy had fallen to its knees, begged for mercy, pleaded insanity and lack of finances, suitable facilities and unfairness to the opposition, and basically reneged on the deal. To ensure there wouldn't be the possibility of a third embarrassing win they'd shoved in an English girl, 24-year-old Ireen Sheer from Romford, as their entry for '74 so that if by any strange chance they did win they could pretend it was really the UK reserve team.

The UK, of course, pompous to the end and always game for a laugh, fondly imagined that impressing the rest of the world with their technical expertise and ability to stage a glitzy, international extravaganza was somehow a contemporary compensation for the loss of an empire and an iffy economy. So yeah, said Britain, we'll bail you out, Luxembourg, we'll take Eurovision off your hands, we've got Katie Boyle to host the thing in a thousand tongues, we've got Terry Wogan to make incredibly funny comments between songs even though he's Irish and we've got lovely Livvy Newton-John to be the perfect woman and show the world we can be great again, even if she was brought up in Australia.

If only it hadn't rained that day. Rained? It looked like the end of the world. Brighton – famous for its aura of fading decadence, pebbly beaches, fish 'n' chip shops and a population composed of ancient grannies and elderly colonels in white hats playing bowls – was almost washed away in the storms. The annual Oxford and Cambridge Boat Race held on the Thames the same day might easily have taken place through the streets of Brighton.

Yeah, if it hadn't been for the weather, Britain could have been great again. Harold Wilson, then showing the strain of his third term of office, would have stayed in power till the end of time, England would have won every World Cup going, and the population would have been healthy, wealthy and wise, living together in perfect harmony for ever and ever amen. And if Livvy had thought of wearing a Napoleon pant suit instead of the ritual Laura Ashley gown, then it could have all been so very different.

Benny, Bjorn, Agnetha and Anni-Frid barely spoke to each other on the way to the Dome, Brighton's charmingly old-fashioned landmark theatre staging the contest that night. For the first time they were discovering the pressures of expectation as pundits grudgingly acknowledged the strength and the very modern brightness of the bold Swedish entry, and the original Euro concept of the song and presentation they'd brought with them. People other than Swedes were actually talking in polite company about the possibility of a Swedish win. Stig Anderson kept saying it. 'We're going to win, we're going to win,' as if trying to convince himself.

The bookies were taking them seriously enough. They'd been quoted at 20–1, but the price was coming down as journalists, TV technicians and nosy old pensioners came away from the rehearsals whistling 'Waterloo'. Anderson screwed up his face and thought back to the rehearsals, trying to pinpoint where the main opposition would come from. There was Livvy, of course, going out at 7–2 favourite, and she was competing on home turf, give or take several thousand miles to Melbourne. But then the Brits were always quoted as favourites, even though they'd only actually won it once when barefoot Sandie Shaw had socked 'Puppet On A String' to the judges seven years earlier. Even Kenneth McKellar had been rated as favourite with the UK entry the previous year, singing some absolute drivel called 'A Man Without Love' and he'd gone on stage in a *kilt* for lawdy's sake. So Livvy was automatically installed as favourite, even though nobody liked her song, 'Long Live Love', and Liv herself sniffily said: 'It's not the song I would have chosen, I'd have preferred a nice ballad. But it's a good, gutsy song and I hope for the best.' That was *before* the contest. Even Sandie Shaw had waited until after the contest before publicly trashing 'Puppet On A String' in a frankly astonishing avalanche of contempt and loathing, and Sandie had *won*.

Stig mused over it all as they cruised along the sea-front, past the chippies, the roaring waves and the smattering of ever-hopeful out-of-season stalls flogging 'kiss-me-quick' hats, candy-floss and windmills on sticks to the crowd aimlessly milling around the Dome. Apart from Livvy and the satanic Mouth & McNeal from the Netherlands, the main favourite was little Gigliola Cinquetti, a passionate Piaf-soundalike from Italy who'd won Eurovision a decade earlier as a jailbait 17-year-old bellowing out the passionate 'No Ho L'Eta Per Amati'. She was back with an equally stirring big ballad and offering charm, sex appeal *and* a voice, she had to be in with a shout. But Stig hadn't seen her frock. It all depended on the frock. If she went for the shimmering, low-cut gown number that had won the day ten years ago then no chance; but if some bright Italian designer were to deck her out in, say, an impossibly tight Napoleon pant suit, then it would be goodnight Irene for Abba and Brighton. The press certainly thought a lot of her, photographing her and demanding to know full details of her sex life and whether or not they should draw any significance from the title of her song, 'Si'. Come Brighton Gigliola was 7–1 second favourite.

Stig reckoned the other main dangers came from old rivals Norway, who were fielding one of their own national treasures, Anne-Karine Strom. Now twenty-three, Anne-Karine had been a child star and was an institution at home. Like Abba's, her connections had made Eurovision a priority in her bid for international recognition and she'd come in seventh in last year's contest in Luxembourg. It was obviously a mistake. The rules clearly stated it was imperative that every year Norway were to be allocated '*nul points*' in revenge for some atrocity committed in Europe by a Norse army several centuries ago and poor Anne-Karine had no more chance of winning the contest than Jamaica have of winning the bobsleigh in the next Olympics. The only way a Norwegian could win would be by posing as a Swede, which if you wanted to be pedantic about it was precisely what Narvik-born Anni-Frid Lyngstad was doing in Abba.

11

Ireland were well fancied too. Their entry was a catchy song called 'Cross Your Heart' by one of their local stars, Tina – Philomena Reynolds in real life – who was looking good on the sympathy vote. Several months earlier she'd been involved in a serious road crash and even now her memory was likely to do a runner at any time. Tina was the press's favourite, chatting to them all like old mates, happily showing off the scar on her forehead to anyone interested (and a lot that weren't) and furnishing the hungry hacks with headline-grabbing minutiae about the crash and confiding that she had to have the words of 'Cross Your Heart' written on her palm in case she forgot them. She hoped she didn't get too nervous and sweaty, 'cos the ink might run and she'd have to make it up as she went along, ha, ha! 'No, I'm not really expecting to win,' she said grinning broadly. 'I'm just pleased to have got here and had the chance of meeting Olivia Newton-John.'

The other main interest among the seventeen competitors was the German husband and wife duo who went out under the name Cindy & Bert. Cindy and *Bert*?!? Funny how they never made it. There was also Piera Martell, a dead ringer for Shirley Bassey, representing Switzerland; the drop-dead gorgeous but entirely hopeless Paulo de Carvalho from Portugal; a pompous Belgian called Jacques Hustin singing some nonsense about the flower of liberty; a dainty, precious young pianist-singer called Carita from Finland stretching the obligatory child prodigy vote to its limits; and Greece, in the contest for the first time with a lady of frightening jackbooted aggression called Marinella performing something titled 'Wine And Sea, My Boyfriend And Me'.

There was no going off down the pub when this little posse of treasures hit the TV screens, eh?

And ole, it was a big night for telly. 'It's become the biggest TV attraction of the year,' BBC head honcho Bill Cotton was saying enthusiastically. 'People may knock it and say it's boring, but they all switch on to watch it.'

Indeed they did. Twenty million in the UK alone. They couldn't all have switched on to watch *Dixon of Dock Green* and forgotten to turn the sets off afterwards. Worldwide television audience was estimated at 500 million in 32 countries. And it went on for hours. And hours. Live.

Police were everywhere. Uniforms. Plain clothes. In disguise. All of them highly conspicuous. The IRA had been making their presence felt with a vengeance. They'd just blown up a coach on the M62 near Bradford killing eleven people and a high profile event like Eurovision was considered a top priority target. Subsequently, security was everywhere. Showtime approached and pandemonium reigned. Benny made some throwaway remark about being arrested on sight for being in charge of offensive costumes, but the others killed him dead with stony glares. This wasn't the time, Benny, this wasn't the time. Humour had got them through a lot. The one thing they could always do was to laugh at themselves and nothing they had got themselves into was more worthy of ridicule than this whole charade, but here they were and, despite themselves, they were excited. They daren't admit it – and had they failed they would have said they didn't want it anyway – but here they were in Brighton and they desperately wanted to win. It got to you like that. Eurovision, Miss World, the Oscars . . . all daft, all meaningless popcorn when you get down to it . . . but here you are backstage at the Brighton Dome and you feel you can touch the mounting excitement. The security searches, the hubbub of chatter, the panic written on the faces of the TV people, the men in suits with grey hair and walkie-talkies, the arriving audience, shrieking and giggling in their Sunday best, the hurtling rush of nerves rapidly taking a stranglehold on the performers, the orchestra tuning up in the background . . . you feel the adrenalin, you see the anticipation, you smell the fear and you gotta *win*.

Agnetha stood still in the tiny dressing room they'd been allocated to wait for the call. She could hear Stig – cool, calculating Stig – in the throes of near-hysteria as he ran through the final details of their performance with their conductor, Sven-Olof Waldoff. She stood stock still. Petrified. She'd've liked to have sat down, but it was physically impossible in the pant suit they'd given her. The wretched thing was so tight she couldn't bend down to scratch her knee without running the danger of the whole thing ripping apart and catapulting her into the front rows. Paralysis was beginning to creep in.

This was a band clearly taking the piss out of the whole Euro ideal. Wasn't it? *Wasn't* it? Or maybe it was Stig Anderson taking the piss out of them, getting them to wear the skin-tight Napoleonic costumes. Even Sven-Olof had been prevailed upon to dress up as Napoleon himself for the occasion. If the organizers needed any confirmation that here was an entry in serious parody mode, then this surely was it. Everyone knew that conductors of orchestras were always white-haired octogenarians in imminent danger of coronaries in black tails and here was bloody Napoleon Bonaparte standing up there waving his baton.

Benny and Bjorn kept their thoughts to themselves. They were ambitious. They wanted their music to be heard. It wasn't the fame or even the money, it was the challenge for them. The drive to advance themselves, to test their own abilities, and to discover exactly how good they were, how far they could go. It was showbusiness. Stupid costumes? So what? This was 1974. An age when communication was all and presentation vital. They *understood*. They could play the roles without any bother because their thing ultimately was the music. They were the ones who put it all together; they'd always laugh off the decorations.

But Agnetha and Anni-Frid; they knew they *were* the decorations. This was Eurovision, this was sex, this was pop, froth and bobtail. They knew all the close-ups would be on them. They knew there'd be hyper-critical maiden aunties at home picking holes in their lip-gloss and they knew they were also fuelling the lusty fantasies of the dirty-old-men fraternity. It was the name of the game and whatever else Eurovision was about, music was scarcely it.

Agnetha couldn't tell what Anni-Frid was thinking. Sweet, complex, tough Anni-Frid, who could be the life and soul of the party one minute and cold as a fish the next. She'd been through a lot already. She never knew her father, a German soldier during the wartime occupation of Norway, and she was orphaned as a baby when her 21-year-old mother died. She was subsequently raised by her grandmother, who moved across the border to Sweden to protect the girl from the inevitable stigma of her background. But she'd overcome the various hang-ups and disadvantages entailed by this difficult start to make her mark as a folk singer, though there were other personal upsets and one disastrous marriage before she was to link up with Benny and Abba. If tonight was to be her crowning triumph she didn't appear too thrilled about it. She looked tense and said nothing. Agnetha wondered if the pressure of it all was crippling Anni-Frid as much as the pant suit was crippling her. No, it couldn't possibly be . . .

But then even the ice queen herself, Auntie Katie Boyle, was claiming to be terrified. 'I've got terrible butterflies,' she confided to the make-up girl. 'Either I get them in my stomach, which makes my face go skew-whiff, or I get them in my legs, which go wobbly, but that doesn't notice. I'm hoping to get them in my legs.'

And who's gonna win, Miss Boyle?

'Ooh goodness me, I have no idea, but I can tell you there are some lovely songs this year. Monaco's got a really good ballad . . . or is it Italy? One of those. Gosh, I'm so nervous I can't remember.'

None of them need have worried.

Dear, dear Katie was an absolute delight, wobbly legs or not, and it was obvious Abba would win as soon as they launched into 'Waterloo'. All their fears, doubts and embarrassment went flying out the window as that man Sven-Olof Waldoff gave them the nod and they were off and flying. This bit they understood. The professionalism in them took an instant hold over all their emotions as they responded to the music, the occasion, the audience and their own ambitions. They had a piledriver of a song and they knew it was a winner as soon as the orchestra launched into it, obliterating the other sad cases that had drifted through to them beforehand from the monitors. They followed the routine finely honed from hundreds of rehearsals and forgot about the costumes and their lungs seemed to grow with their confidence. They couldn't see the audience, but they recognized the warmth coming off them. They knew. They *knew*. That chorus was just too irritatingly memorable, too simple to sing along with. Agnetha and Anni-Frid bumping and grinding was just too erotic, but tasteful mind, to resist. The costumes too brazen to ignore. The whole routine too polished, bright, fresh, bouncy and original to *not* win.

Who else were they gonna pick? Little Gigliola Cinquetti with another heart-rending Italian ballad? Hardly. Cute but bland Livvy Newton-John pretending she was Sandie Shaw? We think not. The huge Slavs with the black beards booming on about shagging sheep in the mountains? Give us a break. Old Rasputin and his Dutch sidekick prattling on about some windmill in Rotterdam? Nah.

No, it was Abba by a street. They retired to the hospitality suite to observe the niceties, bite their nails and pretend they were worried by the threat of Cindy and Bert from Germany, but the judges might just as well have declared a no-contest. Bjorn and Benny had a drink and watched the rest of the pathetic competition with composed smiles on their faces, while Agnetha worried about baby Linda and Anni-Frid started climbing walls.

And those walls in Brighton are pretty high. Then the scores started coming in and it was clearly a landslide. Each participating country had ten judges watching the action in their own studios, who would fight it out to determine their overall position for each song. They then allocated twelve points for their top choice, ten for their second, nine for the third, and so on. That's when the real drama unfolds and Katie Boyle comes into her own, majestically juggling the links and the languages and a ready quip for them all as the spotlight lands briefly in turn on each country's panel to record their score. An outbreak of spluttering at the other end? It doesn't phase

Katie. A momentary breakdown in the telecommunications? It doesn't bother La Boyle. A crossed line and somebody bursting on to the show in Albanian? No worries. Auntie Kate's there to see them swiftly on their way with a bon mot (in their own language, of course) while smiling reassuringly at the rest of us. She just fills that gap with purring competence. She's a real trouper is our Katie.

After two hours of crappy songs and daft frocks, and a bewilderingly incongruous guest appearance by the Wombles as a tension breaker, Katie's in her element, proving herself a genius of mental arithmetic as well as a mistress of international languages. *'Allemagne: huit points! . . . Grand Bretagne: dix points! . . . la Suède: douze points!'* 'Well,' says Katie, the couch potato's friend, 'that's another set of maximum points for Sweden. They're twenty-two points ahead of the Netherlands.'

No pocket calculator for Katie or for Abba. Those maximums just kept on a-coming. They were declaring national holidays in Stockholm even before half the voting had come in. Sweden had never won *anything* before . . .

Bjorn grinned impishly with every volley of votes being hurled their way, while Benny tried to look cool and failed miserably. Anni-Frid was in a state of shock, staring at the scoreboard on the backstage monitor with clenched fists and frozen posture, while Agnetha tempered her natural instinct to jump up and down, conscious of the fragility of the pant costume. Italy were way back, a very poor second, with the Mouth and little Maggie McNeal third, and Monaco, Luxembourg and the UK tying for fourth. They were minor consolation places.

And when it was over they rose as one with as much

decorum as they could muster to hug one another with a passion that made dirty-minded observers wonder exactly who was sleeping with who in this little foursome. Stig Anderson, elated beyond all recognition, was already plotting world domination and poor old Sven-Olof, the conductor, found himself being manhandled in a way that would have resulted in destruction of entire navies had it been perpetrated on the real Napoleon Bonaparte.

Abba were whisked back out on stage for a re-run of the winning song amid wild scenes of international delight, shaking hands and swapping kisses with strangers of a dozen nationalities. Bottles of champagne were produced and consumed with unusual abandon, congratulations flooded in from all over Scandinavia, excitedly banal quotes were bandied at any journalist in sight, and they joined the throng at the official post-competition banquet to shake more hands and kiss more strangers. People kept coming up to them, kept hugging them. Poor Agnetha still couldn't get out of the pant suit. Couldn't sit down all night. They'd been queuing up to pour her into it hours earlier, but there was no one around to help prise her out of it.

They barely saw one another at the party. Afterwards they remembered nothing about it; they just wafted among the crowds in a daze of celebration. The other competitors graciously congratulated them. They were bear-hugged by Belgians, frugged with the French, and kissed (on the cheeks) by Katie.

Headlines appeared in the press next day about a distraught Livvy Newton-John storming out of the party in floods of tears unable to accept the humiliation of defeat, vowing never ever ever to subject herself to the indignity of Eurovision again. A good story. All lies, of course, but a good story. 'No, I didn't storm out and I certainly wasn't in tears. I didn't really like the song I had and Abba deserved to win. The only bit that was right was that I wouldn't ever do it again. I just left normally and went home, that was all.'

Pinned in a corner by the British press demanding to know where Livvy had gone wrong, Anni-Frid diplomatically said: 'I think the song was too similar to a lot of your previous entries, which was the case with a lot of numbers. Our style is what was needed.'

Neutral observers nodded sagely. Abba were already acquiring an influential fan following, who recognized the artistic breakthrough and shift of formula the group had achieved with 'Waterloo'. Bill Martin, co-composer of Britain's first winner – Sandie Shaw's 'Puppet On A String' seven years earlier – said, a mite pompously, 'every British entry since "Puppet" has been watered-down versions of "Puppet". That's why the Swedish win is so good because it opens the thing up to the pop market.' It did that in a way that even Bill Martin couldn't have anticipated, though the token nerd from the *NME* was rather less impressed by the outcome. 'I'm going to need some involved surgery before I start believing that a piece of Swedish glitter dinkum called "Waterloo" is Europe's finest song of the moment,' he announced, while the rest of Europe ran for their dictionaries. Dinkum. *Dinkum?* Vat is zis vord 'dinkum' meaning, pleese?

It all went over the heads of the victorious quartet, high on . . . er . . . life. Presently, Stig spirited them back to the Grand Hotel and they giggled and phoned friends and family at home, and wound down with a few close associates. It was champagne all the way. They even had a bowl of Cornflakes using champagne instead of milk.

They laughed, they hugged, they pulled silly faces, they rolled around on the floor, they shrieked and whooped and tried to reconstruct the barely comprehensible events of the evening just passed. Tonight Abba had the world at their feet. They'd won the Eurovision Song Contest.

It might just have been the worst thing they ever did . . .

2

THE GREATEST

'I'm really glad you came, you know the rules,
you know the game.
Masters of the scene . . .'

'Voulez-Vous'

Abba are the greatest songwriters of the twentieth century.

Not a claim to be made lightly. A claim certainly still guaranteed to send cynics and pundits charging off for the men in the white coats. Too many prejudices. Too much elitism. It's pop music, see. Pop. Not rock, not classical, not jazz, not show music.

History may have shifted attitudes towards Abba, and their memory is largely adored. But still it's for the wrong reasons. A warm expression and guilty grin come over people's faces as they reach for the *Abba Gold* album. 'Oh, I *love* Abba,' you confess behind the bicycle sheds. 'Yeah, me too,' says the bicycle, and you both dissolve into fits of giggles. It's the gaps between the lines that count. The unspoken acknowledgement of the campness involved in any retrospective appreciation of Abba. The acceptance that tackiness is *good*. The very idea that transient pop music for its own sake, unashamed, unpretentious and vacuous, has any lasting worth. There remains a strange defensiveness about Abba fandom that's unique to them, and is wholly unjustified.

Look at musical history, at the supposedly serious, meaningful, cred pioneering musical statements emerging in the wake of *Sergeant Pepper* while the Swedish music industry still had an inferiority complex. Led Zeppelin. Okay, Led Zeppelin *did* pioneer heavy metal and move rock music to a new plane and yes, there was an Australian compilation album in 1993 featuring Rolf Harris and other sundry luminaries performing a bizarre selection of cover versions of 'Stairway To Heaven'. But come on, how many of those hairy monsters playing air guitars to *Led Zeppelin 3* still rush home from their jobs in computer programming to whack it on the turntable? What warm feelings are inspired by Robert's shrieking vocals and Jimmy's scorching axework? How many requests do all these wretched gold radio stations get for the greatest hits of Led Zeppelin?

The answer to all the questions is sod all, right? Led Zeppelin are totally unlistenable to now. They always were but they were deemed cool and they were deemed important and they sold huge amounts of records and gave impetus to a new musical form called heavy metal – a legacy for which alone they deserve instant exile to Van Dieman's Land. Yet critics nodded sagely and students based whole lifestyles on the vision and philosophy of Led Zeppelin and Pink Floyd while Sweet and Mud and Slade were silly bubblegum groups strictly for kids and who made records you'd forgotten before the last note. Which would *you* rather listen to now? Whose records do *you* still remember all the words to?

And Led Zeppelin *were* the best, the most important, the most innovative of the so-called serious groups emerging at the turn of the seventies. It was they who changed pop language. Groups suddenly became bands.

LPs became albums. Pop became rock. Piano became keyboards. Singles became crap. In fact, singles didn't exist if you were a Led Zeppelin fan. The bullshit factor was enormous in the early seventies.

But if Led Zep were the biggest and greatest of the breed, the Beatles of their chosen idiom, what about the rest? Yes? ELP? Wishbone Ash? Barclay James Harvest? Cream? Gentle Giant? Supertramp? Colosseum? Tangerine Dream? Van Der Graaf Generator?!?

Spare us! Give us Smokie, Alvin Stardust and Norman Greenbaum any day! You'd need to be brain dead to want to listen to Van Der Graaf Generator in the nineties. You had to be brain dead to listen to them in the seventies and most people were, that was part of the problem. Loon pants? They laugh themselves stupid at some of the costumes Abba paraded in, but how could you ever take anyone seriously who wore *loon pants* and played tracks that lasted fourteen minutes? There's a school of thought that anyone caught entering a record shop attempting to buy a Van Der Graaf Generator album should undergo instant euthanasia and, let's be fair, it's kinder that way.

And while we're on the subject, what about Quintessence? A society that elevates Quintessence to even marginal stardom is unquestionably terminally sick. It was all George Harrison's fault, of course. All that skiving off to India having tea and yoga with the Maharishi and then including the truly abominable 'Within You, Without You' on *Sergeant Pepper*. How on earth did someone so domineeringly pragmatic as Paul McCartney allow him to get away with it? Why didn't John Lennon just chin him and tell him to stop being so stupid? Too busy being high on life, apparently.

And they accused Abba of nonsense!

After all that garbage, by God we *needed* Paper Lace and Gary Glitter. Maybe we didn't need the Bay City Rollers, but you can't have it all ways. Others were smarter. Bolan, Bowie, Elton John ... they skilfully managed to disguise their own simple, bubblegum pop in an ingenious shroud of mystique and inventiveness. All image and no trousers, they eluded dread Zep-inspired scorn with extraordinary sleight of hand and breathtaking guile. Especially Marc Bolan. His songs were nursery rhymes. Stupid, nonsensical rhyming couplets over a primitive three-chord strum and a strangulated whine designed to cause grown dogs the utmost distress. But Marc also had this magic wand to weave a mesmerizing spell over his audience which hoodwinked even the high priest of cool, John Peel. If Peelie – who'd after all established his own untouchable reputation on pirate radio with readings from *The Perfumed Garden* – thought Bolan was the messiah, then what were a few dumb songs with daffy lyrics to call him a liar?

Marc seemed to hypnotize the entire nation. So that when his image as cultural youth guru reached critical mass and he suddenly burst among the kiddiewinkies as an unapologetic fully-fledged pop star with screaming girls and everything, he got away with that too. Bolan threw himself into the role of pin-up teen hero with such abandon that even Peelie had to recoil, but few others batted an eyelid. His songs were still crap, but without any discernible shift in the goalposts or his own game plan, he'd leapt from underground hero to pop icon in one giant bound. It was the most astonishing lie in pop history, but with the sheer, breathtaking brashness of the bound, he managed to execute it without discernible damage to life, limb or image. Extraordinary.

Even Bowie and Elton couldn't muster quite as much front, sometimes painfully juggling their roles of serious artists, pop darlings and laboured court jesters. They shielded their exploding ambitions and desire for the whole rock 'n' roll dream with humour, daring outrageousness and chameleon disguise. Bolan's unashamed gall must have taken their breath away and made them hugely envious. Both got there in the end, of course, but it was a wholly more tortuous process of media manipulation and audience delusion before they were finally accelerated into the rarefied atmosphere of pop stardom.

This was the sunlight into which Abba emerged, blinking, without guile, subtlety or subterfuge. Their success was in spite of the embarrassingly inept styling with which they were lumbered throughout their career. It was in spite of the stigma of being forever associated with Eurovision and its proud history of fleeting crassness and five-minute fame. In spite of being Swedish and therefore at the mercy of the musical jingoism rampant throughout Britain and the States, for so long engaged in their own private Ryder Cup for control of the international charts. In spite of playing pure, unabashed pop music without the remotest sense of apology, deceit or pretence that it was anything else at a time when out-and-out pop acts from Bolan to Sweet to Gilbert O'Sullivan, for Godsake, had to couch their intentions in some mask of art or earnestness.

And so Abba's music wasn't taken seriously in their lifetime and while time has reflected kindly on their image and their memory, the music still isn't taken seriously. Not as seriously as it should be.

'The Winner Takes It All' is pure gold. A wonderful,

heartbreakingly beautiful song, with moving lyrics and classic melody structure that ranks alongside anything put together by Lennon and McCartney. Or Cole Porter. Or Irving Berlin. Or George Gershwin. Likewise 'Fernando', 'Knowing Me, Knowing You', 'Chiquitita', 'The Day Before You Came'. And even 'When All Is Said And Done', one of the last tracks they ever recorded from their final album, *The Visitors*, and never released as a single, but a stunning song.

You won't hear any of this from music historians, of course. The thinking goes that Abba were of the seventies and the seventies were crap, therefore Abba were crap. But, of course, the basic premise of that argument is seriously wrong in the first place. This romantic rose-tinted idea that the sixties were the golden age of pop is unadulterated bullshit.

The sixties were a crucially significant decade for youth culture and pop music played a role in that. Not especially for the quality of the music – though, of course, the enduring magic of the Beatles, the Stones and all things Motown is not to be dismissed lightly – but just by being. Youth was invented in the fifties but if Bill Haley, Elvis Presley and Buddy Holly were its icons, then Monroe, James Dean and Marlon Brando were part and parcel of that revolution. It was also almost entirely an American phenomenon.

But if the fifties invented the teenager, then the sixties in general – the Beatles and the Stones in particular – made it accessible to everyone. Having established that there was something called a teenager, the sixties beat boom created an environment where it was not only possible, but essential to be one. Teenagers had a voice and the natural order of things declared that that voice should be used in rejection of and rebellion against all that had gone before. Long hair, electric guitars, pirate radio, blues riffs, surly looks; all were ingredients of the highly necessary anti-establishment stance that has been the staple diet of youth culture. Everything changed once 'Please Please Me' hit the top of the charts. The whole balance of pop power shifted from the States to Europe, groups had to write their own material or be considered helplessly uncool, and you had to rail against the status quo to have any chance of survival.

Yet because the whole thing represented such a huge shift in youth culture and therefore society, the historical importance given to the music has been out of all proportion to its worth. Because the Beatles were so brilliant, everyone assumes the music around them was of almost equal value. Well, there was the Stones. And who were next in the pecking order? The bloody Dave Clark Five, that's who! By no stretch of the imagination could anyone call 'Glad All Over' or 'Bits And Pieces' classics. Then we had the dear old reliable Hollies, honest plodders who made passable radio fodder and built a lasting career out of half-decent tunes and Everly Brothers harmonies, but seriously missed the boat when they were dishing out glamour, charisma and excitement. The Hollies were as thrilling as an over-ripe tomato.

Manfred Mann had a cracking singer in Paul Jones and a healthy interest in Bob Dylan until they started to believe in themselves as the beat boom's answer to Duke Ellington. And who were the other leading heart-throbs trailblazing this heroic new era of rock? Freddie and the Dreamers and Herman's Hermits, both marginally less juvenile than Noddy and Muffin the Mule; and Billy J. Kramer, more wooden than Pinocchio, whose only decent songs were written by Lennon-McCartney. Bless 'em all, bless 'em all, the long, and the short and the tall. But a vintage decade they do not make.

And then at the end of the era we had the Beatles taking too many drugs and the whole soppy peace and love and it-doesn't-matter-if-I'm-crap-cos-I've-got-a-flower-in-my-hair-and-I'm-not-frightfully-keen-about-killing-Asians-in-Vietnam drippy hippy home-spun scenarios. Lots of serious dullards preaching at us and thinking they'd found the meaning of life in a tab of acid and then we were into that whole disgraceful time when the three-minute time limit was removed from singles and artists were allowed to indulge themselves to painful degrees.

So no, the sixties weren't as great as you may think they were. Nobody believes it, though. History reckons the sixties were an undiluted diet of fab fab fab and therefore the seventies were dire. But turn on the radio and thrill to those golden oldies. Which tracks still sound fresh and alert and make your toes turn up in pleasure? It's the only sure way of discerning lasting quality and – trust us – the seventies come out of it *glowing*. Those tracks were bequeathed by all those artists who were dismissed at the time as throwaway bubblegum pop bands, all plastic smiles and no trousers. Bowie, Slade, Elton John, 10cc. . . great, great records virtually every time they entered the studio. And the kings of the castle were, of course, Abba.

The seventies weren't the only decade to get a rough deal. Nobody will ever admit it, but the mid-eighties was a golden age for pop, too. 'Freedom' by Wham! Fabulous record! The trilogy of Frankie Goes To Hollywood number ones were superb, too, though more for style and Trevor Horn's production than for actual song content. 'True' by Spandau Ballet – wonderful song. Then there's all the Culture Club hits: 'Do You Really Want To Hurt Me?', 'Church Of The Poisoned Mind' and 'Karma Chameleon'. Let's not forget, either, the pioneering synth-pop audacity of those stirring Human League hits: 'Love Action', 'Mirror Man', 'Louise' and 'Don't You Want Me Baby?', the trash Motown parody to end them all.

Then, ushering in the end of the decade with hilarious arrogance and opportunism, there were Stock, Aitken & Waterman, using the dance floor as a vehicle for the basest pop instincts. Naturally enough, S/A/W were roundly reviled and despised by anyone over thirteen, but listen to those records now. They stand up! 'Never Gonna Give You Up' by Rick Astley thunders out from the speakers with a heart-warming thump and a joy that'll surprise even the harshest eighties cynic. 'Oh, I love this, what is it?' you begin to say before stopping suddenly as you realize exactly what it is . . .

And those Jason and Kylie records, *especially* the Kylie records. 'I Should Be So Lucky', 'Especially For You', 'Je Ne Sais Pas Pourquoi'. A soundtrack to youth and a decent one at that, even if the S/A/W philosophy relied as much on production techniques as it did on pure songwriting skills. In years to come there will be a radical reassessment of Kylie Minogue records. They will be hailed as pop classics in the way that Abba's hits have come to be accepted, even though the reliance on production meant Kylie's records were timepieces much more than Abba's ever were. But Mike Stock, Matt Aitken and Pete Waterman understood the fundamental rules of classic pop music. Simple chords, irresistible choruses, lively singing, dancey beat, undemanding lyrics, warm atmospherics and nothing, but *nothing*, beyond three minutes.

Maybe it's the lot of great pop that it's discounted as meaningless and transient when all the evidence is there for everyone to see that truly *great* pop has to appear that way to be great, but in fact lasts for ever. The sheer consistency of Abba's output has to put them at the very top of pop's golden greats. They did it and they did it and they kept doing it for over a decade and, lest we get too wound up defending the seventies and imagining they were some cute period piece, we should emphasize that they continued to produce superb songs – in fact probably produced their best songs – in the eighties.

So we say that Abba were the best, the greatest songwriters of the twentieth century. Who else do you make a case for? Lennon/McCartney, for sure. But their impact and their whole appeal owed a lot to other matters, too . . . like the cultural revolution they helped to bring about, and the innovations they made via musical experiment and studio development, *Revolver* onwards. Analyse the songwriting alone, though, and you get a slightly different perspective. Mostly they were still brilliant and mostly they survive the ultimate acid test of whether the songs themselves – stripped of extraneous studio technique, period mood and contagious hero worship – would still be hit songs today. Mostly, probably, they would, and they even managed to break the most sacred pop rule of them all – never go over three minutes – and come out smelling of roses with 'Hey Jude'. Yet they were erratic and there is a surprising amount of drivel in their back catalogue, too. 'Ticket To Ride'. Not what you'd call a great song, is it? Or 'She Loves You'. Dreadful rubbish.

With The Beatles was their best album. 'Eight Days A

Week', 'I'm A Loser', 'I'll Follow The Sun', 'No Reply': terrific songs beautifully performed. But *With The Beatles* also included four makeweight Lennon/McCartney efforts – you can't really make a case for 'What You're Doing' or 'Every Little Thing' as classics – as well as material by Buddy Holly, Chuck Berry, Carl Perkins and Leiber and Stoller.

And later on they simply stopped writing songs for their own sake. *Sergeant Pepper* did have 'With A Little Help From My Friends' and 'She's Leaving Home', but its genius was largely in the way George Martin made sense of outlandish ideas resulting from mind-expanding drugs. Once they found it worked – and more than that, it furthered pop music and their own perception of themselves – they didn't really want to be bothered with the frivolity of pop for its own sake any more. Inevitably, a few classics did subsequently emerge along the way, but they were almost incidental to the whole changing picture and it was only later, after the split, that Lennon and McCartney returned individually to mother earth and the pop idiom. And – precluding the odd 'Imagine' or 'Live And Let Die' – there were elements of self-parody about this supposedly sophisticated turn of events climaxing with the embarrassment that doesn't dare speak its name. Simply because it was released weeks before his death and it was his comeback album, John Lennon's *Double Fantasy* album has been spared the judgement we all know it really deserves. With the exception of 'Starting Over', which showed Lennon at his Shirrelles-remembered best, *Double Fantasy* stunk. To high heaven. But you're not allowed to say that. 'Sentimental' and 'romantic' and 'sweet' and 'lush' are the nearest you can ever get to damning *Double Fantasy*.

And then there's the Stones. Great band. For about three years. But let's be honest, they haven't come up with anything remotely classic or original since 'Satisfaction' in 1965. For three decades they've lived off Jagger's wit and Keith Richards' rebellious image. After 'Satisfaction', the first and best Stones' roll continued through 'Paint It Black' and 'Ruby Tuesday' until the work turned on the Stones and they found their name blackened in the same thick black print that had them tied to success. 'Cept now it was excess, petty and serious drug busts, sex and death scandals, before retiring as a great band and returning as 'the greatest rock 'n' roll band in the world'. It's only rock 'n' roll so we fake it.

But pop translates as having sold enough records in Australia so that every home has your record, an Abba record. That's the school we grew up in and we believe the fab four and naughty five attended the same school.

In truth there aren't too many others in the same league on the pop side. Bacharach and David? Leiber and Stoller? Holland-Dozier-Holland? Stevie Wonder? Bob Dylan? Elton John? David Bowie? Elvis Costello? Michael Jackson? Prince? Fabulous songwriters all, but did they ever achieve the level of consistency and sheer volume of success of the songs of Bjorn Ulvaeus and Benny Andersson?

For real competition we have to look at the acknowledged greats of stage and screen. Rodgers and Hart/ Hammerstein. Stephen Sondheim. Irving Berlin. Andrew Lloyd-Webber, Cole Porter. These are rarefied heights and why not? It's impossible to compare 'I Have A Dream' with 'I Get A Kick Out Of You' – how can anyone ever judge the merits of one song above another (even though it's how Abba came to our attention in the first place)? But, lyrically, melodically, emotionally, 'I Have A Dream' most certainly lives with 'I Get A Kick Out Of You'. In another age Frank Sinatra or Nat King Cole or Ella Fitzgerald could have sung 'I Have A Dream' and it would have sounded the most natural thing in the world. So yeah, Ulvaeus and Andersson are in that league and why should we feel embarrassed about acknowledging it?

Because they recorded supposedly frivolous pop songs and wore ridiculous costumes and nobody took them seriously, that's why. But they didn't sell seven million copies of *Abba Gold* a full decade after any real active service purely on the basis of some kind of camp nostalgia trip. Ask any songwriter – simplicity is the most effective and most difficult quality to successfully construct in music. When a song sounds like it was slotted together like a five-piece jigsaw in a matter of seconds, then that's a recipe for extravagant, enduring success. Think about it. 'Yesterday'. 'Mull Of Kintyre'. 'Rocket Man'. 'The Young Ones', 'I Got You Babe'. Classics of sorts, all sounding ludicrously simple. You could almost imagine Paul saying to John: 'Look, I've written this new thing, it's so easy I'm not sure I can play it to you' and John howling with laughter when he heard it. 'We can't sing that, Paulie, nobody would take us seriously again, they'll think we've gone soft in the head or summat!' And, of course, the Beatles didn't play 'Yesterday'. The song was unveiled in a brief Paul solo excursion during a Beatles set on *Sunday Night At the London Palladium*, ending with John wandering on to give Paul a bouquet of flowers as his own sardonic comment.

Abba achieved this memorable simplicity in their work again and again and again. It was one of their traits and it was one of the reasons they were widely derided, but it was also one of the reasons their songs were so memorable and their success so enduring.

And can their work really be elevated up there in the echelons of the great musical songwriters, the Rodgers and Hammersteins of the world? *Absolutely!* In this respect Ulvaeus and Andersson might even be considered in the infancy of their careers, having dipped their toes into the torrid waters of stage musicals with the Tim Rice collaboration *Chess*. It was a totally new area for them and a big leap from hit singles to the London stage. But *Chess* was a major success and produced a succession of wonderful songs, notably 'I Know Him So Well', cleverly tackling the thoughts of two people as a counterpoint to one another in a grand ballad, and taken to the top of the charts by Elaine Paige and Barbara Dickson long before *Chess* opened.

The continuing Benny and Bjorn story will doubtless confirm it, but meanwhile we have no doubts. They're the greatest songwriters of the twentieth century.

3

THE GIRL WITH THE
GOLDEN HAIR

*'I was an impossible case, no one ever can reach me
But I think I can see in your face, there's a
lot you can teach me'*

'The Name Of The Game'

One night on tour in the States in 1979 it all began to get out of hand.

Agnetha – nervous, fretting and irritable – wanted out. She was becoming, as she more and more frequently was these days, racked with guilt. She was homesick, she was paranoid about flying, the pressures were mounting, there was no time for anything any more, and even the gigs weren't that great any more.

Where were they? Washington? Chicago? Philadelphia? She scarcely knew and she certainly didn't care. She was worn out, lonely and desperately missing her kids. What was she doing here? There was no point to it. No fulfilment. Few compensations. Money? She didn't care about money. She really never cared about money.

And she was on her own. She and Bjorn had officially split on Christmas Eve 1978 and while the painful, official announcement had taken the heat out of the tension that had existed between them for so long, it was still hard watching him skate through it with barely a hiccup. They hardly communicated any more. Why should they? There was no marriage. No friendship. No love. No joy. No *nothing* any more. Even the audiences brought her scant comfort, not here. Here more than anywhere they demanded their pleasures on a plate and would dismiss you disdainfully with withering indifference should you fail to deliver the dish they'd demanded of you. She loathed the whole baggage of touring. The whole process of getting from one place to another exhausted her, the thought of setting foot on a plane terrified her, even the idea of singing in front of an audience filled her with dread now. There was so much to think about, so many chances of things going wrong, so much responsibility. All those people, all that expectation. Pressure, pressure, pressure. She hated it.

This was the States, the worst place in the world to get the blues, where the winners really do take it all. See that beggar on the sidewalk? Tough shit, kid, I gotta fur coat to buy! The States had always been hard for Abba, despite the outbursts of mini-hysteria that had swept 'Dancing Queen' to the top of the charts and had them pegged in the disco strait-jacket to be mentioned in the same breath as the Bee Gees. Agnetha had started to wonder if she was now a member of a new supergroup, the BeeGeesand-Abba, she heard their names linked so often, without ever understanding why. Who needs it, eh? It's one thing to be twenty-one and shooting round the world for the first time and discovering everyone adores you and life is a minestrone. It's quite another to be grown up, and a mother, but alone in your hotel room, being carted from one anonymous city to another to be poured on stage and perform your party piece like some travelling circus act. If you're lucky they shout and cheer, and then you're put back in your box, stuck away in some gloomy room for the night, and marched off the next morning for the next instalment. Was this what it had all been for?

Not for the first time, Agnetha decided this was it. She'd quit now. Get on the next plane to Stockholm. Maybe not even tell the others. Just leave a note and go. What could they do? What *would* they do? The way she felt right now Agnetha doubted they'd even notice. She knew they'd carry on. Frida would take centre-stage the way she'd always wanted and become the heroine of the day, and Agnetha would be the villain of the piece (again), hounded by the press (again) and she'd get even more confused and guilty about the whole situation (again).

That night she did her stuff like a good girl. She swished and shimmied and shook and smiled in the time-honoured fashion. She smiled wryly. The consummate professional. The show must go on and all that. She milked the applause, but came off – adrenalin pumping.

Frida got off on the fame. She loved the attention and responded to the importance it lent her. Frida seemed born to it and barely disguised her scorn for what Agnetha knew she regarded as her smallmindedness.

There they were, being whisked back to the hotel, the scene a perfect microcosm of the cavernous rift between them. Agnetha, sullen and brooding, muttering that this was it, she wanted to end this tour *now*, didn't want any more to do with Abba.

And there was Frida, high on life, animatedly discussing where they were off to now. A couple of guys from the record company had mentioned a really great restaurant. Slightly out of town, a bit of a cab ride but worth it. They had cabaret some nights, hey let's go party!

Agnetha was intent on basking in her solitude, looking only to phone home, maybe watch a late-night movie in her room. Whatever, she'd end the night miserable. Inevitably an argument ensued.

With the resigned air of seasoned peacemakers, Bjorn and Benny began to calm them down, though both had had their own fill of the enmity between the two girls. The whole thing was falling apart around their ears and they knew it. Just get through this tour without scandal, nervous breakdown or mass murder and it would be a bonus. A bloody miracle, more like.

So Agnetha went to her room alone, miserable. Frida went out on the town, delirious. The guys hit the bottle, with a vengeance. Grudging truces were made and wounds were bandaged and the girls kept their distance for the sake of peace and perceived harmony. Abba was effectively over. From here on in it was all a sham.

Agnetha and Frida had long disliked one another. Two girls from very different backgrounds, with radically different attitudes and sharply clashing temperaments had been thrown together in a cauldron of closeness as a direct consequence of being with the men they loved. They weren't friends, they couldn't ever be friends. They were like two in-laws making polite conversation at a wedding reception without any real affection or interest in one another. Except the other guests all suddenly disappeared, leaving just the four of them together in the middle of the dance floor lit by floodlights for the amusement of a baying audience. It seemed like a set-up, certainly a trap to Agnetha. Frida and Agnetha certainly got to know one another a whole lot better in the interminable waltz that followed, but they never made it as far as friendship. Eventually, as the novelty wore off and the pressure moved up a gear, all pretence at cordiality went out of the window and the cold war gave way to outright hostilities.

They were just so different, Agnetha and Frida. If they'd been at school together, they would have ignored one another, arranging their own groups of friends around them to gossip and moan about the other. Agnetha's friends would have been reassuring her, looking after her, building up her confidence, avoiding her tantrums; Frida's friends would have been out partying, laughing about the funny blonde girl in the corner, who was always sucking up to the teacher and somehow seemed to think she was a cut above them. Each would have thought the other a snob. And each would have had a latent, unspoken jealousy of the other. Frida for Agnetha's looks, figure, popularity with boys, and her obviously sensible nature. Agnetha would have envied Frida's *joie de vivre*, her self-assurance, happy outgoing nature and her daring.

Opposites certainly didn't attract in this case, though they were central to the charisma and intrigue that held the world's infatuation for over a decade. Were they lesbians? Did they swap partners? Was there real chemistry between them or was it a trick of the light? No, no, no, *no* came back the answers and that made the pairing all the more interesting. There was something . . . there was definitely *something* unexplained about them. Something beyond all accepted devices of image-making and pop formulae. Something remarkable but indefinable that made them very special. Nobody ever twigged it was that they hated each other.

Agnetha. Dear, gorgeous, complicated, mixed-up Agnetha. The archetypal shop-girl who really only ever wanted to grow up ordinary. To fall in love, raise kids and live happily ever after. She never craved fame, she never wanted to be a millionaire, she had no use of adulation. But she had a talent and she got lucky. All her dreams came true and more but she found them difficult to cope with.

Jonkoping is an industrial city in the south of Sweden, close to Lake Vattern, about 100 miles east of Gothenburg. A busy, if unprepossessing place with a population today of 107,000, it has a thriving community built around an army of factories. Machinery, shoes, chemicals; all are the staple diet of life in Jonkoping. Its most celebrated industry, though, is matches. Safety matches. They started a mechanized production line in matches back in 1845 and haven't looked back. Dear lord, there's even a match museum in the city to prove it.

All that work needs a fair bit of play to go with it. Ingvar Faltskog was a prime ingredient of that playmaking. He enthusiastically involved himself in local amateur dramatics, acting, directing, even writing sketches for numerous productions, energetically organizing dances, plays and revues for local societies, old people's homes, community events. Anything going, really, and Ingvar would be in the middle of it.

His daughter Agnetha Ase was born in Jonkoping on 5 April 1950 and was instantly sucked into this mini-showbiz community. Ingvar adored her – and who wouldn't? – smothering her in the smell of greasepaint almost as soon as she could stand.

The story of her first stage appearance when her dad coaxed her on stage for a Christmas show when she was five and she stole the show when her pants fell down became a staple anecdote in later years. She also had piano lessons as a toddler, though these weren't enough and she'd badger the next-door neighbour to let her practise on their joanna. She was a nice enough kid and they usually let her, though her persistence and reluctance to leave became wearing, and it was a relief all round when the Faltskogs finally acquired a piano of their own when Agnetha was seven. She played fugues on the harpsichord in the local church, and by the time she was thirteen was appearing regularly on stage, either playing piano, acting or singing.

By now she was harbouring ambitions of a singing career. She was a huge fan of Connie Francis, doing the usual mirror-in-the-bathroom trick to belt out 'Who's Sorry Now?' when she thought no one was listening, and taking an avid interest in the pop revolution emerging in America. Yet her father's influence hadn't been in vain, giving her a good grounding, too, in classical music, jazz and show tunes. Agnetha loved it all, determinedly grabbing all the opportunities available to her to get up in front of an audience and do her thing. And in Jonkoping in the early sixties there were plenty of these.

She became a local celebrity, the Jonkoping child star. Inspired by the all-girl vocal harmony groups springing up in the States she formed a short-lived Jonkoping version, performing covers of the hits of the day at small-time shows, though increasingly she was invited to sing with more serious semi-pro big bands performing dance tunes and standard ballads.

She quit school at fifteen and took her first job as a telephonist in a car showroom, living for the weekends when she sang with the Bengt Enghardt Orchestra from Huskvarna. It was an incongruous sight. The formal, mainly middle-aged orchestra playing proper dance music for proper dances for a regular clientele of the suited and booted; and in the middle of them the striking teenage blonde who sang with a maturity beyond her years, but disappeared at the first stroke of midnight to magically transform herself into a humble telephonist and be at work at 8 a.m. on Monday morning.

It got harder as the orchestra undertook more and more work, through the week, travelling further distances. Everybody who's ever been in a band and attempted to hold down a full-time job at the same time has a story of staggering home at the crack of dawn just in time for a shower and a bowl of cornflakes, before heading off for work. And, of course, they always fell asleep over the lathe, or the filing, or the accounts, or the classroom, or whatever, and were sacked on the spot. Agnetha wasn't sacked but plenty of would-be clients at the car showroom found themselves re-directed to the public toilets rather than the sales department.

Never reckless, Agnetha hung on as long as she could – encouraged by her parents who loved seeing their little girl on stage but never seriously believing there might be a career at the end of it. But Agnetha was young, glamorous and exceedingly talented. She knew that because everybody she met told her as much and in the slightly starchy environment in which she now predominantly operated she stood out like a glittering diamond. Thrilled by the whole idea of music, *any* music, she was even writing her own songs before she was seventeen, starting off almost exclusively writing about the highs – and ultimately the desperate lows – of her first painful love affair. It was to be a forerunner of many hurtful affairs to follow.

Such was her youthful ebullience, she wasn't even self-conscious about her own songs, confidently performing them with the orchestra. Bengt Enghardt decided they should try to make a record with Agnetha and they recorded demos of a couple of her songs 'Folj Med Min' ('Follow Me') and 'Jag Var Sa Kar' ('I Was So In Love'). That demo was heard by a colourful character called Little Gerhard, himself a former Swedish pop star and now a producer, and talent scout for CBS/Cupol. Gerhard summoned Agnetha with some good news and some bad news. He loved the song. Loved Agnetha's voice. Hated Bengt Enghardt's orchestra. He wanted to sign her . . . but not the band.

Agnetha was disconcerted by this unexpected dilemma which pitched loyalty against ambition. But if *you* were seventeen with stars in your eyes and some hotshot producer said stick with me, kid, I'll make you a star, what would *you* do? The gutters are littered with embittered souls left to fantasize about what might have been had their lifelong pal, the blood brother they'd taught to play guitar and massaged into the spotlight, not been scooped up into the big time.

Hey, it's nothing personal. This is business, right? And it's the biggest, most volatile, most thrilling business in Christendom, so sure there's gonna be a few casualties along the way. And for every painful BEATLES SACK PETE BEST story, there's a Slade to restore your faith in rock star nature. Don Powell, Slade's drummer, was left more dead than alive in a horrific car crash on American Independence Day in 1973. His girlfriend Angela Morris was killed outright and Don was in hospital for six weeks unable to recognize even his nearest and dearest. He was to suffer dire memory lapses for years afterwards, and Noddy Holder, Jim Lea and Dave Hill had patiently to re-teach him the Slade set night after night when they eventually went back on the road. It must have driven them bonkers and it didn't do Don Powell much good, but they wouldn't hear of him leaving. Slade are from Wolverhampton where you lay down your life for someone who buys you a pint when you're broke. For richer, for poorer, for better or worse. Slade stuck with Don Powell, just like Def Leppard stuck with their drummer Rick Allen after his left arm was ripped off in a terrible car crash near Sheffield on New Year's Eve, 1984.

If it wasn't so tragic, it would be hilarious. How could Def Leppard even contemplate continuing with a *one-armed drummer*?!? Surely, Def Leppard, cried a non-comprehending rock world, you cannot be serious! They were perfectly serious. A special drum kit was built, months of agonizing physiotherapy followed and at the end of the day, Def Leppard went back on the road with their one-armed drummer. It didn't do them any harm, either. Ghoulish curiosity being what it is, and the daily rags lapping up a great human heartbreak triumph-over-adversity tale when they sniff it, Def Lep returned to competitive action in a blaze of publicity and sold-out gigs. See, it's not all vicious bastards, greed and ruthlessness.

Agnetha Faltskog, though, did what anyone would do in the circumstances. She blew Bengt Enghardt a big kiss and caught the next train to Stockholm to go see Little Gerhard. Gerhard honed in on the fraught, emotional 'I Was So In Love' and the shellshocked vulnerability of Agnetha's vocals. He had her re-record the song with a lusher backing from the orchestra of Sven-Olof Waldoff, the man who was subsequently decorated in garish Napoleonic guise to share in Abba's greatest/worst moment down in Britain six years later. There was no suggestion of any of this then, of course. Agnetha, wide-eyed and breathless with excitement about it all but desperately inexperienced, had few long-term aspirations about singing. She could scarcely entertain the prospect of having a record in the charts, but ruefully saw the whole thing as a way of gaining some comfort, a small degree of revenge and a little compensation from the ex-boyfriend who'd broken her heart.

Agnetha duly signed a deal with Cupol and 'I Was So In Love' was released as her first single to instant acclaim and mass airplay. She was perceived as the ideal Swedish girl. An ordinary blue-eyed blonde from Smalltown, Sweden, who was well-scrubbed, loved her family and smiled sweetly while showing a touching fondness for nature in pictures. She looked pure and virginal, with a touch of the outrageous flirt in the way she tossed her classic flowing blonde hair and vivaciously lit up her surroundings in inevitable micro-skirt and kinky boots. All this *and* she was nursing a broken heart. 'I Was So In Love' was topping the charts within weeks.

Other hits followed in rapid succession. Excited by every new experience – radio shows, TV appearances, mixing with celebrities, being fawned over by record company lackeys – Agnetha was on fire, writing prolifically and enjoying her fame without any of the hang-ups that were later to dog her. The Swedish record industry is hardly huge, but success when it hits you for the first time is overwhelming in any language. She wrote all the tracks on her first album, *Agnetha Fältskog*, which included three other hits almost as big as the first – 'Utan Dej' ('Without You'), 'Forsonade' ('United') and 'Allting Har Förändrat Sig' ('Everything Has Changed'). They were straightforward, romantic pop songs constructed basically around Agnetha's delicate emotional state, her childhood adoration of Connie Francis and her lively love life.

Scandinavia was in love with her and while the second album, released in 1969 and imaginatively titled *Agnetha Fältskog Vol. 2*, didn't deviate remotely from its predecessor, it underlined her arrival as one of the hottest properties in Scandinavia. A succession of other hits followed: 'Snövit Och De Sju Dvargarna', 'En Gang Fanns Bara Vi Två' ('Once We Were Two'), 'Skal Kara Van', 'Hjärtat Kronprins' and 'Zigenarvan', all draped in perfectly executed images of girlie charm on the picture sleeve. If there had been a Swedish version of *Neighbours*, Agnetha would have been in it, lending an ear to all the problems of the locality in Ramsaygatan while her own boyfriends did the dirty on her. She was Kylie Minogue before her time.

But she was still unknown beyond Scandinavia. She was still not overtly ambitious or demanding, but frustrations and irritations were creeping in. Everything is wonderfully thrilling when it's new and different, but second and third time around the paint begins to fade. She'd sung at virtually every decent venue available in Stockholm, she'd done the whole media circus and she'd met most of the leading music biz luminaries in Sweden, including – in passing – one Bjorn Ulvaeus. The limitations of her genre and her environment began to grate on her and she wanted, needed something, *anything* to break the mould. International success was something that she could scarcely think about coveting as she seemed to believe the fulcrum of her popularity was centred around the heartfelt emotions of her own songs and at this time she had neither the incentive nor the confidence in her own mastery of other languages to write in anything other than Swedish. This was, after all, the fag end of the sixties when only Frank Sinatra and no-hopers recorded cover versions. You recorded a score of somewhere slightly below *entirely useless* on the credibility-meter if you couldn't write your own songs and Agnetha clearly could – she had the gold discs and the big, fat bank account to prove it.

Then she fell in love. Again. His name was Dieter Zimmerman, a German songwriter and producer with a dashing air, a knowing worldliness and a deep, deep admiration for Agnetha. He told her she was brilliant. That she had a stunning voice, a brilliant collection of songs and a glittering future. He talked of a glittering future for them together, insisting there were no limits to what she could achieve as a singer. She had a rare talent and an incredible beauty and, given the chance, the world would love her. She was too good to stay cooped up in Sweden. She should tour in Europe, make films, record fabulous records, have babies with him.

Agnetha needed to hear it. Despite her runaway success, her insecurities were seldom far from the surface and she constantly sought assurance about her worth. She had, after all, left the bosom of her family in Jonkoping to be a pop star at the tender age of seventeen. A couple of years on she still felt strangely lonely in the midst of all the glory which was beginning to assume a slightly tainted edge and without the closeness of her family around her she needed regular cajoling, encouragement and loving to function.

Dieter Zimmerman was saying all the right things. She listened and she believed. Dieter had the answers. Dieter was the Svengali who'd come along to look after her and transform her life. They announced their engagement and went off to Germany, first base in the projected international breakthrough to follow.

In 1969 Zimmerman set Agnetha up in the studio for the first onslaught in what was intended to be a painstaking international campaign. She sang for the first time in a foreign language – German – on a selection of songs initially written by her but drastically re-structured by Zimmerman. The German market was huge, he assured her, much bigger and more credible than that in Sweden. Who, after all, had ever heard of an international pop star from Sweden? Agnetha failed to ask the key question: how many international pop stars were there from Germany, Mr Dieter Zimmerman?

Together they recorded eight specially tailored Euro-songs subsequently released as singles by Metronome and CBS, mainly in the German language: 'Robinson Crusoe', 'Komm Doch Zu Mir' ('Do Come To Me'), 'Mein Schönster Tag' ('My Loveliest Day'), 'Concerto D'Amore', 'Wer Schreibt Heut' Noch Liebesbriefe?' ('Who Is Writing Love Letters Today?'), 'Fragezeichen Mag Ich Nicht' ('I Don't Like Question Marks'), 'Ein Kleiner Mann In Einer Flashe' ('A Small Man In A Bottle') and 'Geh' Mit Gott' ('Walk With God'). There was even one English language record resulting from the sessions: 'Golliwog', backed with 'Here For Your Love'.

Germany, though, was distinctly underwhelmed. The rest of Europe yawned. They never even got a sniff of the UK. There was no media support, no airplay, no live performance to back any of it up. The whole exercise was a hopeless, miserable flop. Germany had enough unknown singers of their own scrabbling for a foothold without worrying about some blonde Swede. Failure was a new and galling experience for Agnetha, used to seeing the streets turn to gold as soon as she set foot on the pavement, and she could scarcely conceal her disappointment.

Dieter hadn't delivered on his promises and clearly wasn't the superman she so desperately wanted him to be. When she heard the records she didn't recognize herself, rueing her trust in the confidently expressed advice of others. The killer about being insecure is that you are instantly in awe of anyone with confidence. Confidence is a surprisingly elusive commodity in creative people – resulting in constant paranoia about the very idea of public performance in the first place – and leading to a dangerous belief in the power of others who exude it. Failure should be on your own terms – there is nothing remotely worse than failure as a result of foolish adherence to the advice of others blindly followed in the absence of self-belief. First rule of life: follow your own heart, your own instincts. If you blow it, then you've only got yourself to blame.

Agnetha failed in Germany because she thought Dieter Zimmerman had a magic wand. As she quickly realized he didn't – or if he had he'd forgotten how to use it – they began to fight and the relationship briskly tumbled in a mire of squabbles and accusations. Their engagement was abruptly broken off and she returned home, where her reputation had been soured as an indirect consequence of the German experiment.

Stars that leave home in search of greener grass are considered fair game for a knife in the back. In later years Agnetha was to become accustomed, if never hardened, to the open warfare the Swedish press later declared on Abba in general and Agnetha in particular, but that initial backlash cut her to the quick.

Sweden at the time was up to its eyes in vigorous debate about what the people perceived as the gipsy problem. Politicians and media programmes were turning the spotlight on travellers in a big way in the wake of a series of hysterical horror stories circulating about damage, crime and general nuisance supposedly perpetrated by gipsies. This in turn produced a spirited defence of personal freedom and the alternative lifestyle chosen by the travelling community.

It was at this point that poor, unsuspecting Agnetha was relaunched in Sweden after the German disaster. By this time Agnetha had seemingly lost her grip on her own career – she'd constructed the music but not the lyrics for the song selected as the new single, a track off her second album which had obviously been written, recorded and initially released in album form long before there had been any whiff of controversy about gipsies. But, as luck would have it, the song was called 'Zigenarvan' – 'Gipsy Friend'. As soon as it was released – at the height of the gipsy controversy – all hell was let loose. Agnetha was crucified for the record. TASTELESS EXPLOITATION! CASHING IN! A SICK JOKE! The headlines roared their disapproval at a hapless Faltskog, still only twenty and totally bewildered to discover the same people who'd been loudly adoring her now suddenly pillorying her for what she saw as a gently romantic and completely innocuous ballad. Agnetha was barely aware of the gipsy thing, let alone incensed enough about it to gamble her whole career on making a political statement in a song about it.

She was distraught about the whole thing. The record was a relative failure and her image took a severe pounding. In six short months the smiling innocence of her arrival at the top of the Swedish charts had been replaced by a sullen worldliness as she lived through a lonely, humiliating failure in Germany; a difficult break-up of her engagement; and now a painful mutiny from her own ranks of fans. She'd been forced to grow up and didn't like it. Her inner paranoia surfaced and she was convinced her career was finished. She prepared to limp back to Jonkoping to lick her wounds.

It got worse before it got better. Agnetha's third album, *Som Jag Ar*, was released and the ultra-smoochy slow dance number 'Om Tarar Vore Guld' ('If Tears Were Gold') came out as the first single from it. It was a beautiful if unashamedly slushy song, which became a big hit and seemed to have restored the sensitive Agnetha to national favour. Enter Per Hvid to spoil the party.

Per Hvid was a Danish bandleader and composer who started making some very public threats about plagiarism, claiming Agnetha had stolen the main melody line from a tune he'd written a couple of decades earlier. Nobody took it too seriously, but ol' Per proved to be persistent if illogical, and was determined to drag Agnetha through the courts. Once more Agnetha was bemused. Per Hvid wasn't exactly a household name in Jonkoping and she'd never heard of the tune he reckoned she'd liberated for 'If Tears Were Gold'. Where exactly, she asked, was she supposed to have encountered this long-forgotten classic? On a tour of Sweden he performed a while back, said Per. How long a while back, enquired Agnetha. Er . . . twenty years a while back, said Per. You didn't need to be Einstein to work out the flaws in Per's case. Agnetha was supposed to have attended Per's concert, remembered one of his tunes and stored it away for use two decades later, even though she was still a babe in arms at the time. Oddly enough Per didn't manage to make his charges stick, though he was later still insistent that it was *his* handiwork behind Agnetha's voice as the gropers rose to pay their own respects to the smouldering epic at the end of a heavy night on the dance floor.

Her career was back on course. Sort of. Another big hit, 'Ta Det Bara Med Ro' ('Go Slowly') followed the 'If Tears Were Gold' case, and then there was a well-received duet with Jorgen Edman, 'Sjung Denna Sang' ('Sing This Song'). On a professional level it seemed like business as usual and Agnetha appeared to have settled for the domestic front after those shattered illusions about making it abroad. Wounds from it, though, were never far from the surface as her love life continued to let her down. She still hadn't found what she was looking for.

Bjorn and Agnetha were an ideal match. Their paths had crossed as strangers in the night on various occasions, but they got it on when they appeared together on a TV show in Stockholm. Bjorn, sensible and sensitive, offered the psychological support that Agnetha's increasingly fragile ego desperately needed. She fell in and out of love with alarming ease and habitually gravitated towards self-assured, powerful men who'd dominate and protect her. Bjorn was a solid and reliable character, who'd already been through the star trip with his group the Hootenanny Singers and so understood the pressures plaguing Agnetha; but unlike Agnetha, his own success had left him with a confidence and security about himself which she found irresistible. He excited her, he inspired her, he comforted her, he loved her without any of the mind games executed by most of her boyfriends, some of whom were in total awe of her while others treated her as a glamorous trophy on their arm.

Agnetha in turn was thrilled to be involved with somebody whose musical accomplishments outstripped her own and whom she regarded as a brilliant musician and songwriter. She never saw him competitively, instantly ready to bow to his greater experience in all matters of music and life. She had scars from her previous relationships and was well aware of her appalling track record in affairs of the heart, but couldn't help herself. Bjorn seemed to understand her . . . he was gentle and caring yet also commanding and decisive.

News of the relationship slipped out to an ecstatic press. This was Sweden's closest equivalent to rock royalty, and the country seemed to be holding its breath awaiting The Announcement as their private relationship shifted into professional. Neither Bjorn nor Agnetha actively courted such attention – they were not the two, after all, who went out partying and enjoyed seeing their pictures in the gossip columns – but equally they had the lovers' pride in their own good fortune not to have any reason to hide it. Agnetha's heart glittered on her sleeve.

They were engaged in 1970 and Bjorn duly produced Agnetha's next album, *När En Vacker Blir En Sang* (*When A Beautiful Thought Becomes A Song*), a palpable revitalization of her talents with the inclusion of several tracks co-written with Bjorn. Two of them, 'Kongens Vakt Parad' ('King's Parade') and 'Han Lamnar Mig For Att Dommer Till Dig' ('He Leaves Me To Come To You'), subsequently emerged as singles.

Agnetha was happy to be sucked into Bjorn's world of muso friends and high intellect. She trusted him absolutely and was in complete awe of his understanding of studio technique. Initially there was no thought or suggestion of twining their musical fates together and Agnetha had no intention of sacrificing her own career on behalf of Bjorn's, yet being so comprehensively in love also had the effect of dulling her own personal ambitions.

It always happens. If you're happy, you don't need any artificial stimulants like fame and glory. When somebody's done the dirty on you, the best possible therapy is to get on out there and prove yourself. Don't get mad, get ambitious.

If all the bandleaders in Denmark suddenly emerged to accuse her of plagiarism then Agnetha would smile sweetly and tell them to go take a hike. The power of love. Private nirvana. Professional disaster.

With this sort of euphoria gliding around her, if Bjorn had introduced King Kong to her as his best mate, then she wouldn't have noticed anything amiss. In this case it wasn't King Kong, but Benny Andersson, already a familiar face from his role in the Hep Stars, Sweden's very own answer to the Beatles, who had dominated the Swedish charts in the sixties. Benny was by now into the early stages of a formal partnership with her fiancé. No problem. She liked Benny. Everyone liked Benny. He was funny. He was the life and soul of the party. He was easy to get along with. And he was Bjorn's best mate. It was enough.

She wasn't quite so sure about Benny's fiancée. Anni-Frid was outgoing, friendly and funny too, but there was something about her that made Agnetha uncertain, brought out her insecurities. Agnetha had an inferiority complex which she thought long buried, but which imperceptibly nudged into view whenever Anni-Frid was around. She had all the characteristics of self-assurance and strength which Agnetha knew she herself lacked and it irritated her. She felt dull, nondescript and stupid around her.

No worries. It wasn't a problem. Frida was only Bjorn's best mate's girlfriend, after all. It wasn't as if they therefore had to be close friends too, or see each other every day, or become partners and work together, too, did it? *Did it?!?*

It did.

It was a joke at first. A one-off. The last thing anyone considered was a union as a career move – they all had, after all, their own highly successful individual careers. And not one of them imagined in their wildest dreams that any substantially grander success might be on the cards at any stage. The last thing these four sharply disparate characters figured was that it might be achievable by pooling their resources.

As chance, fate, luck, fluke would have it, the accidental linking of four individual but firmly local stars unwittingly developed into the biggest international success story of their era. And, of course, it threw Agnetha and Frida together in an intimacy that would have been unthinkable had they met in any other profession or walk of life.

For a long time their differences were smothered in the pure, simple shared joy of success. Their adventure was unprecedented, certainly in Sweden, certainly with two couples. While the girls' relationships with their respective husbands blossomed, they had more than enough fulfilment not to bother unduly about the tensions between them. But once they'd visited every country in the world, once they'd had Number Ones from Arbroath to Argentina, once they'd sold out the biggest concert halls in Christendom and fun had given way to the constant gruelling grind of their work schedule . . . that's when individual foibles came bursting to the surface like ugly cold sores.

Agnetha's inferiority complex rose once more like a

colossus to sour her attitude to the group as a whole, and Frida in particular. The wholesomeness of the imagery which they'd carried with them since Brighton merely provoked her agitation further – there's nothing worse than being unhappy, except pretending you're not. The gradual decline of her marriage to Bjorn mirrored her sinking morale and fading self-confidence. She was riddled with insecurity, illness and guilt about whether or not she was a good mother. Suddenly the Abba camp was an awkward mess of rows and backbiting.

Frida was never one to swallow her tongue, and reacted angrily to what she saw as Agnetha's whingeing and sniping. Stories emerged of their eternal battles, mostly verbal, but a few of them physical. Once after an awards ceremony Agnetha and Frida were reputed to have been slugging one another with gold discs. And still they had to smile and present themselves as the perfect family group with unblemished reputations – shining examples of the modern happy family, and role models for the new Europe. That's a dangerous time bomb to have ticking away in your pocket.

And yet Agnetha and Frida's relationship represented the very crux of the world's infatuation with Abba. Probably it started as a mainly male obsession, but women too were to become engrossed in the Great Abba Intrigue surrounding the Blonde One and the Other One. The Blonde One was, of course, everybody's Nordic ideal with her flowing blonde hair and fresh-faced beauty . . . the very essence of health and efficiency. Let us not forget she also had the finest bum on God's earth.

The Other One was in popular public perception cast as the baddie in the partnership. All devastating twosomes are required by convention to have a goodie and a baddie.

Anything resembling an equal partnership provides an irresistible opportunity for observers to take sides and pitch one against the other. John versus Paul. Jimmy Page versus Robert Plant. Nigel Benn versus Chris Eubank. Pinky versus Perky. Likewise you couldn't possibly be a fan of Elvis Presley *and* Cliff Richard. Or Bjorn Borg *and* John McEnroe. Or Ayrton Senna *and* Alain Prost. Or Robert de Niro *and* Al Pacino. Sides, always sides. It only works when the cards are evenly stacked and the competition is fair. You couldn't pitch Mick Jagger against Keith Richards because they never competed for our attention – Keith knew his place and was a knowing complement to Mick's craven narcissism. And you couldn't play Bjorn against Benny because while musically they *were* Abba, they silently acknowledged – and possibly fostered – the deal whereby the whole image of the group rested on them as secondary to the glamour on the front line. And those up front giving good glamour had to be played off against one another in the public perception – that was the only way it could work.

Frida held a deeper mystique and certainly had her own fan club in the Abba beauty debate, but human nature being what it is, most people grabbed the obvious option in the alternative and struck out for the World's Greatest Bum. Even had Agnetha and Frida been soul sisters with ne'er a cross word or an ounce of jealousy between them, such a weighted public view was bound to have strained their relationship. As it happened they had nothing in common and didn't like each other at all, and allowed themselves to be dragged along with the game without revealing in public a single chink in the idyllic veneer that was deemed essential to the Abba myth. Even so, Bjorn and Benny made absolutely sure the two women got an equal number of lead vocals on every album and had an equal share of the spotlight on gigs and in videos to keep the peace. Maybe, just maybe, they would have garnered more credibility had Agnetha's fierce temper and Frida's impatience been exposed to public gaze; but then the very coldness and refrigerated formality of the partnership provided its own enticement.

The way the videos interminably focused on the two girls close up led to many assumptions. Agnetha and Frida eyeball to eyeball. Agnetha and Frida back to back and (the perverts fondly imagined) rubbing bottoms. Agnetha and Frida dancing. Smiling. Laughing. Winking. Agnetha and Frida. Team Abba. Were they? Could they possibly be? Surely? They *must* be!?!

The guys at the bar downing their lager tops were insistent on the Great Abba debate. The Blonde One and the Other One were lesbians. Had to be. There was a sexual chemistry between them that could only be explained in the bedroom. It was the perfect solution. The guys at the bar were convinced about it. They were making it together and – the icing on the cake – they were screwing each other's husbands too. At the same time.

Regrettably none of it was true. Agnetha was too soppy about men to have the remotest lesbian inclination and Frida would no sooner have kissed Agnetha than gone to bed with a duck-billed platypus. But these were the perverted fantasies that gripped the pubs of Europe beyond the immaculate gloss of the Abba machine. Just as men fantasize about posh well-bred Roedean girls suddenly downing spectacles, bunned hair and knickers and turning into raving nymphomaniacs, so the country craved for real people beneath the unyielding correctness. Not a platitude out of place in their interviews. Not a dab of make-up smudged on their faces. Not a note out of tune in their singing. Fabulous melodies and sweet harmonies were the cornerstone of Abba's enduring appeal, but surely they were people too? Didn't they ever get the urge to launch into 'Why Don't We Do It In The Road?' in the middle of 'Fernando'? Weren't they suddenly overwhelmed with the desire to leap from their security blanket and start stuffing microphones down throats when asked the inevitable question about babies and their hairdos at those awful, embarrassing press conferences? Hadn't they any inclination to throw televisions out of windows and gob at doormen when they arrived at a posh hotel in another foreign town which they would never get to see?

Yep, but we never saw it. They argued. They fought. They laughed like drains. They got unspeakably drunk. They told bad jokes. They played practical jokes on waiters. They swore. They slammed the phone down on nuisance callers. They had hangovers. They looked awful in the mornings. They belched. They sat on the toilet. They were just like everyone else.

But you'd never have believed it. You were never allowed to believe it. And so you had to invent your own scenario.

Agnetha and Frida had an unspoken agreement to hide their differences and perpetuate the myth. Time after time they swallowed their pride, bit their tongues and got the hell on with it. They'd somehow convinced themselves it was worth it. But they were never sure.

4

GIMME! GIMME! GIMME!

'There's not a soul out there, no one to hear my prayer'

'Gimme! Gimme! Gimme! (A Man After Midnight)'

It was pushing midnight when Abba tumbled wearily off the plane at Arlanda Airport on that chilly Thursday night in 1974.

The effect of anti-climax on the emotions is underestimated. The low after the high can chill you to your bones in the traditional empty manner of cold turkey drug withdrawal. Agnetha had been rudely reminded exactly how much she hated flying, while Benny and Anni-Frid sat on the plane engrossed in a therapeutic game of chess.

For five days they'd been drinking champagne. For five days they'd been treated like royalty. For five days they'd been trailed by press and television and revealed the answers to everything from their favourite singers (Stevie Wonder, Stevie Wonder, John Lennon, Stevie Wonder) to favourite TV programmes (*Monty Python*, documentaries, adverts, anything with Stevie Wonder) to sexual habits (pass, best bum in the world, pass, Stevie Wonder) to food and drink (yes please, as often as possible). For five days they'd been lords of the universe, beyond time, sleep, age and all mortal reality.

It seemed to them the world had been halted in mid-spin while all heads turned in their direction to applaud, admire and adore. Surely nothing else could possibly be going on in the world while they were receiving this sort of attention. They glided from Brighton to London in a haze of euphoria. Life was a mesmerizing transportation from one media shindig to another; one bottle of champagne to the next. They couldn't sleep, they had no need for such trifles in the haphazard whirl of snatched conversations whizzing round befuddled brains and smiles comprehensively superglued to their faces.

They were wined and dined by their record company, fêted by fast-talking strangers with satin tour jackets and sub-human egos who wouldn't have bid them good morning had faceless juries from Holland, Germany and Monaco not awarded them '*douze points*' in Brighton. Most of those doing the fêting weren't really anticipating having to bid them good morning for too long. This was the way of things with Eurovision winners. All good, clean, stupid fun. A chance to get one trivial pop record away into the charts, a shortlived celebrity status for the lucky winners, a few bob in the bank for all concerned, and goodnight Irene. Don't knock it. A painless diversion from the arduous toil of breaking bands on endless route marches around the country, and winning Eurovision had to be better than not winning Eurovision. A lucrative belt of fun, but once 'Waterloo' had keeled over and died six weeks on, Abba's name would be consigned to the netherworld of triv quizzes and Eurovision history. 'Mabel, what *was* the name of that funny Scandinavian band who wore those stupid pant suits at the Eurovision Song Contest that time?'

Such thoughts may have begun to sift into Abba's

consciousness as they flew out of London four days after Eurovision. They broke the trip home to stop off at Hamburg for yet another performance of 'Waterloo' on yet another TV show and somehow the magic was broken. As they hit the plane afterwards for the home-coming to Stockholm, they felt reality returning and exhaustion began to set in.

Stig Anderson only ever saw Brighton and Eurovision as the beginning, but it was hard to counter the unspoken assumption of the entire music world that this was where it all began, started and finished. There was no precedent for a previously unknown Eurovision winner to sustain an international career on the back of it. Not unless you count Dana from Ireland, who drifted into a comfortable career as a female Cliff Richard doing God spots and Christmas singles, but she had a gap in her front teeth and a ready audience in women's magazines. Old Jean Claude Pascal from Luxembourg didn't exactly keep the juke boxes swallowing coins after his triumph in 1961, did he? And where is the Dutchman Teddy Scholten (1959 winner) now? Or the Austrian Udo Jurgens (1966)? Even gorgeous little Gigliola Cinquetti from Italy (the 1964 winner) was forced into a Eurovision return ten years later in search of glories past. Few ignominies can be greater than having to represent your country in the wretched contest *twice*.

So nobody outside the Abba camp believed they had a serious international life beyond 'Waterloo'. But Stikkan Anderson, he believed. He *always* believed. There was not the slightest, tiniest, minutest *crumb* of a scrap of doubt in his mind. Abba were his destiny. He didn't know it when he started, but they were the golden carrot that had lured him into this whole thankless business in the first place.

He just knew it. He knew it after Brighton. He knew it before Brighton. He knew it the previous year when those prats on the selection committee had voted against 'Ring Ring' in the '73 Eurovision qualifying competition. There was just no talking to him about it. He knew Abba were it, and he'd move heaven and earth and a whole lot more besides to make it happen with them.

And people listened to him. Stig was no fly-by-night kid fuelled on personal ambition, outrageous ego and dodgy white powder. He was a primary school teacher from Hova, a tiny town close to the banks of Lake Vanern, 200 kilometres southwest of Stockholm. He left school at thirteen and went to work for the local athletic club, but while this was in the fifties, pre-Beatles, pre-Elvis, pre-Buddy Holly, pre-*everything*, he still felt the beginnings of something gnawing at his soul, slowly but surely taking an iron grip on his whole being. Hova wasn't exactly a hotbed of music, but Stig felt an unreal surge of excitement and anticipation whenever he got within several hundred yards of a real live instrument or something came on the radio.

When the whole rock 'n' roll type thang began to take shape, Stig was off and running like a bat out of hell. His first band was called Stig Anderson and His Mashed Creampuffs. History, sadly, sheds no light on the artistic strengths of this imaginatively titled little combo – and Stig isn't volunteering too much information on the subject these days – but we confidently imagine they'd blow your socks off.

In time he found a more natural niche for himself as a songwriter. He wrote songs fast and often, with the brash fearlessness of a stunt rider taking on a parade of double-decker buses. None of your sentimental clichés in Stig's couplets – his songs were bright, vivid, imaginative, daring and funny, if a little too racily eccentric for mass consumption. The hit of his youthful enterprise was a cryptically knowing little ditty called 'The Girls Who Know Are Found In The Country', though through the sixties and seventies he estimates he wrote something like 2,000 song lyrics. But not all of them were as meaningful as 'The Girls Who Know Are Found In The Country'.

Restless, impatient, ambitious, incautious . . . Stig could never be content with parochial when he knew national was up for grabs. And he certainly wouldn't settle for national when there was international just around the corner. And what's the use of international when there's global a couple of steps ahead? Stig wrote his songs in English because nobody ever got to be a millionaire catering just for Sweden. You feel you need to be a millionaire to live there sometimes, but Stig hungrily eyed the big, wide world from the outset, even before anyone started taking him seriously.

His first big success, in 1959, 'Rockin' Billy', gave him golden records not only in all the Nordic countries, but also in Holland. At the time he was teaching, but he decided to publish this song himself since he had written both the music and the lyrics and he placed it with different Scandinavian artists. So, all of a sudden, and quite unintentionally, he was in the music publishing business.

He named the company, with admirable grandeur and self-importance, Sweden Music. Head office was in his tiny kitchen, but hell, Trivial Pursuit started with a couple of broke, starving Canadians trying to stave off total ruination with increasing desperation in a front room, and in due course, Stig Anderson's kitchen publishing company became the root for the richest, most profitable empire in the history of pop music. Life's funny like that.

From Sweden Music, Stig set up Polar Music three years later, met Bjorn and then Benny, started writing with them and then began the whole colossal avalanche that was Abba.

If the truth be told, in the Abba camp only Stig truly believed there was life after Eurovision. Bjorn, Benny, Agnetha and Anni-Frid were living in faith and blind hope, but if they searched their hearts thoroughly they didn't seriously believe for one second that 'Waterloo' was but the prelude for countless glories to come. This was it, for the members of the group. International acclaim. London. Fame all over Europe. An instant hit in a dozen different countries that they'd never visit. Champagne on tap. *Anything* on tap, if they'd wanted it. This was it, all right. The summation of their wildest ambitions. For fifteen minutes.

Now, perhaps, time was being called on that fifteen minutes. Agnetha was sick, they all suddenly felt dog tired and a strange flat calm descended over them, like the pain of real life kicking them in the upper groin as the plane hit the tarmac in Stockholm. It was cold and late and there was no welcoming committee cheering their triumphant homecoming, no waving crowds lining the streets, no hordes of kids demanding locks of hair and autographs. The party was over.

They just quietly sloped back to their Stockholm flats. Agnetha and Bjorn back for a long, reassuring cuddle with baby Linda and straight to bed; Benny and Anni-Frid to a measured reconstruction of the week's extraordinary events and the by now customary bottle of champagne before bedtime. Fame always rested more comfortably on the Andersson-Lyngstad part of the equation than it did on family Ulvaeus.

Morning came for all of them with all the classic hangover symptoms . . . and their headaches were to last for several months as the awkward practicalities of being public property came to haunt them. It was one thing being godlike in your own country, it was quite another to be nearly godlike and potential has-beens in the rest of the world, all in the same breath. They already had reasonable careers in their own right pre-Eurovision and they had to decide whether the demands and sacrifices necessary to keep the momentum going beyond Eurovision, with no real probability of coming up trumps, would actually be worthwhile. Agnetha, for one, a joyful and devoted mother, was uncertain; Bjorn was happier planning the strategy rather than actually doing it; Anni-Frid wanted it *all*; and Benny went with the flow.

In the event there wasn't time to even question it. As far as Stig was concerned there were no decisions to be made. They'd finally reached first base and there was to be no stopping now. Stig created such a frenzy of activity and excitement in his planning that the band were swept up in it, barely questioning the absurd rush of promotional activity being asked of them. They just kept on smiling and wearing whichever barmy outfit they laid hands on; and with each dumb answer to each dumb question fired at them in a succession of languages, any remnants of possible musical credibility slipped through their fingers.

'Waterloo' duly sold a million in 1974 and Stig went into overdrive, sending Abba on a fleeting visit to the States where the record eventually snuck up to Number Six during a four-month run in the charts. This *and* a chart-topper right across Europe – even by normal

Eurovision winner standards this was a biggie. Yet still nobody really expected them to hang around too long to enjoy the spoils, least of all the Swedish press.

The Swedish satisfaction at having taken on the rest of Europe and swept the floor with the Brits at their own game in their own back yard was displaced by a weird sort of collective snobbery about Abba's success. While the Hep Stars – Benny's band – and the Hootenanny Singers – Bjorn's – and Agnetha and Anni-Frid were having huge local hits every day of the week they were canonized by the Swedish media, however crappy the records may have been. But one half-decent hit single in the UK, Germany, USA and every damn place else and suddenly they were seen to be heaping international embarrassment on the country. Sure, it was those costumes doing the serious damage here – and the Swedes had a point – but in the absence of any previous major pop breakthrough (unless you count the Spotniks, whose version of 'Orange Blossom Special' scraped into the British Top Thirty in 1962) a little more pride might have been in order.

But in an interesting form of inverted elitism that is by no means exclusive to Sweden, Abba were scorned for having the temerity to be successful abroad where they'd been widely admired for being successful at home. Now they'd made it internationally – however shortlived this might prove to be – they were considered fair game. No great national pride was taken in Abba in these fraught early days of their fame – or at any period in their lifetime as a band, come to that. Once they stopped doing it, of course, it was all very different again and the name Abba is to be breathed only in hushed, reverential tones with the word 'fabulous' statutorily prefixed before their name. But way back when, the snipers were off and running from day one. It hurt them, too. They had enough credibility problems with the national comics laying into them at every conceivable opportunity.

Stig was particularly outraged. 'If we were English we'd be getting honours from the Queen by now,' he said at one point, 'but in Sweden they don't like you to be successful.' It was the start of a long-running local feud between Abba and the press, who were quick to tease and parody, but almost pathological in their reluctance to offer any praise. It wound Stig up enormously – his pride in the Abba beast was such that it withstood no carping.

The basic argument the papers had with Abba was over political unsoundness. Stig's undisguised passion for the big, bad commercial world and all the capitalist values it embraces clashed violently with the left-wing viewpoints being widely embraced in Sweden in the seventies.

The . . . erm . . . *undemanding* lyrics provided by Stig and Bjorn fuelled the scorn directed at them in an age where the country's youth demanded social awareness and appropriately antagonistic lyrics. Protest song and the avant-garde were also in vogue at the time and the lightweight pop of the Abba sound was seen to be an insult to society. The press had no qualms about saying as much and Abba and their manager stood accused of empty-headed greed. It might have been more fitting for the students who shaped this argument to stand accused of being cultural morons, but there you go.

Abba were unlucky that their international break-through coincided with a stringent re-examination of Sweden's own social values. Student revolts of 1968 had a knock-on effect of rejecting established teenage culture and a snowballing socialist music movement arose from left-wing youth organizations sprouting up all over

Europe. International solidarity movements organized demonstrations against American warfare in Indochina, and there were plenty of local causes to campaign against. One of them was pop music. The whole pop circus was seen as a brainwashing exercise conspiring to rob youth of opinion and individuality. Even while Abba were preparing for their first assault on Eurovision in '73 there was a growing body of opinion in direct and bitter opposition to the values it and they were to come to represent.

There were protests and demonstrations aimed at the crass 'Teenage Fair' in Stockholm and local music societies – Music Fora – were set up throughout Sweden to combat the vacuous evils of pop idolatry and plan a long-term strategy under the umbrella of a movement they called Kontaknatet.

The mood of rebellion swept the nation. The most active of pop's opponents set up their own 'anti-commercial' independent labels like Musiknatet Waxholm, Silence and Nacksving, all receiving substantial support in their avowed policy of using all profits from their best-selling records to finance other more worthy, politically correct and culturally motivated work. Successful rock bands like the Hoola Bandoola Band and Nationalteatern emerged from the movement which also ran its own record distribution companies and even its own magazine, *Musikens Makt* (*The Power of Music*).

Musical styles previously on the fringe like jazz, blues, reggae and avant-garde classical were suddenly propelled to the forefront of public consciousness and the pure pop songs tumbling out of Stig's Polar label courtesy of Bjorn and Benny could scarcely have been considered more unfashionable given the rise of the new breed of right-on heroes like the experimental Samla Mammas Manna, blues star Peps Blodsband, musos Jan Hammarlund and Fria Proteatern, and a whole stable of folk-rockers, Arbete & Fritid, Kebnekaise, and Norrlatar.

Swedish culture and Swedish lyrics were backed to the hilt by this movement, which even spilled into national radio resulting in a significant reduction of pure pop music being played and a rule that only original Swedish compositions would be included on the hugely popular *Svensktoppen* show. This form of cultural culling reached its peak with Abba's triumph in Brighton – the country's guardians of aural quality dominated to such an extent that no newspaper or magazine went with Abba to England to follow their fortunes at first hand. Even in their hour of triumph it went on . . . some journalist called Stig in his Brighton hotel room from Stockholm making charges of tastelessness against him for using the imagery of a war in which 40,000 people were killed for their stupid song. Somebody else was on the line accusing Benny of stealing the 'Waterloo' melody from the Foundations' 'Build Me Up Buttercup'.

Both received very short shrift from Stig, acerbic at the best of times and in this, his moment of glory, beyond reasoned argument on either matter. He slammed down the phone and laughed like a drain, but the mood of sniping at Abba's achievements was to continue right through the early years of Abba's career. There was a storm of protest against Sweden staging Eurovision the following year in the normal custom of the contest – a protest that had the support of many Swedish TV executives who were sympathetic to the accusations about it being a mass exercise in crassness and in any case felt they were totally ill-equipped to handle such a huge technically demanding occasion. In the end the Swedes did their duty and duly staged Eurovision '75, though it was held side by side with a vigorously supported 'Alternative Festival Song Contest' held in direct opposition.

The press didn't have to wait long for the opportunity to turn on Abba with all guns blazing. The group had been advertised to do the usual two-month stint on the Swedish folk-park circuit in the summer of '74, just as they had all been doing in their individual private lives for the past few years. The folk-parks are a summer institution in Sweden involving open variety shows up and down the country, but one look at the messages and offers on the table back at Polar immediately persuaded Stig to take folk-parks off the itinerary. Holland, Germany, the USA, Australia, Japan, albums, singles, international tours, promo visits . . . this was the future, not trudging up and down Sweden banging out dance music for pocket money in some obscure country town on a bill with middle-aged orchestras and cute teenage starlets.

None of the group argued with him and Stig cancelled the folk-parks. All hell broke loose. Abba were letting the fans down, they were letting their country down, they'd got big time about it all, they were worthy only of abuse and contempt. In a way they were right. They *were* getting big time and quite rightly so . . . it was the only way. Had they fulfilled their obligation to the folk-park tour the Swedish press would still have played merry hell with them and their credibility as potential international stars would have been left irreversibly in tatters.

Such logic cut no ice, though, with their own press, now on a runaway crusade of anti-Abba propaganda. Turncoats! Traitors! Greedy! Selfish! Immoral! Thoughtless! Unreliable! But who cares, they're rubbish anyway, right? There was talk of legal action against them and all manner of emotional blackmail about the legions of broken-hearted fans left twiddling their thumbs up and down the country waiting to welcome their heroes.

None of which cowed Stig Anderson, now with the bit firmly between his teeth. 'Working for small fees in the folk-parks while Europe is waiting to be conquered just doesn't make sense,' said Stig baldly. Abba pulled out and, almost to add insult to injury, Stig arranged for the group to be replaced on the tour by Mouth & McNeal, the Dutch duo they'd vanquished at Eurovision. And that was that, though Abba carried resentment with them for several years afterwards and the group themselves – less convinced than Stig that Europe was ready to roll over and have its tummy tickled – were privately concerned about burning their domestic boats in the search for something grander which there were no guarantees that they'd find. The cautious Agnetha was specially concerned about the way they appeared to be risking everything they'd achieved already in this search for the holy grail. But she saw the crescent while Stig saw the whole of the moon.

Stig did make one conciliatory gesture, promising Abba would be back to fulfil their obligations to the folk-park circuit the following year – and they did, though it was very much on their own terms. Delayed by another of Agnetha's recurring illnesses, it turned into more of a triumphal march around Sweden than a traditional folk-park event, with Stig demanding – and getting – a major slice of the box office. He argued his corner eloquently enough and the tour was ultimately considered a great success, but it didn't prevent the flak flying.

'Waterloo' went on to sell nearly six million copies and

was a hit in virtually every country in Europe, as well as America and Australia. Abba found themselves on that mad roller coaster of television shows, interviews and other promotional activities in a succession of faceless cities and incomprehensible languages. It was exciting and it was fun. They scarcely had time to draw breath, let alone worry about the folk-parks, or the press . . . or *where the next hit was coming from*.

This was crucial. Some interviewer posed the question in the lounge of a hotel in London. 'How are you going to follow up "Waterloo"?' Here was the most vexed question of them all. All their dreams and Stig's plans hung on that very point – how *do* you follow up a record that has sold six million copies?

Pop history is littered with colossal sellers, *classics* even, creating a standard of sales or quality that proves too intimidating to emulate. Norman Greenbaum, 1970, 'Spirit In The Sky'. What a record *that* was! But who the hell was Norman Greenbaum? Where on God's earth did he come from? And more significantly, where did he *go* to? Who knows? We certainly don't. All we can tell you is that ol' Norm came from Boston and once fronted a group called Eggplant, which is more than anyone needs to know about Norman Greenbaum. 'Spirit In The Sky', though, remains one of the greatest pop records of all time. Don't argue, it *is*.

The Greenbaum effect is a recurring one. Men At Work. Had a smash in nineteen continents playing professional Aussies with 'Down Under', but could they come up with anything remotely as good or commercial afterwards? Nope, nope, nope. Who else? Ken Boothe and 'Everything I Own'. Mr Bachman, Mr Turner and Mr Overdrive and 'You Ain't Seen Nothing Yet'. Terry

Jacks and 'Seasons In The Sun'. Kajagoogoo and 'Too Shy'. Procol Harum and 'A Whiter Shade Of Pale'. Scott McKenzie and 'San Francisco'. And going further back . . . Unit 4 Plus 2 and 'Concrete And Clay', Peter & Gordon and 'World Without Love'.

The same old story. Every musician has one smash hit in them, just like everybody has one novel in them. Same as the second-album syndrome. You spend all your life going through the experiences that combine to produce the material on a brilliant first album . . . and five minutes coming up with equally powerful material to follow it up.

The popular method of following the impossible in the old days was simply to take the formula that had achieved success in the first place and copy it exactly. Just change the words around a bit and maybe switch a couple of the notes in the chorus and trust there to be enough clout in the image and the voice to see it through. It was a lazy theory – why change a winning formula? If people liked it that much to buy it in droves in the first place, then they'd be perfectly happy to buy it again . . . just as long as you disguised it superficially enough to fool them into believing what they were getting was development and progression rather than a shameless action replay. It was also a theory born out of desperation – contrary to popular belief most bands in the sixties didn't have an original thought in their head and were incapable of coming up with anything different, in which case plagiarizing themselves was a useful method of buying time to keep the name around long enough to enable somebody to come up with an exciting new scam.

It was a problem that suddenly hit Abba hard when the reporters started asking them about follow-ups. Apart from the folk-parks, Bjorn and Benny had a series of pre-

Eurovision studio commitments booked for Polar. They were heavily involved in producing an album for Ted Gardestad, now a big star in Sweden, as well as an album for Benny's old Hep Stars partner Svenne Hedlund, now recording with his wife Lotta. These weren't involvements to be tossed into the air like the folk-parks tour – Bjorn and Benny had seen writing and production as the future and were realistic enough to believe that this still might be the case, however much Stig insisted otherwise. The studio was the one domain they took seriously above all others, and they prided themselves on their professionalism and technique. They'd been anxious to build up their reputations in the studio and besides, these were their friends who were working with them – they weren't about to sell themselves or anybody else short on this one.

Fine, but it didn't leave them a great deal of time to come up with a new blockbuster to match 'Waterloo' and stuff everybody's 'one-hit wonder' jibes back down their throats and perpetuate Stig's plans to conquer the world. They had enough material in hand to polish up and rush out the *Waterloo* album in 1974 which did well enough without giving any serious indication of the riches in store.

It remains a curious mismatch of material, including discarded attempts at creating something Eurovision-friendly like 'Hasta Manana', a couple of Beach Boys homages, 'Suzy Hang-Around' and 'King Kong Song', and a smattering of the totally bizarre, like 'What About Livingstone?' along with the previous year's failed Eurovision attempt 'Ring Ring'. It did, though, inspire that age-old practice of the cover version – their 'Honey Honey', being released by a little-known English duo, Sweet Dreams, reached the British Top 10 and reassured

Bjorn and Benny that *somebody* thought there was life after 'Waterloo'.

It didn't solve the problem of the all-important follow-up. There were one or two desultory attempts to get the muse off and running in chart mode and a lot of silly ideas were broached. You can imagine it. 'Hey guys, I got it, let's do a love song about . . . *Agincourt*. Or hey, what about *Trafalgar*? Benny could have a patch over his eye and an admiral's hat on and pretend he was Nelson.'

Ultimately, in Britain and several other countries, at least, they went with 'Ring Ring'. Stig had an unreasonable faith in the song despite its stigma of failure. It had topped the charts in Sweden and Stig had invested a lot of money, time and effort in the song in the conviction that this would be the track to get them away. Neil Sedaka and Phil Cody had been rowed in to provide the English lyrics and, largely on that basis, had got a British release through Epic. The single flopped miserably, though it did chart in several countries, including South Africa and Australia, and Stig remained convinced that 'Ring Ring' was a smash hit given the right conditions. And what better conditions could there be than coming in off the back of a six-million-selling single? There may also have been a sense of vengeance in his thinking – the original decision of the Swedish Eurovision jury to reject the song in 1973 still rankled and Stig couldn't resist one more stab at rubbing their noses further in it. Besides, Stig figured, the vague familiarity that accompanied 'Ring Ring' through its previous release would surely make it easier for radio stations to latch on to it and audiences to sing along with it, especially given a brand, spanking new re-mix. The theory sounded fine . . .

Less than a month after 'Waterloo' had finally departed

the charts, 'Ring Ring' limped into view to replace it. It stumbled at No. 32 in the British charts and limped away again in disgrace. In the States they went with 'Honey Honey' and that didn't exactly set the world on fire either. They briefly went into the studio to record some fresh material and came out with 'So Long', a feisty bopper which Bjorn and Benny were particularly pleased with and which they felt confident would shock people out of their Eurovision preconceptions and give them a big, fat, juicy Top Tenner. Nobody gave it the time of day and 'So Long' didn't trouble the chart compilers *anywhere*. The gloomiest predictions about one-hit wonders appeared alarmingly real.

Still they had little time to reverse the decline. Stig was adamant that to maintain the momentum of 'Waterloo' they had to hit Europe with a concert tour, and he wasn't talking Swedish folk-parks. It was to be a tour befitting their new status the like of which they'd never undertaken before, involving huge lighting rigs, massive PAs, an army of roadies, and a gigantic financial gamble. Anni-Frid and Agnetha were dispatched for dancing lessons and Bjorn and Benny locked themselves away working on new material and rehearsing their band for their first major tour.

It started in front of a full house in Copenhagen on 17 November 1974 . . . and went downhill from there on. The sweep of hits Stig had anticipated following 'Waterloo' and leading into the tour just hadn't happened; widespread apathy and cynicism began to seep through and the grand concert halls that had been booked for them at various cities through Austria, Germany and Switzerland seemed hopelessly ambitious. Stig's original gameplan had been to climax the tour with five triumphant Christmas concerts in London, but it rapidly became obvious that this was disastrously fanciful. Six months on from Brighton and they were already a footnote in pop history as far as English audiences were concerned – they'd be lucky to pull enough people to justify one night at a pub in Hammersmith, let alone five nights at a prestigious concert hall like Hammersmith Odeon. The English leg of the tour was put on ice for a while. Quite a long while, as it turned out.

It all inevitably fuelled the tensions in the band, magnifying the teething troubles on the tour and the considerable problems they were facing as a band adapting into a full-blown rock outfit, with all the showbiz trickery and electric stage presence this requires.

At this point they still harboured pretensions of being good, cred rockers and the guys, especially, felt disgruntled by the images of bland pop they were being saddled with . . . though having agreed to go to Brighton in those costumes it's difficult to see why. When Abba went on the road it was a band ill at ease with itself, unsure of its direction or destiny. They thought of themselves as a rock 'n' roll band, but they were easily tempted by the great prostitute of commercialism and the pull of their marketing machine was difficult to resist. And so they set foot on the road with yet another wardrobe of daft costumes, all skin-tight pants, satin flares, ludicrous platform boots, glittery tops, white miniskirts and acres of flesh. Every perceived ingredient of excitement wrapped into one wardrobe.

None of them were natural stage performers, either. Agnetha was the best – she was acutely aware of the sly grins, the provocative pouts and the sidelong glances that seduced audiences. Anni-Frid froze on stage – awkward, wooden and stilted and the most ungainly dancer this side of Nellie the Elephant, though she learnt to overcome it and eventually became the best stage performer of them all. At the death she was the only one who enjoyed live performance at all. Benny sailed through it with his customary carelessness, but Bjorn went through his paces with evident discomfort. They were to learn and they got better, but Abba's forte was never live performance, and a few nights into that premier tour and they began to believe it.

It was a difficult time for them. The euphoria of Brighton and the hilarious fun-filled round of promotional romps round Europe now seemed like another life. Suddenly the jackpot they'd just won on the one-armed bandit looked more and more like fools' gold. The drudgery they'd come to accept as an occasional by-product of their work now began to dominate their days, feeding the frustrations and resentments that were to explode in their faces every time they attempted a tour, and which is one reason they were to risk it so rarely.

They split the tour into two parts to allow time to stay at home for Christmas and returned, refreshed, to play for more enthusiastic Scandinavian audiences where their following wasn't governed so exclusively by 'Waterloo' and its subsequent offshoots. They played the Stockholm Concert Hall and sold it out, winning an ecstatic ovation with their slicker – though dangerously contrived – show. Their beleaguered morale took some encouragement from the Scandinavian concerts, but they were still crucified by most of the press reviews, which spotlighted their stage-managed hysteria, twee choruses and facile lyrics as damning evidence of their overall uselessness.

British and American critics pride themselves on their skill at sticking the knife in, but they're pussycats compared with the Swedish crucifixion of Abba. 'Abba,' declared one writer, 'are as dead as a herring.' This coming just a few months after they'd topped the charts in almost every country in Europe.

'Deplorable . . .', 'meaningless . . .', 'emptyheaded and devoid of opinions . . .', 'plastic . . .', 'moneygrabbing . . .', 'stupid beyond belief . . .', 'the best thing about them is Agnetha's bottom . . .' The insults flew thick and fast in their direction. The more militant of their opponents even made the sinister allegation that they were actively *dangerous* in promoting vacuous images and putting daft romantic ideas into kids' heads. Yeah, they shot JFK as well.

That's critics for you. They think of a witty one-liner on the way to the gig and build the rest of the review around it. The press had presented a united front in their Abba-baiting, and in such a unilateral declaration of enmity few journalists are going to break ranks.

Despite a few small battles won, the war appeared to be a rout of Abba. Bjorn and Benny began to take an interest in their independent studio projects again, Agnetha absorbed herself in motherhood, and Anni-Frid wondered about a solo album. It had been a gas, but it wasn't happening. It really wasn't happening. Not in the greater picture. They could see it. The press could see it. Their various record companies could certainly see it. Stig never saw it.

Stig's belief that Abba were on the verge of becoming something wholly extraordinary was unshakable. He told everyone he met that Abba would be the biggest band in the world. They laughed at him, so he told them again.

Louder. Few people argued with Stig when he talked louder.

The first episode of Operation World Domination hadn't gone well. Okay, so 'Waterloo' had become a full-blown phenomenon and their bank balances were grinning handsomely back at them, but it felt like they were taking two hard-earned steps forward for every three wind-assisted leaps backward. They were shocked by the amount of vitriol and jealousy flying around their heads at this level of fame. Gentle Scandinavian superstardom in their youth had not prepared them for the volume of hatred you inspire just by being *known* around the rest of the world . . . and they certainly hadn't expected the scorn being heaped on them by newspapers and magazines which had previously been metaphorically sucking their toes at every available opportunity.

Stig, anxious to keep the ball rolling, wanted them back on the road at the earliest opportunity, but the others wouldn't hear of it. This last tour had been a chastening experience and another one in the immediate future would have been over Agnetha's dead body. There were times when the other three thought that might not be a bad arrangement, but Bjorn was insistent that the answers lay with Benny's blossoming flair in the studio. Jolted by the unexpected failure of 'So Long', they resolved that at the very least the whole world now knew who they were and the only way they would live down 'Waterloo' would be to come up with a whole bunch of material that was better.

So Bjorn and Benny, joined by Stig whenever he could manage it, buried themselves away on Viggso, one of the mesmerizing network of islands surrounding Stockholm, and their professional equivalent of the treehouse in the garden where kids retreat to do their homework and dust down their thoughts in times of stress. Viggso was Abba's escape valve and became their creative nerve centre with the Ulvaeus-Andersson team hunched around a piano for hours on end plotting lethal melodies. Eventually they were forced out of Viggso by persistent fans and nosy journalists but found a new hideaway on another island further out.

For now, though, they retreated to Viggso. Bjorn and Benny slobbed around, cracked open a bottle of Scotch, chainsmoked, talked and knuckled down to it. There was nothing for them to do but work. Which was just as well. If there was a single distraction in the area, then you could bet your last dollar that Benny would find it. The only time he felt truly fulfilled was sat in front of a piano and he loved to come to the island, where he could pursue his passionate love affair without interference or explanation or bills or nagging women or nagging record companies. It was heaven. Just Benny, with Bjorn – unshaven and proud of it – egging him on, nudging him in the right direction, shaping and polishing and chipping away at the tunes until they were ready to emerge, gleaming, and he could set about the more gruelling task of applying words to them.

Different strokes for different folks, but for somebody who resisted it and refused to acknowledge its existence during practically every aspect of his professional life, pressure had a startlingly creative effect on Benny. The flops had a more stimulating impact than any of the successes, focusing his mind and developing his crafts-manship. And if Benny is a craftsman, then Bjorn is his workmate doubling as foreman.

Benny and Bjorn duly started pulling out the aces

during those slovenly weeks out in Viggso in the early days of '75, and pieced together the songs that would combine to create the album they titled – with stunning imagination – *Abba*. One of the first things they put together was 'Bang-A-Boomerang', a song even dafter than 'Waterloo' which read and sounded like a Eurovision parody . . . and which they wrote and produced specifically for their old friends Svenne & Lotta Hedlund to have a go at Eurovision in '75. It was a joke. We *hope* it was a joke. But, blessed with the Abba magic, how could it fail? 'Bang-A-Boomerang' duly won the Swedish nomination – was there any doubt – but failed to impress the voting panels when the Stockholm finals took place. After all, wasn't the thumping 'Waterloo' designed to get rid of all the boom-bang-a-bang garbage that had previously littered Eurovision? Er . . . no. Eurovision '75 was won by something Dutch and something dreadful called 'Ding Ding A Dong' by Teach In. *So* much more sophisticated than 'Bang-A-Boomerang'.

Crass as it was, 'Bang-A-Boomerang' did get them off and running and gradually the classics began to take shape. They began to put melodies together imagining the dramatic effect the girls' voices would have on the action, thinking laterally, arranging as they went. They began to get more confident, advancing their style, spreading their range; a dabble into reggae on 'Tropical Loveland'; a grand pseudo-classical keyboard instrumental in the great traditions of Keith Emerson and Rick Wakeman on 'Intermezzo No. 1'; a probing, mildly introverted bout of self-analysis on 'Man In The Middle'; an explosive burst of all guns blazing on 'Rock Me'; and a mighty treasure-chest of choruses on the likes of 'Mamma Mia', 'Hey, Hey, Helen' and 'SOS'. Stig was still collaborating on the lyrics of several of the tracks, but the success of this batch of songs virtually signalled the end of his creative input as the business end of Team Abba took a firmer grip on his time.

Any further self-doubt disappeared when they started fleshing out the songs in the studio, where the benefits of the tour became apparent in the confident contributions from Anni-Frid and Agnetha. Making the album seemed interminable, but its evident flourishing drove them on to add ever more layers and textures. If this one didn't happen then they might just as well dig out that contract for the folk-park tour. Abba were delighted with their work. This one *would* happen. This one *had* to happen. But pop music was a lottery. Since when did justice ever come into it?

'I Do, I Do, I Do, I Do, I Do' seeped into play as a preview of the album. A pretty song, but one hardly done justice by the coy performance and limp production. Abba-ologists were to argue themselves senseless for centuries over the release of 'I Do' as the flagship for the *Abba* album. It was such an obvious makeweight alongside the likes of 'Mamma Mia' and 'SOS', but there was real pride in it from Benny and Bjorn, who felt the big band arrangement was daringly different and obtuse and would win them respect for their maturity, as well as airplay for novelty value. Sergeant Pepper's bastard son and a total contrast to both 'Waterloo' and the previous overly aggressive flopperoonee, 'So Long'.

In fact it achieved neither. All it did was send their record company promotions and marketing departments into blind panic. 'I Do, I Do, I Do, I Do, I Do' was greeted with yawning indifference by radio producers and public alike and the Epic promotions team – having had the importance of getting the single away hammered into them ad nauseam – resorted to laughably desperate tactics. Publicity stunts are an honourable part of the promotions man's stock-in-trade. A good publicity stunt will never put a record in the charts but it will always win the heart of a harassed hack and pop history has a glittering array of great stunts, the best of them usually involving a bottle of champagne and a visa. Ancient journos still talk fondly of the legendary Brinsley Schwarz trip when a plane-load of writers were plied with bubbly (and a few other things besides) all the way across the Atlantic in order to be placed in a decent frame of mind to witness the debut gig of the then unknown Brinsley Schwarz. They were shovelled off the plane at the other end in various states of disarray, and arrived at the gig extremely happy, but very late. Brinsley Schwarz apparently played a great gig that night, but none of the journalists were on hand to witness it, so the whole junket was a complete waste of time. Or was it? The fact that it's still discussed today suggests a weird kind of reverse psychology may have been brought into use with effective results.

It certainly beat the appalling practice common at the time of dispatching dreadful singer-songwriters who thought they were the new Elton John into newspaper offices where they would creep up on the unsuspecting hacks and ply their wares with an acoustic guitar and awful shrieking ballads about the iniquities of love and feeling depressed at train stations while their boot heels start a-wandering. Depending on whether or not they'd been down the pub beforehand, the hacks would either studiously ignore this hapless hopeful and make a grab for the phone; or they'd disembowel the poor creature on the spot. What *possesses* a record company to send an unknown artist into an office full of cynical reporters to try and sing a supposedly sensitive song? If the chap survived the disembowelling he would undoubtedly go straight home and hang himself.

A & M pulled a nasty trick once when they invited a group of journalists to lunch. No strings, they said. Just a lunch. Talk about a few things. We've got a new artist you might be interested in, blah, blah. Come the day lunch is served along with a quiet, mumbling Irishman in the corner. The new artist. Ha! Seems like a nice boy. Lives in a castle in Cork or somewhere. Could make a gossip item. Just give us a tape and we'll all go home. Then with the creme caramel and the brandy comes the pay-off. Waiter brings acoustic guitar and presents it to lad in corner. He grabs it and for the next twenty-five minutes wails his way through a weird old song about the devil. Ladies and gentlemen, we give you Chris De Burgh.

The Epic promotional budget for Abba sadly didn't stretch to such extravagances as wining and dining plane-loads of media persons on trips to New York. Or even Stockholm. A much tackier approach was necessary. In the event Lewis Rogers, who spearheaded Abba's UK promotional campaign, and his colleagues resorted to dressing up in top hats, tails and wedding dress, and drove around London in a Rolls-Royce, stopping off at every radio station they could find to enact the wedding ceremony. Lewis Rogers in drag in full white wedding kit, his mates in top hat and tails, bluffing their way on air to read out their wedding vows in front of a bemused presenter fretting about the next jingle. All because the title of the song they were plugging happened to be 'I Do, I Do, I Do, I Do, I Do'. Is this an utterly ridiculous industry or what?

Epic did everything they could short of blackmail and grievous bodily harm to get 'I Do, I Do, I Do, I Do, I Do' into the charts, aware their prize Swedes could be about to pull a pint at the last chance saloon. They failed miserably. They got the airplay, the publicity and the media attention, and sacrificed themselves as a laughing stock in the process. And *still* the record couldn't crawl any higher than Number Thirty-eight in the British singles charts. The *Abba* album – ready and waiting for launch on the back of what everyone had confidently believed would be a super-soaraway hit single – suddenly looked very sorry for itself in its shrink wrap.

It was, perhaps, the lowest point in Abba's professional lives. They immediately sent the world an SOS.

5

THE OTHER ONE

*'I saw myself as a concealed attraction
I felt you were robbing me away from
the heat of the action'*

'One Of Us'

I t was the satirical English television programme *Not
The Nine O'Clock News* which wickedly but accurately
pinpointed the widespread public perception of the Abba
Girl Debate. In an unkind but nevertheless hilarious skit
on Abba, they sang 'One of us is ugly, one of us is cute,
one of us you'd like to see in her birthday suit!'

No equivocation there about which one they deemed
ugly and which one they thought cute. Agnetha had that
vulnerable beauty, the shy, girlish smile destined to give
camera lenses multiple orgasms, a look later adopted and
patented by Princess Diana. Winners and losers. The good
and the bad. The beautiful and the ugly. The princess and
the chancer. That's the way the system works and if
Agnetha was the beautiful one, then Anni-Frid *had* to be
the ugly one. It's the nature of pop, it's the nature of life.

Anni-Frid resented it – as anyone would. Frida was five
years older than her more obviously glamorous colleague
and light years beyond in maturity and experience of life.
Where Agnetha had been cosseted, Frida roughed it. And
she enjoyed her success far more as a result. She always
looked more worn and knowing. More calculating and

therefore more cynical. More uncomfortable with the foolish costumes she was required to wear. More erratic with her haircuts. Why is it that women in rock who change their hairstyles more than once in their careers are subjected to such public scrutiny? David Bowie does it once a week and he's colourful and ingenious and innovative and witty and manipulative and a rock icon. Even when that bloke from the Human League emerged sporting that crazy style covering just one side of his face while leaving the other half free – the most obscene haircut in Britain since Bobby Charlton's hopelessly uncontrollable World Cup winning bald spot camouflage – he was given credit for his publicity acumen. Once the Human League started getting hits, Phillip Oakey adopted a more conservative accountant's crop and refused to do interviews for a couple of years, so shamed was he by his former, blatant opportunism.

But if girls come out parading daffy hairdos – or even *different* hairdos – there's at worst a sense of outrage, and at best, shifty unease. Sinead O'Connor arrived wielding attitude baldness and was tagged by some of the tabloid press as a trouble-making, pro-Republican leftie. None of which was, of course, remotely true – ol' Sinead's just a crooner who loves to sing and on occasion makes comments without really thinking, but the law clearly states that stereotypes must be strictly adhered to at all times, especially if you're a singer and particularly if you're a woman.

So Frida's hair was always a problem. Red for a start. That's *very* dodgy. Redheads are always Irish girls with long claws and fiery tempers that explode without warning at the tiniest provocation. And hey, whoever heard of a redhead from Scandinavia?!?

Then there was the perm. In the whole horrifying scheme of Abba fashion unconsciousness, the Lyngstad perm has to rank as the greatest disability of them all. The tacky trappings surrounding the enterprise were the crucial factor in their credibility-lacking career yet paradoxically contributed to the perverse charm and period appeal that has subsequently made their whole character so enduringly memorable.

But that perm was something else. A real suburban shopgirl shock that would have been inappropriate in its rightful spiritual home with a middle-class housewife from Essex desperately trying, but uselessly failing, to look young and trendy. We were in an age where naffness was at the core of society and even footballers were trotting out to matches sporting unsightly frizzes – they were making designer toilet brushes out of Kevin Keegan's haircut at one point.

All of which should have scared Frida right away from having anything to do with perms. The first rule of pop imagery is to *lead* High Street fashion, not to follow it. Fans strive to imitate their idols and not the other way around. The moment Essex girls saw this suspicious redhead with a perm Abba became something of a joke. Traces of such a strategic mistake were to dog them for the rest of their professional life. After all, even Essex *boys* had noticed the nation's propensity for perms, and when you're so far behind the game as all this, then you slip beyond even cliché. Unless you can somehow intimate that you're deliberately doing it as a joke to send up the whole silly business, which was how people like Elton John, Gary Glitter and even Sweet managed to survive so long on platform heels – in which case the stakes get higher.

Abba never even attempted to use such an audacious escape route for the folly. Privately they had rampant senses of humour and in the early years especially they spent a lot of time together laughing at the whole sorry business, but here again the styling and presentation let them down. Maybe their lack of confidence in their English precluded them from revealing their true selves; maybe it was their basic insecurities as Swedes gate-crashing the Anglo-American domain of pop stardom; maybe they were just following orders.

Whatever, their interviews were few and far between and when they came, they were a study in blandness. Humour, unfairly, was deemed to be totally absent from the ingredients of the Abba package, so any suggestion of irony in the Abba wardrobe in general and Frida's perm in particular was dismissed out of court. No jokes please, we are Swedish.

In truth, the Lyngstad perm was shortlived. But it made a couple of appearances at critical times and even while the tumbling volcanic lava look that tended to be a favourite with Frida's hairdresser the rest of the time wasn't exactly the height of chic, the sheer awful tastelessness of that perm had long-running consequences. It was there at the beginning at Brighton, on the *Waterloo* album sleeve in those early heady days of glory, and it lent an unnerving, surreal edge to the whole thing which seriously complicated subsequent bids for acceptance on musical grounds.

It sounds crazy. It *is* crazy. But one misguided trip to the hairdressers was a major factor in the criminal neglect of Abba on purely musical grounds as the greatest songwriters of the twentieth century.

As for Anni-Frid, she had a rough ride the whole way

through. She was a vibrant, colourful personality, exploding with zest and humour, and always much more comfortable and easy with the pressurized realities of fame – and indeed her role within the framework of the group – than the insecure and temperamental Agnetha. There were times when her resentment got the better of her and she betrayed her jealousy of Agnetha, who she came to regard as an irritating small-time girl with no real place in the cut and thrust of stardom. If you can't stand the heat you should go home to Jonkoping and shut the hell up, that was Frida's attitude to the throat problems, the illnesses, the fear of flying, and the nervousness about singing live which she saw recurring from the other.

Frida regarded herself as a professional. She saw no problem about pretending she and Agnetha were bosom buddies, or with the bizarre costumes, or the constant travelling, or the punishing work schedule. She appreciated that this was what she'd always wanted and dreamed about and striven for. Nobody said it would be a breeze. Work hard, play hard, that was the Lyngstad ethos and she kept to it throughout the lifetime of Abba.

She didn't have the greatest bum on earth. She drew the short straw in the Agnetha/Frida dream ticket and never quite forgave Agnetha for it. In another group in another age in another life in another country, Frida could have been the supreme rock goddess. A good singer, grittier and more powerful than Agnetha. Good temperament. Strong personality. And yeah, forget how you've been brainwashed all these years, she looked great too.

Of all of them she could have been cred. Not quite a Janis Joplin, but a Grace Slick certainly. She could have done it too. Frida had the confidence and the front to convincingly carry off any scenario. The mid-seventies were not merely the era of glitter-rock, they also witnessed the evolution of heavy metal as a valid musical form in its own right in the aftermath of Hendrix and the development of Led Zeppelin. Frida in jackboots and leather studs strutting her stuff in front of howling guitars and hairy monsters? Absolutely! Why not? It couldn't have been any more preposterous than the gipsy dresses and baubled blouses she was dressed up in to bill and coo with Abba.

Frida was always going to be the outsider. For a start she was born not in Sweden at all, but in Norway. No problem there. Norway, Sweden. What's the difference? It's all Scandinavia. Just like England and Scotland are both part of Britain. Local rivalries inevitably run deep.

Norway and Sweden are joined at the hip. Ruled by the Danes from the fourteenth century, Norway was part of Sweden from 1814 to 1905, when it gained independence. The border between the two lands stretches over a thousand miles and the two peoples have clearly defined cultural identities. It still jars slightly with Swedish pride to note that a quarter of one of the country's greatest institutions emanates from the wrong side of the border. It's almost as if Sweden can't fully celebrate the achievements of Abba because of the stray Norwegian among them. It's not racism as much as a private joke, but it tarnishes the perfection and it did Frida's image no favours at all in the overall scheme of things.

For the Scandinavian hierarchy decrees that Norway has traditionally played second string to Sweden. A smaller, more rugged, less famous, less prosperous country altogether, Norway has a long history of poverty behind it. North Sea oil and gas has changed all that and it is now one of Europe's most prosperous nations, offering political stability, beautiful scenery and thriving industry – though it's still nowhere near as rich as Sweden. Its past as the Nordic wasteland frequented by mad Vikings, impenetrable islands and fjords, long dark winters and eccentric people is never forgotten, not least by the proud Swedes.

At one point in the frozen north, well into the Arctic Circle, the country narrows to such a point that it is a mere four miles in breadth. It's around this point that you find the port of Narvik, on Ofotfjord, east of the Lofoten and Vesteralen islands, but where the harbour miraculously escapes the ice you find almost everywhere else in the area. Life in Narvik is centred on the harbour and the allied fishing and shipping communities.

At the outbreak of the Second World War, Norway was intent on maintaining its traditional policy of neutrality. Hitler, though, was frightened that the Allies would use Norway as a launching pad for a counter-offensive in Europe and invaded in April 1940. There was little resistance from the weak and ill-prepared local army. Vidkun Quisling, who'd formed the Norwegian National Rally in imitation of the Nazis, was appointed leader of a new regime during the German occupation . . . and found himself reviled by the rest of the world while his name entered the English language in reference to the most despicable acts of treachery.

The Nazis poured north into Narvik, seen as a significant strategic landmark and a vital base for refuelling in the battle for Northern Europe. Within a couple of days of the German invasion, British destroyers sailed into Narvik Fjord and launched an all-out onslaught on the unsuspecting German navy in the harbour. In a cataclysmic four-hour battle, the Allies caused havoc. Six German supply ships and eight destroyers were sunk. But soon the Nazis took France, Norway's King Haakon fled to England and the Allies were forced to pull out of Norway as the Germans took a stranglehold. It was a horrific time for the people there. There had been a strong ground-swell of opinion throughout Norway that the country should have thrown in their lot with the Allies from the outset and the resistance movement rapidly moved into gear to sabotage the Germans at every opportunity. This instantly resulted in a hardening of attitude from the German forces and Quisling – operating on orders directly from Berlin – presided over an atrocious regime whose brutality intensified with every act of sabotage from the highly active resistance.

Narvik was an animated and frightening port through-out the occupation, which lasted for almost the entire duration of the war. You had to learn to survive it somehow in your own way. Whatever it took. And remember that the Germans – some of them kids barely out of school – were often as frightened, insecure and miserable as the Norwegians. At least they had the comfort of home territory. The German boys were far from home, suffering the cold and the dark, living among people who despised them and wished them dead – many of them doing their damnedest to cause that very eventuality at every conceivable opportunity.

The affair between Alfred Haase and Synni Lyngstad was a clandestine union. Both of them knew the shame, scandal and disgust that would be heaped on them should it become common knowledge. Sleeping with the enemy was not a wartime occupation approved of by anybody in the equation, but since when did love follow any rules of logic, reason or public opinion?

Alfred Haase was a baker from Karlsruhe, an industrial city in the Rhine valley, northwest of Stuttgart, who cared little for Nazi ideology, but did what he was told. And what he was told to do was keep the Norwegians in order in Narvik.

There were worse places to be a German soldier. Haase didn't regard himself as a Nazi, he saw little direct action, he wasn't called upon to kill anybody and he somehow felt impersonal about what was going on in the rest of Europe. He was widely respected by his colleagues, and he became an officer. But he was lonely, he was homesick and if the truth be told, he was scared too. He was married with a wife living back home in Karlsruhe.

Synni Lyngstad was an impressionable 19-year-old living with her mum in the tiny village of Bjorkasen, just outside Narvik. From the moment she met the handsome German officer she lost all reason and control over her emotions, instantly falling hopelessly and completely in love with Haase. He was her first and last lover.

It was a tragic affair. Snatched moments in secluded hideaways, whispered conversations and secret rendez-vous. Long partings and stilted conversation with very substantial language and cultural barriers between them.

It was doomed from the outset. Love affairs are a wretched business at the best of times, but it's impossible to imagine a more disastrous set of circumstances for an affair than those surrounding Synni and Alfred. It was a romance fraught with danger and could have yielded so little joy in compensation. They must both have accepted the horror and condemnation that awaited them should word of it escape in the town and they must have both known it was wholly doomed from day one.

But they made absurd promises to each other about

the future and probably even believed them. As the tide turned, the Allies marched back into Europe and headed towards Berlin and the end of the war approached, Alfred Haase was recalled to Germany and left on a troop ship from Narvik almost without warning. No time even for tearful farewells, and because of the unquestionable wrongness of the liaison and the unanimous disapproval it would inevitably inspire, Synni was denied the comfort of sympathy and understanding from others.

It destroyed Synni. A few weeks after Alfred had disappeared she discovered she was pregnant with his child and any pretence of innocence in her relationship with the German officer was exposed once and for all. The family were virtually ostracized in Bjorkasen and Synni barely set foot outside her house again. Old morals were still the order of the day in this close-knit northern community and Synni knew the stigma of having an illegitimate baby would forever haunt her here, even without the additional abhorrence to society of surrendering her honour to an officer of the despised Nazi occupying forces. Synni, young and vulnerable, couldn't live with the shame.

Her daughter Anni-Frid Synni Lyngstad was born in Bjorkasen on 15 November 1945 – six months after the liberation of Norway and when revulsion at the emerging catalogue of German atrocities was at its height. Anni-Frid, Synni and her mother were outcasts in their own community.

Synni clung to the hope that Alfred would return. She hadn't known he was married and the one thing that kept her going was the increasingly forlorn belief that he'd be returning to Narvik for her. He never came. Synni's mother made various energetic attempts to find him, but was eventually informed that the boat taking him back to Germany from Narvik had been sunk and Alfred Haase was officially listed as one of those lost at sea.

It was too much for the frail Synni. Her deep depression sank into a grave illness and she died in abject misery shortly after the war. She was twenty-one.

The memories were far too painful for Synni's distraught mother – Anni-Frid's grandmother – to stay in Bjorkasen. The stigma of the whole tragic episode drove her to take the baby in search of a new life across the border into Sweden. It was the only way to give Anni-Frid a chance in life and rid herself of the curse of the war and the Narvik occupation. Herself left alone, she had little money and few friends, but she did have a tremendous strength of character and will to give Anni-Frid as decent an upbringing as she could possibly manage.

So they crossed the border and trawled around Sweden as Mrs Lyngstad sought work to keep them alive. She was an accomplished seamstress and through her skill and blind determination she managed to find enough temporary work to survive for a while until it was time to move on to the next place. Money was scarce and security non-existent, but Mrs Lyngstad showed extraordinary resilience in the face of extreme hardship and bred in the child a fierce independence and inner strength that was to serve her proud in later years. The full breadth of difference between the apparently orphaned Frida's early poverty-stricken nomadic life and Agnetha's secure, cosy family life in comfortable Jonköping were all too evidently apparent in their respective infant years.

Ultimately Anni-Frid and grandmother gravitated south where Mrs Lyngstad finally settled down after finding a regular sewing job in a factory in the industrial city of Eskilstuna, beside Lake Malaren, just seventy miles west of Stockholm.

It was still hard, but Frida's grandmother cheerfully worked all hours to give the girl a proper schooling, while at nights they made their own entertainment singing traditional Scandinavian folk songs. They'd made it. Frida had survived intact with the sort of character and mental strength that only comes out of adversity. Her grandmother had defeated all the odds. The curse of Narvik had been eradicated.

There was an intriguing addendum to the story of Frida's childhood several years later while Abba were at the peak of their fame. Frida, herself hazy about all the facts, felt no sense of shame about it all and was justifiably proud of her grandmother, but didn't feel the need to broadcast it to the world. She was at ease with herself and had come to terms with her parentage and as far as she was concerned it wasn't anybody else's business.

But in 1977 a German journalist started digging around in Narvik and revealed the true facts of Anni-Frid's birth and the scandal of the German officer who'd fathered her. The juicy story was, inevitably, retold in various papers and magazines around the world where Abba were by now huge. But far from being the shock-horror-stunner it might have appeared a few years earlier, no stigma was attached to Frida as a result and the story touched a nerve and inspired much support and sympathy for Frida. The Germans, particularly, starved of the remotest whiff of international pop success and by now coming to terms with their own role in the past, were thrilled by the idea that one of the biggest stars in the world was of German stock and splashed the story loud and proud in the best-selling *Bravo* magazine. The conclusion remained the same – that Alfred Haase had drowned between Norway and Germany.

A German Abba fan called Andrea Buchinger read the story avidly and was startled when she read about Alfred Haase. It was her uncle's name. She knew he'd served in Norway during the war and instantly phoned her cousin Peter who questioned his father about Narvik and Synni Lyngstad. Yes, he said, he was that soldier.

The official information had been wrong. Alfred Haase had made it back to Germany and Karlsruhe and settled down again with his wife and they raised two children. He had no idea that Synni had been pregnant and had a daughter, though he claimed he had tried to write to Synni after the war, but the letters must have been lost.

It was an unlikely tale and something that the battle-hardened, deeply suspicious Anni-Frid found hard to stomach when Alfred Haase attempted to get in touch with her. His initial enquiries were met with incomprehension – basically he spoke only German, and his claims to be Anni-Frid's father were met with acute disbelief. It would be a big shock for anyone to suddenly be confronted by a guy claiming to be the father they'd been brought up to believe had died before they were born. When they knew that guy had been wearing a Nazi uniform many wouldn't have wanted to have known him anyway, even if they were convinced he was who he claimed to be.

Anni-Frid's case was further complicated by fame. When you have money and glory, the world is full of charlatans only too ready to rip you off with every outlandish story known to man or beast. It's funny how many long-lost friends and relatives come crawling out of the woodwork once you start making a name for yourself and are assumed to have money. It was relatively late in the game when John Lennon's dad emerged pleading poverty and wanting hand-outs, even making a record on the back of the family name, though he'd abandoned and disowned John when he was a small kid. Now John Lennon didn't want to know him and was pilloried for it in some papers, though even the most charitable, forgiving Christians must have felt a surge of satisfaction seeing John showing his long-lost father the door.

Frida's difficult upbringing, also, had given her a skin tough enough to protect her against such opportunism and she could see through those intent on taking her for a ride. You had to work hard to win the trust of Anni-Frid Lyngstad. But she was not vindictive and she was intrigued. She checked the story out. It was true all the time. Alfred Haase was everything he claimed to be and Frida quietly acknowledged that he was indeed her father.

She overcame her reservations and arranged for him to come to Stockholm to meet her. The past was past and she saw no threat in the sudden discovery that she had a father alive and living in seeming prosperity in Germany with his own family. It gave her a feeling of stability and comfort after all the years of rootlessness. Suddenly she had a family, a past, a character. It made her feel better than she ever imagined it could have done. She'd never dwelt on the respective fates of her parents, accepting the realities of her situation and idolizing her grandmother for her strength. Now she had something more spiritually solid to lean on and the warmth she felt from that overrode any latent bitterness she may have felt about the circumstances of her own birth.

The actual meeting with her father was inevitably difficult. The press were agog as news of the meeting leaked out and the awkwardness of the initial encounter was further exacerbated by the language problem that had existed between Alfred and Synni and now made communication with her daughter halting and stilted. But for all that it was a successful meeting and while they met only occasionally, Frida and the white-haired, bearded Alfred Haase kept in touch.

Frida's obvious singing talent was supported and encouraged all the way by her grandmother. The one luxury they had at their home in Eskilstuna was an old wind-up gramophone which played only 78 rpm records. But they had a few jazz records, which they played constantly to be imitated note-perfectly by Anni-Frid.

She was eleven when she made her public debut singing jazz standards in the style of her prime musical heroines Ella Fitzgerald, Sara Vaughan and Peggy Lee at a Red Cross Bazaar. She was to remain a huge Peggy Lee fan throughout Abba and one of her greatest thrills of their first American visit was meeting Lee backstage at one of the concerts in 1974. Her grandmother's legacy had also been a deep love of folk song, but her single-minded ambition was to be the singer in a jazz band. Everything she did was geared to that objective, listening, learning, practising.

She was a confident, earnest kid, too. By the time she was thirteen she was singing professionally with a local swing band led by Ewald Ek playing every week at an Eskilstuna restaurant. There were rules about that sort of thing, but Frida was no academic and had no qualms about accepting the gig, lying about her age to give up school and follow her heart. She certainly looked a whole lot more than thirteen, with the looks, the voice, the assurance and the behaviour of someone several years older. She was good too and slipped easily into the role of jazz singer.

It can be a grimly exacting lifestyle, especially for a woman, singing in dark, smoky clubs and restaurants at unsocial hours with half the audience legless and the other obliviously talking loudly amongst themselves. But Frida took to it like a member of the royal family to skis. She loved it all. The music was taken as read – this was her music, she'd been practising it for most of her life and she saw it as her destiny. But she also loved the whole lifestyle, the entire *atmosphere* of the whole thing. She loved being around musicians, sharing their jokes and animated muso discussions, joining in fully with the drinking and partying. She was a natural.

She was also frenetically driven by ambition. It didn't matter that she was barely sixteen, she knew more about the realities of life than many twice her age, and there was nothing – from the heckles of the drunk at the bar to the wallet-waving fat man crudely coming on to her at the end of the night – that she couldn't handle. There was no way she'd be content to stay in a small-time outfit for long and when she got the chance to sing with one of Eskilstuna's busiest and most highly rated bands, the Bengt Sandlund jazz big band, she was gone like a shot.

This was even more exciting. So much scope and range. Bigger audiences. Greater prospects. People loved her for her youth, vitality and exceptional rapport with audiences, but mainly for her superb singing over a broad range of material. It was obvious to all that it wouldn't be too long before she outgrew the Sandlund band too. The band was playing everything from Glenn Miller to Roberta Flack, but by now Frida was also into Frank Zappa.

One night she hooked up with Ragnar Fredericksson, the Sandlund band bass player. He adored her from her first night with the band. It was obvious then she was special and that she was going places. He'd never encountered anyone with her drive and love of life before. Ragnar was a trustworthy character, full of charm and humour, and older than Frida; he offered her the stability and male influence that had been missing from her life.

They both quit the Sandlund band to form the Anni-Frid Four, and the reputation of the redheaded sensation continued to thrive in the looser, more intimate four-piece line-up. They became a big draw in Eskilstuna, still concentrating primarily on jazz, but broadening the net to encompass popular standards. Her career, though, began to drift after she married Ragnar Fredericksson and went on to have two children, Hans, born in 1963, and Lisa-Lotte, born in 1967.

But the strongly independent, free-spirited Frida wasn't cut out to settle down. Not then, if ever. 'Ninety-nine per cent of my time is spent on my career and the other one per cent is on partying,' she commented on one famous occasion during the Abba years and her ambition wasn't to allow her to rest at home with Ragnar and the kids. Everything in her life had been focused on a career as a singer and while she got out as many evenings as she could to sing, she was inwardly frustrated by the opportunities passing her by while she sat at home. She was barely out of her teens, still evolving as a person and a singer and somehow knew she wasn't meant to spend the rest of her life in domestic bliss in Eskilstuna. The tension resulting from this thwarted ambition sparked an irreversible friction between her and Ragnar. She did her best to settle down and be happy like normal people, but there was a streak within her, gnawing at her, unsettling her, haunting her, convincing her she should be some place else doing something different.

The odd restaurant or club gig did little to assuage this rampant musical bent and she went to a voice coach and took to entering talent competitions as a potential short-cut to national fame while circumventing the drudgery of trying to get a record deal. One of these was a competition organized by a children's charity based on the old *New Faces* idea.

She went through a series of local heats and chose a ballad, 'A Day Off', for the finals, held on 3 September 1967. The competition was a huge event, the biggest of its kind in Sweden, and hyped to the hilt. It was held in Stockholm – in Skansen Park – in front of a large audience which fired Frida to a passionate performance. She won by a mile.

There was a surprise prize for the exhausted winner – an immediate live performance on the mass audience Lennart Hyland television show. This was the night Sweden switched from driving on the left to the right and the television stations had a high profile schedule specifically designed to keep potential motorists indoors glued to the box instead of outside causing untold carnage. So Frida, tired after the Skansen Park contest and nervous as a kitten at this unexpected turn of events, was trooped out for another rendering of 'A Day Off'. A different medium, but the same adrenalin. Frida – already the supreme pro – once more rose to the occasion. And it was quite an occasion. Viewing figures for the show, which featured a whole galaxy of Scandinavian stars, were phenomenal. It was estimated that virtually the entire nation had been watching the show. Before she'd finished singing, every record company in Sweden was queuing round the block to sign Anni-Frid Lyngstad.

There was little hope for the marriage after that. Frida had too much passion and fire within her to go after the opportunities suddenly opening up before her with anything less than 300 per cent. Ragnar knew it too. The writing had been on the wall for a long time before this – Skansen Park was merely the confirmation she needed that this was the big one. And it allowed no room for a husband and family.

When the dust settled later on, Ragnar accepted the inevitability of their marriage breakdown. He was no mean musician himself, but he was always ready to opt for what he already had. Frida wasn't like that. She constantly wanted the bigger picture. There might be a great painting on the wall in front of her, but she was always haring away intent on seeing the next one round the corner. Progress. Development. Fulfilment of potential. Achievement. That's what it was always about with Anni-Frid and her frustrations were intense whenever she felt she wasn't following her heart. She went through violent mood swings in the course of a day, from black depressions to rampant ebullience with little warning of the changes. Ragnar felt the brunt of these swings. He worshipped her, but he knew he'd never hang on to her. He was enormously proud of her that night at Skansen Park, but he also knew it signalled the end of the marriage. By the time Frida signed with EMI she'd already left Ragnar, Hans and Lise-Lotte at home to become a star.

In black and white terms, a Lyngstad had once more defied public convention. Once the Abba story came to be told, eyebrows were raised about the decency of a woman who could walk out on her children, but nobody who knew her was surprised or outraged.

Frida didn't just abandon her kids without a care in the world. It was a gradual rather than a clean separation as Frida became sucked once more into career mode and the final severence wasn't made until she met Benny Andersson and knew there was to be no going back. In the meantime she managed to sustain a relatively cordial relationship with the understanding Ragnar, now working as a carpet salesman as well as part-time bass player, and who was far better equipped to raise the children. During her travels she made regular visits back to Eskilstuna to see – and maintain a good relationship with – Hans and Lise-Lotte from the launch of her solo career right through the duration of Abba.

But she did base herself in Stockholm, launched her recording career with a couple of well-received, though hardly blockbusting singles, 'En Ledit Dag' ('A Day Off') and 'Din' ('Yours'), and gleefully set off round the country to work the cabaret clubs, revue theatres and folk-parks that were the staple diet of the Swedish music scene.

She never achieved the kind of solo success enjoyed by Agnetha and nobody complimented her much on her bum, but Frida's determination, resilience and will to succeed are a shining example to all. It's one of the reasons why she could never muster much patience or empathy for Agnetha, who in her terms had been born with a silver spoon in her mouth but discovered it was making her choke. After what she'd come through to achieve even minor stardom at the end of the sixties, it's small wonder she later found Agnetha such a trial.

After the first batch of EMI records, Frida signed with

Columbia and had another couple of minor hits – 'Simsalabim' and 'Mycket Kar' – but it wasn't enough. She was avidly curious about every musical form she heard, ranging from traditional folksong to modern jazz, and she went to extraordinary lengths, working herself to a frazzle to improve her technique and forward her career. Later she was to involve herself in all aspects of the Abba package. She helped design clothes, she art-directed album sleeves, she came up with ideas for marketing and videos. She even offered suggestions for songs, though they never seemed to be taken up.

The grander scheme was always on her horizon. She took full advantage of all the cultural possibilities opening up to her, like a starving man stumbling across a luxuriant picnic hamper. She developed a passion for opera, ballet, high art, studying everything she could conceivably find on a subject once she'd discovered it. She had a lust for learning that's unique to those denied sophisticated schooling in their youth. People had assumed that her hardened attitudes and streetwise understanding of life indicated a primitive brain. But Frida was sharper than most and, whatever else, she wasn't thick. She avariciously studied anything and everything to prove just that, reaching a point of such advanced self-education that she could hold her own in any high-brow political debate, ultimately taking a deep, deep interest in matters of social concern and latterly vigorously involving herself in environmental issues while enjoying a society lifestyle. Yet still she retained the old street-fighter's slogging toughness. Nobody crossed Frida lightly.

No matter how many knocks she took, how many dives she appeared in, and how many drunks abused her, she remained fiercely undeterred from pursuing the goals she continually set herself. Frida Lyngstad was going to be a huge star all right, and a pox on anybody who tried to get in her way.

One night in 1969 Frida appeared at a night-club in Malmo. The Hep Stars happened to be playing at another club in town the same night and after her own show, Frida popped along to see them. It was the night she met Benny Andersson. Niceties were exchanged and she was on her way. A few weeks later their paths crossed again and they had a drink together. Then they found themselves appearing on the same panel of a radio show featuring celebrities commenting on new releases. The outgoing Benny treated it as a huge joke, and Frida found herself responding to his humour in a way that surprised even herself.

Afterwards they fell into deep discussions about music, discovering similar feelings, ambitions and hopes in one another. She was captivated by his knowledge and understanding of music, his humour and his mesmerizing personality. They talked well into the night. They got drunk together. And they became lovers.

Ragnar's lingering hopes of a reunion with his wife went out of the window. Within weeks Benny and Frida were living together, planning, talking, learning, writing and partying. They were almost uncannily matched.

Life could never be the same again for either of them.

6

THANK YOU FOR THE MUSIC

'I have a dream, a song to sing
To help me cope with anything'

'I Have A Dream'

If they were going to jack it in the least they could have done was give us a proper funeral.

Legends have a duty to go out in dramatic style, they shouldn't just not bother to do it any more without telling anyone. Nothing wrong with leaving your options open but, hey, tell everyone you're splitting, do the farewell tour, flog the live album for all it's worth . . . and you can always change your mind and come back next year for an equally well publicized comeback. Happens all the time. Gary Glitter. Status Quo. Frank Sinatra. Frank Sinatra. Frank Sinatra.

It's one of the things that miffed Stig Anderson most. All that uncertainty. It's so . . . *messy*. Stig, the ultimate marketing machine, cursed the missed opportunities. It was bad enough that the buggers weren't still actually making wonderful music together any more and looked unlikely to be doing so again this century, without denying the opportunity for one final mother-of-all killings. A triumphant farewell tour. A last studio album. A live album of the tour. And then . . . who knows?

Maybe they'd come to their senses and start doing it over.

Had Abba played the game properly and done all these things, then there was only one song which would have served as their final number on their final gig. It would also have been released as their final single. It would have gone straight to Number One, would very possibly still be there now, and there wouldn't have been a dry eye in any stadium or living room where it was played. The song is 'The Way Old Friends Do'.

It's an anthem, see. A real tear-jerking let's-all-clasp-arms-I-wish-you-were-my-brother sentimental terrace hymn of nostalgic overkill into which they threw everything *including* the kitchen sink. Recorded live at Wembley on the '79 tour, it was a track on *Super Trouper* which only belatedly saw the light of day as a single in 1992 as a trailer for *More Abba Gold*. It's 'Auld Lang Syne'. It's a Scottish folk song. It's amazing. Kitsch and tacky, *naturally*, but that's partly the point. It's class tack and it's a million miles from the crap tackiness on which they originally launched their career together in the early seventies.

There were always a lot of distractions with Abba; crap telly shows to ugly divorces. But they were mere sideshows to the main event, which was the music. Great pop music will always instantly define a time, a place and a person, bringing old deeply buried emotions, flavours, colours, moods roaring back into focus the second they're heard. And if they're really, *really* good, then you can also listen to them as pieces of music in their own right and they still sound fresh and alive and current. Abba's claims to greatness lie resoundingly in the unerring ability of the songs of Bjorn Ulvaeus and Benny Andersson to meet all these criteria.

Bjorn and Benny travelled a long way with Abba. 'Honey Honey' to 'The Winner Takes It All'. 'Ring Ring' to 'The Way Old Friends Do'. Their very best work occurred at the tail end of their career together when everyone assumed their creativity had been battered into non-existence by all the extraneous problems. On the contrary, those problems and pressures merely stripped away the superficialities clogging up their early writing, and turned them into the greatest songwriting and production team of our age.

The song that defined the Abba sound was 'SOS'. 'Waterloo' was something they'd plucked out of thin air to win them Brighton. They thought they'd done it the previous year with the execrable 'Ring Ring' – it was bright, catchy and nauseating enough in the grand Euro tradition. At that point Abba weren't a group at all in the accepted sense. They were Bjorn Ulvaeus and Benny Andersson being helped out by their girlfriends Agnetha Faltskog and Anni-Frid Lyngstad. Bjorn and Benny were the act and Agnetha and Anni-Frid the trimmings that would project them. Stig was always clear about that and when they performed 'Ring Ring' at the Stockholm heat of Eurovision in 1973 when Agnetha was nine months pregnant, they weren't Abba, they weren't a proper group at all, they were just Bjorn, Benny, Agnetha and Anni-Frid. There was no masterplan, no battle strategy set beyond Eurovision. And certainly there was no identifiable sound.

In that year between the two contests they weren't looking for a sound or a style. All they wanted was a song. A hit song, neutral enough to please the whole of Europe, with an agreeable sound and international lyrics. Stig, who'd turned crass trivia into an art form, was the dominant force in hoisting Abba into a direction of bubbly Euro-twaddle. It was Stig the realist who insisted that Bjorn and Benny had to record in English to stand any sort of chance of breaking out of Scandinavia; and it was Stig the eternal Mr Fixit who initially took charge of that corner of the operation. His lyrics were universally awful, but they *were* universal. Benny couldn't do it to save his life and in the first instance Bjorn wasn't so hot either. Writing song lyrics can be pretty difficult in your own language without attempting it in a foreign tongue. Plenty of lyricists *sound* like they're writing in an unnatural language, so Stig was probably safe enough in thinking he could get away with it. This, after all, was a lyricist who'd built his early reputation on the back of something called 'The Girls Who Know Are Found In The Country'. And for those early Euro purposes he more or less did get away with it – nobody ever bought a record purely on the strength of its lyrical content (why aren't poetry books at the top of the charts if that's the case?) and mostly people don't even take any notice of the lyrics.

It's one of Bjorn's most magnificent achievements that he mastered the art of songwriting in a foreign language to such an advanced degree, maturing spectacularly from thoroughly hopeless to sort-of-okay to – ultimately – something approximating deep and meaningful.

Way back then, though, the height of their ambition was, *'Honey, honey, how you thrill me, uh huh/Honey honey, you nearly kill me, uh huh.'* Well, it worked for the Archies, who topped the charts with 'Sugar Sugar' amid similar lyrical shorthand in 1969 and *they* were just a cartoon strip. In the final countdown for Eurovision '74 it was a straight toss-up between 'Waterloo' and 'Hasta Manana'.

Just titles with international connotations randomly plucked from the air with tunes around them specifically tailored to meet the perceived Euro requirements. Lyrics were tagged on at the end of that, almost as an afterthought.

There was a strong body of opinion that they should go with 'Hasta Manana', that 'Waterloo' was too modern and upbeat for the fragile ears of the judges and that the more soothing, melodic 'Hasta Manana' was what the doctor ordered. But 'Hasta Manana' was also more similar to the defeated 'Ring Ring' and Stig was eventually persuaded that Europe was indeed ready for a blast of Napoleonism. Who knows what would have happened had the vote gone instead to the mellifluous balladry of 'Hasta Manana'? It would have been strictly sombreros, cowboy boots and ponchos, with maybe a tassly slit skirt to provide the obligatory daring.

And if it had been 'Hasta Manana' instead of 'Waterloo' which carried them to glory, then they might as well have forgotten about any aspirations towards any jiggery rockery altogether and settled for a life of gentle balladry and serene smooch. The hits would maybe still have come, but the emphasis would have been almost entirely on singing and beauty, and the Ulvaeus-Andersson studio machine shackled at birth. If, if, if . . . pop is all about if.

Stig Anderson rejects all of this, of course. He still maintains that Eurovision was peripheral to Abba's rise. He's not to be shifted on his opinion that Abba would have made it internationally with or without Eurovision. It may have taken a little longer, but talent like that is not to be denied and would have won the day eventually come what may. His faith in pop justice is touching, if misplaced. Bjorn and Benny may well have come through ultimately as a red hot songwriting/production team – and the ease with which they turned into disco fiends with the *Voulez-Vous* album suggests they could have been Europe's answer to Nile Rodgers and Bernard Edwards. But there almost certainly wouldn't have been an Abba as we learned to love and obey them were it not for success at Eurovision.

Agnetha and Frida were originally only makeweights in the arrangement, a touch of glamour, some light and shade in the music. It was with some reluctance that Stig gave them any acknowledgement at all on the first recording credits, and then as individuals, as if this was not something that was going to happen regularly. People continued to refer to them as Agnetha, Bjorn, Benny and Anni-Frid until Stig started referring to them by the initials of their forenames for brevity. It was only when someone gently suggested that Agnetha, Bjorn, Benny and Anni-Frid might prove a little complicated for Katie Boyle to get her teeth round at Eurovision '74 that Abba came into play as an official title . . . and even then only after ratification from a radio poll.

So there was no rehearsed strategy. They had no idea what Abba was or indeed *if* it was. They could have no long-term ambitions, no *future* at all unless they got another hit before all remnant of credibility and momentum dripped through their fingers. Style, consistency, feel, character . . . none of it mattered as long as they proved they could come up with something to follow 'Waterloo'.

In the process they drew blatantly on all the influences and hit-making formulae they'd been privy to down the years. 'So Long' is now barely recognizable as Abba. It sounds like any number of sixties rock songs by any number of sixties girl groups lifted by some strident electric guitar to get the local dance floor hopping. An effective live number – especially as a boppy show-closer, but not a hit single. Here was a band shooting in the dark, perhaps attempting to shake off the stigma of Eurovision with an out-and-out rocker but succeeding only in creating confusion among listeners with its desperation tactics.

When it missed the mark by several miles, they plundered even more ancient pop history, rediscovering a fifties style in a sax solo and merging it with ballroom dance smooch on 'I Do, I Do, I Do, I Do, I Do' that might even have been considered clever pastiche had they produced it with more conviction. A nice tune, but a hopelessly pallid complexion which made it a sworn enemy of radio play. On the back of it was 'Rock Me', an attempt on basic knee-trembling raunch which came out more Little Bo Peep than Little Richard. Abba were in trouble. Sliding fast and clutching at straws. No sound, no style and, apparently, no idea.

Then came 'SOS', Benny's intricate pseudo-classical interlude sculpting the main melody, a yearning, melancholic verse building towards the classic onrushing chorus that comes at you all guns blazing, marching triumphantly off with your brain cells. There was considerable media indifference towards Abba by this time. Their records couldn't get arrested and while the residue of 'Waterloo' was still sufficient to maintain them as a hot property in various outposts of Europe, the CBS promotions team in Britain was in overdrive attempting to keep their career alive. 'SOS' may have been their last shot. And it was a lethal one.

Everything from here on stemmed from 'SOS'. The whole *mode* of Bjorn's and Benny's songwriting changed as they settled into a groove they found to be satisfying and – more importantly – ultra-commercial. Virtually everything they touched in the next couple of years conformed to the formula they had stumbled upon in 'SOS' – the atmospheric intro, the moody build-up, the electrifying chorus suddenly lighting the whole thing like a beacon with the girls' harmonic vitality. Other elements came to characterize their work – the repeated use of fairground music in the arrangements; the hugely effective heavily accented vocals; the cascading production on the chorus lines; the unashamed babble of Europop; and the unerring cleanliness of the Polar studio sound, nurtured by their engineer Micke Tretow.

Having at last got a proper grip on the baton, Bjorn and Benny became gloriously efficient songwriters, energizing one another, developing a perfect rapport, and instinctively reacting to each other's mind patterns.

It's a rare occurrence in a songwriting team. It's rare in *any* team. There's usually one dominant partner and this inevitably provokes jealousies and recriminations, but no such hang-ups pervaded the Andersson-Ulvaeus partnership. They quickly outgrew the gimmicky parochialism of the Stig Anderson school of songwriting to smooth a classy, shiny veneer over an innate pop sensibility. It wound a lot of people up, but it was brilliantly effective and ultimately it was transformed into something much more rare and significant.

Mostly they wrote on a grand piano on their island hideaway, tinkering around with strands of tunes, searching for the trigger to send them off into those famous, crushing choruses. They always wore their influences loudly and proudly, using other people's styles to positive effect as reference points in their own distinctive sounds.

The Beatles, the Beach Boys, Leiber & Stoller; recurring heroes, recurring tributes in their own music. 'On And On And On', a B-side as late as 1981, was so stylized in the fashion of the Beach Boys it could only have been a deliberate homage.

'I really don't know where it comes from or why it ends up a ballad or a rock 'n' roll song,' said Benny in an interview with *Songwriter* magazine, attempting to put some sense of logic into the wholly illogical process of songwriting. 'That's why we spend so much time with it because you never know what's going to happen. I spend a lot of time alone playing the piano or synthesizers and it's more like therapy, just to be prepared.'

Once they had the basic melody knocked into shape, Bjorn would hack out a rough lyric to go with it, and then they'd go in and record the basic instrumental. It was at this point that they'd invariably begin to panic about the need for words and with everything else complete, Bjorn would be dispatched to hell to come up with something that fitted the mood of the song *and* made sense. This he'd then float at Benny, and his reaction would determine whether or not they could go ahead with the track and safely alert Agnetha and Frida. They were always brutally honest about each other's contributions and if either had misgivings about something then it would automatically be scrapped, irrespective of how brilliant its creator felt it to be. That was the measure of the respect between them and the fact that this closeness and intensity never caused even the beginnings of a crack in their relationship, either professional or personal. Both knew they'd be nothing without the other and their readiness to recognize the fact was a crucial factor in their stability and consistency as a writing force.

'If we get stuck,' Benny told *Songwriter*, 'we go away and we eat, sleep and write twenty-four hours. It opens your mind. It's very easy to get stuck, but there's nobody on our backs. No record companies or agents or managers or lawyers. We just relax because we know that if it's not good enough, we don't release it. It eases the tension a lot when we realize that it's not for anybody else but ourselves.'

Maintaining such rigid standards duly resulted in an awful lot of wastage and the further they went the harder it got as they strove to develop and stretch themselves. The trick was always making it sound simple, and Bjorn and Benny would spend weeks perfecting something which sounded like it had been knocked up in five minutes. Later, as they deliberately tried to make their music more complex and demanding, notably with *The Visitors* album, their commercial clout suffered as a result and they immediately showed dangerous signs of self-consciousness and uncertainty.

But the run they had was unparalleled in modern times. And for Bjorn and Benny the ultimate joy was producing a great song. Not in the studio recording it. Not playing it on stage in front of a rapturous audience. Not watching it hit the top of the charts with an almighty crack. Not even observing the cash tills ringing as the song earned them yet another small fortune. But that moment at the end of all the sweat and swearing when no one else was around and Benny would slump back and smile contentedly at Bjorn in silent acknowledgement of another job well done. Not necessarily another hit – though that seemed automatically to follow – but another satisfying piece of craftsmanship. Anything that finally came up to scratch to match their own rigorous standards of quality and design was a racing certainty to receive a hero's welcome from their public around the world.

'There's a lot more to life than success,' says Benny. 'It has nothing to do with the creative process.'

And yet, they freely admit it, creativity comes out of personal experience and influences. They do acknowledge their debt to Lennon/McCartney and Brian Wilson, as well as Stevie Wonder and the Eagles and . . . everybody they ever heard in their lives. The same with any songwriter. It only becomes effective when you infuse it with a sound and style specifically your own. This Abba only started to do with 'SOS'.

Trying to accurately convey the particular magic and appeal of a certain artist in words is always impossible. It's all mood and feeling and touching a common nerve. 'I think,' Bjorn once told *Songwriter* magazine, 'our world-wide success is because we have such a broad tradition when it comes to music. We were brought up on American and English rock 'n' roll at the same time as we were brought up on German schlagger and Italian schmaltz. I guess we've taken the best out of different worlds. Also we're very conscious about the structure of the song. Once that part is there, all of a sudden it's a whole song. And each part is equally important, whether it's an instrumental interlude, a bridge or the chorus. Just because we think we have a hell of a chorus we don't give up on the verse.'

It's probably grossly inaccurate but tempting never-theless to draw some conclusions about the first cracks appearing in Bjorn and Agnetha's relationship from 'SOS'. *You seem so far away though you are standing near/You make* me *feel alive, but something died, I fear.* Bjorn always denied his lyrics contained any specific personal emotional outburst, but they were protestations that became increasingly half-hearted as he became ever more comfortable in his command of English as a writing language, and ever more worldly and heartfelt in his use of it.

Of *course* the songs were personal. How else does a lyricist write if not by drawing on personal experience? Unless, of course, you're Kate Bush and you read loads of heavy books. Personal nostalgia and difficult affairs of the heart, that was Bjorn's forte throughout Abba's career, sad songs generally having more impact and meaning than happy ones. 'I'm fed up, the bastard has gone and I'm gonna kill myself' generally wields a little more emotional power than 'Everything is perfect and I am awfully happy, thank you very much'.

Bjorn's words were to reach an astonishing level of maturity and emotional conviction in the later stages of Abba, but 'SOS' once again set the tone for these outbursts. A tortuous private life is always a great recipe for a good lyricist and the mental torment of the grief between him and Agnetha served him well.

'SOS' brought them back from the dead. It wasn't to be one of their hugest hits, but it restored them to the charts of Europe, reaching Number 6 in Britain in 1976, and proved there was life after 'Waterloo'. And it established a solid pattern they were to perfect and ultimately elaborate on with such accomplishment over the next few years. It was their first single released with an accompanying video, a medium they were to pioneer as it became obvious to all at Polar that here was another short cut begging to be exploited. The videos became an important means of creating the glamorous aura that came to be associated with them.

Given a second crack, there was to be no holding them now. Bjorn and Benny had finally found their range and went full tilt. Excess subtlety never got a pop group anywhere – who needs to be considered classy when you can have *hits*? Ask Deacon Blue, or Prefab Sprout. Bjorn and Benny found a groove and they tucked right into it. The next single 'Mamma Mia', was 'SOS', but more so. That annoying 'Puppet On A String' fairground jingle tingled away in the background, burying its claws deep into your brain, there was a vigorous coda and a chorus that *flew* out of the traps all lush and fresh with Agnetha and Frida's harmonies and a vastly more streamlined arrangement and production job. More angry lyrics, too, though you wouldn't know it from the cheery expressions on the artists' faces: *'I've been cheated by you since I don't know when . . .'* they wailed. Anger, defiance, bitterness – and true love reigning in the end. Abba had well and truly cracked this pop lark.

'Mamma Mia' ultimately had a bigger run at the top than 'Waterloo'. It was a smash all over Europe, topping the charts through the early weeks of '76, and belatedly dragging with it the *Abba* album from whence it came. It also bore the definitive Abba video, closing in on the lips of Agnetha and Frida at opposing angles in a filming technique that was to be repeated with huge success on different parts of their anatomy down the years. And in her white flared costume and frizzy dark hair, Frida even bore an uncanny resemblance to Brian May of Queen, an ironic similarity given Queen's own dominance of the charts and the video field with their own all-conquering 'Bohemian Rhapsody'. 'Mamma Mia' sounded like the perfect pop record. Still does. But then so does everything else they put out over the next three years.

It also resolved the dilemma over Abba's long-term future. They'd gone into Eurovision on a partly experimental basis, just to see what the wind blew up. None were as convinced as Stig about the group's long-term international potential, least of all Agnetha and Anni-Frid, both still keeping their own solo careers simmering. The post-Eurovision flops seemed to confirm their doubts and misgivings and while supposedly committed to Stig's Abba dream, they were never that convinced about their own long-term roles in it, and both went ahead with solo albums in Sweden in 1975. At this time Agnetha was still contracted as a solo act to CBS-Cupol in Sweden, fulfilling her part of the deal with a mildly feminist effort called 'Eleven Women In Our House'. And poor Frida, who'd striven so long and hard to get any real credit with her solo material, suddenly found herself with massive hits in Scandinavia. Her *Frida Ensam (Frida Alone)* album portrayed her as a sex kitten and suddenly she and not Agnetha was the nation's darling. The album (which included the original Swedish language version of 'Fernando' and 10cc's 'Wall Street Shuffle') topped the Swedish charts and, having worked and waited so long for this level of breakthrough in her own right, she was anxious to take it to its limit. Basically she wanted out of Abba to be the solo star she'd dreamed of being for so long.

Love and Stig eventually changed her mind. She would have more success than she could possibly dream of if she stayed with Abba, Stig told her, and Stig is rarely wrong. Even when he is, he doesn't *appear* to be. The combination of Stig's insistence that she must stay to give Abba her full commitment and her natural desire to be with Benny as much as she could put her solo ambitions in abeyance. Just, she emphasized, for the time being.

Agnetha, too, was a problem. She still wanted a solo career, and there was some more hard talking from Stig before she was persuaded to fly to America with the rest of the band for a promotional tour in 1975. Her fear of flying and the prospect of being parted from her daughter Linda set her against the trip. She eventually relented, taking Linda with her, but it was an unhappy trip that appeared to have little immediate benefit to the Abba cause. Agnetha's future with Abba seemed as uncertain as Anni-Frid's towards the end of 1975.

But the release of 'Mamma Mia' in December 1975 buried all the doubts. There was no more talk of splits and solo careers once 'Mamma Mia' had taken a hold, belatedly hitting the top of the British charts after an epic grapple with Queen's 'Bohemian Rhapsody'. It was the same story throughout Europe, while 'Mamma Mia' was also the record that caught the imagination of the Australians. Abba went on their first promotional trip to Oz in 1976 where they made an embarrassingly coy TV special involving intimate conversations with koalas and parading a succession of what looked like gaudy pyjamas. It didn't matter. Abba were fêted wherever they went in Australia and the full force of their international appeal was starting to become apparent. The Americans were still largely sceptical, but then that's Americans for you.

Buoyed by the success of 'Mamma Mia', Bjorn and Benny went into the studio full of confidence as they prepared material for their next album, *Arrival*. They put out their own English language version of 'Fernando', the song they'd originally written for Frida's solo album, and made use of all the pomp and dramatic solemnity that only a military drum can provide. It sounded more exotic and grand than it actually was, but a hit song is a hit song, and Bjorn and Benny had proved they could step at least some way beyond the 'SOS'/'Mamma Mia' school of bubblegum mayhem and still get hits. 'Fernando' duly became another massive hit all around the world in 1976 and cued Abba up for the avalanche that Bjorn and Benny were frenziedly putting together for *Arrival*.

They were smitten by success by now. For the first time they had supreme confidence in their own ability to knock out international hits. Bjorn and Benny reached a purple patch of composing and the twin rewards of money and ego-boosting acclaim were artistic aphrodisiacs. Frida had a million ideas for costume and image, Agnetha prided herself on singing and harmonies, Bjorn and Benny were exploring new adventures with melody and technique by the day, and they found that success fuelled rather than dulled their own ambition. They used to think Stig was potty with all his dreams and talk of international stardom in every continent; now his dreams were their dreams too.

In the summer of 1976 they played at a highly prestigious ball in Stockholm in front of King Carl Gustaf on the eve of his wedding to Silvia Sommerlath. Anybody doubting the depth of ambition now raging within Abba should check out their performance at the ball. They showcased 'Dancing Queen', a song widely interpreted as having been written in honour of the future queen – a notion Stig did nothing to discourage – although Benny, Bjorn and Stig had actually put it together six months earlier. They bowed and beamed and decked themselves out for the occasion in unbelievable period costume that made them look oddly like something out of a Shake-spearean sonnet. Agnetha and Frida were all heaving bosoms and hair in ringlets, billowing velvet frocks,

decorative bonnets and frills a-go-go. This was breath-
takingly embarrassing, but it was nothing to how the boys
looked. Benny managed to hide most of his own hideous
attire behind his piano, but Bjorn's discomfort was there
for all to see . . . a ridiculous bow in the hair and . . . wait
for it . . . white *tights*. This was a group wondering why
they weren't accorded their due respect and complaining
that people didn't take them seriously enough as an
albums band?!? No, this was a group caught in the very
heart of obsessive ambition, prepared to expose themselves to any embarrassment or indignity in pursuit of the
treasure trove of rewards beginning to reveal themselves
in front of them.

'Dancing Queen' duly smashed the States for them,
and inadvertently later became a disco classic, too; Bjorn's
simple story of a dancer unwittingly anticipating the disco
age. A fluke, of course, but the slightly grubbier
production helped give it a life beyond Abba and all its
connotations of era, style and timing. Like 'YMCA' by the
Village People, like 'I Will Survive' by Gloria Gaynor, like
'Ride On Time' by Blackbox, 'Dancing Queen' became
submerged in some weird kind of shadowy secret life,
having divorced itself completely from the saccharine
image which at the time still plagued its creators. More
atmosphere than style, more beer than froth, it may also
have altered a few attitudes about Abba en route. The
crucial power of the backing track inspired all the
members of the group to excel themselves and it was one
song on which Agnetha and Frida displayed real rapport
and comradeship in the performances on record and on
stage. Much later Frida went on record as saying that
'Dancing Queen' was her favourite Abba song of them
all.

It hit the top of the charts everywhere in 1976 from Austria to Australia, Switzerland to South Africa, selling three million copies and preluding the release of the *Arrival* album, which confirmed that Benny and Bjorn were now completely on fire. Their first world tour had been announced to heighten the unlikely frenzy now surrounding everything touched by Abba. *Arrival* yielded two other smashes, 'Money, Money, Money' and 'Knowing Me, Knowing You', as well as another couple of songs destined to play a prominent role in their stage performance, 'Tiger' and 'When I Kissed The Teacher', which Bjorn later regarded as one of his favourites.

'Money, Money, Money' certainly marked a departure. A video depicting Agnetha and Frida in thirties-style flapper dresses, with feathers in their hair, was as surreal as anything they'd done and the song itself could have been right out of Lionel Bart's score for *Oliver. 'I work all night, I work all day to pay the bills I have to pay,'* growled Anni-Frid seductively in the manner not of Fagin from *Oliver* but Sally Bowles from *Cabaret.* Unless you count 'I Do, I Do, I Do, I Do, I Do', it was also the first time they revealed a more cinematic approach to writing, boldly splitting verse and chorus to a cavernous degree and also revealing for the first time the sense of irony in which Benny Andersson, particularly, privately excelled. How can you sing *'There never seems to be a penny left for me'* with any degree of sincerity when everyone's saying your company's earnings are second only to Volvo? It was the first, but not the last time they were to take the rise out of themselves in this way, though few saw the joke. Few others saw, either, that 'Money, Money, Money' would lead them eventually towards a long and winding road into the realm of musicals. Nobody thought they were capable of it. But armed with such a formidable armament of success, Bjorn and Benny were themselves starting to think along those lines. And 'Money, Money, Money' was the first step up that ladder.

'Knowing Me, Knowing You' was different again, a giant leap into maturity, both musically and lyrically. Several leagues on even from 'Mamma Mia'. Stig was still getting credits on the songwriting, but this was surely the moment Bjorn gave vent to his inner soul and Abba started to give an imitation of real life rather than cartoon comic strips. *'No more carefree laughter, silence ever after . . .'* sang Agnetha mournfully on a lyric that retrospectively spoke volumes about the human condition as seen through the eyes of Bjorn Ulvaeus, and specifically about his collapsing relationship with Agnetha.

Melodically, too, it flowed with none of the rasping poppery and self-consciousness that afflicted many of their earlier songs. Their one gimmick in 'Knowing Me, Knowing You' was the grunting 'a-ha' at the end of the first line of the chorus, from which the Norwegian pop icons of the mid-eighties took their name (we don't think). If you're talking class and sheer quality, then 'Knowing Me, Knowing You' was their best to date and still stands up to scrutiny both as a song and an arrangement. It's the sort of song that could be interpreted in any style by any act in any era . . . that's the mark of a good song. But whatever anybody ever does to it, Abba's version will always be definitive and that fact alone is a mark of their emerging stature by this time. Nothing they'd done before this could stand up to either challenge.

'Knowing Me, Knowing You' was another Number One, knocking 'Chanson d'Amour' by Manhattan Transfer off the top of the British charts in February 1977.

Which makes you wonder a bit about the late seventies, frankly. Despite all the protestations about punk revolutions, Abba were knocking *Manhattan Transfer* off the top of the British charts?!? The most notable thing about Manhattan Transfer was that they had a red-headed singer called Laurel Masse who was nine feet tall and was loved and adored in every gay bar in New York. 'Chanson d'Amour' was still a crap record, though.

Despite the way history has been rewritten, punk was still relatively small fry in commercial terms. It was only later when people like the Clash and the Jam and the Stranglers and the Police and Elvis Costello began to emerge from its entrails to discover that while it had 'ENEMY SCUM' written all over it, the much-maligned tradition of good tunes did have some decent characteristics. Like it was more likely to get you in the charts and make you lots of money. Nobody believed all that garbage about overthrowing the music industry and creating musical co-operatives – they just wanted to get rid of Genesis and Yes so they could get a wedge for themselves, a process severely complicated by the need for tunes.

Abba, reviled as they universally were by every cool dude on the planet, had a greater influence on music than the Sex Pistols ever did for all their antagonistic posturing and unrelenting publicity. Bjorn Again weren't the first group to come along playing old Abba hits. Loads of people were doing it at the time. Brotherhood of Man, for one. They just changed the tunes a little and altered the titles. Brotherhood of Man were an odd one – they originally came together and had a couple of hits in 1970, the most famous of them being 'United We Stand', which sounded like a football chant but in fact became adopted as an anthem for American gay liberation groups. After Abba had won Eurovision with 'Waterloo', Brotherhood of Man magically reappeared in 1976 with the same double couple line-up to sing 'Save Your Kisses For Me' to win the contest with the biggest margin in Eurovision history. They were Abba, but *more* so. Leather jackets, double chins, silly hats . . . *and* they were English. A marketing man's dream – the English Abba. It's like boxing promoters looking for a white heavyweight champion.

Brotherhood of Man, it was swiftly revealed, weren't on the same planet. If Abba coughed, Brotherhood of Man would be in the studio doing the same thing with a few more splutters and an extra choke or two. But they were fools' gold. The Swedishness had become part of Abba's magic, those accents an integral part of the appeal; their total absence of taste in fashion an essential ingredient of their kitsch irresistibility; their lack of hipness itself an unwitting conspirator in their cult status. Brotherhood of Man were merely masquerading in the role of great white hopes, though it was a lucrative, if short-lived masquerade. After Abba had come out with 'Fernando', Brotherhood of Man emerged with 'Angelo', a tearjerker about some Mexican kid who falls in love with a rich woman and dies. Just like that.

But Abba had Bjorn and Benny and Brotherhood of Man had Tony Hiller, who somehow wasn't quite as good. And where Abba moved effortlessly on from 'Fernando' to 'Dancing Queen' and 'Money, Money, Money', Brotherhood of Man stuck in the same Latin groove for 'Figaro'. It went to Number One, but Abba were by now out of sight and the contest was over. There were other, lesser challenges but they were too little, too late. Abba's class was now seeing off all invaders.

By the end of '77 Abba's flame lit up the firmament.

The world tour had been successfully negotiated. It drained them emotionally but it set up enough gushing momentum to carry their star soaring into the following year with the release of the movie and the coinciding *Abba the Album* and its own treasure trove of hits. 'The Name Of The Game' was the first. It's another great song, immaculately constructed and produced, offering yet another intriguing insight into their psyche. It's a song of cautious triumph, while openly proclaiming confusion and insecurity. It also finely displays the subtle, yet powerful contrast in the two girls' voices. Frida's was always technically better – deeper, sultry, textured, more controlled, more versatile and flexible. Yet Agnetha's was consistently the more lethal pop weapon – occasionally shrill, sometimes even flat, yet never less than emotive and evocative, perhaps the single most effective tool in the Abba arsenal. Despite (or maybe because of) their personal differences they were voices that blended well together whether in unison or harmonizing, when Frida's voice would invariably be more effective in the less glorified anchor role. But when they got to the real gut-wrenching material late on in their career like 'The Winner Takes It All' and 'The Day Before You Came', Agnetha's more heart-on-the-sleeve style was always favourite to carry the song . . . and your soul with it.

Abba the Album also gave us the classic 'Take A Chance On Me', with its wonderful parrot-style backing vocal from Bjorn and Benny and the video that looked like a game show. Four squares, four faces. Pick the face that winks and win a bungalow in Tahiti. Oops sorry, madam, it's not Benny this time, it's Anni-Frid. Come back next week to see if you can SPOT THE WINKER. That's *winker*, okay?

They were heavily into the studio by now with all the tricks and toys at their disposal. No credits for Stig this time, just a long soaring chorus, an intricate meandering verse, and some gorgeously lush arrangements to carry it all along in a wave of euphoric passion. There were other big songs on *Abba the Album*. The whole of 'The Girl With The Golden Hair' segment from the live shows for one, including the anthemic 'Thank You For The Music' which became one of their most famous songs, though it wasn't released as a single until four years later. There were worries at the time that the song would be misinterpreted outside the context of 'The Girl With The Golden Hair' and might dump them into an unwanted area of the market in AOR. They might have been right, too, though by now they should have been way beyond worrying about image and their position in the marketplace. 'Thank You For The Music' is, of course, overly sentimental, but the polish of the craftsmanship in its construction is unmistakable enough to lift it beyond such unworthy pedantics. 'Thank You For The Music' flew the flag for their bid for Broadway, while 'Eagle' at the other extreme was pure California in thought and deed. Just glide on to the LA Freeway, open the roof and let her roll.

'Eagle' became a firm favourite within the band because it showed another dimension to their style, a freer, more modern country-rock style that collided favourably with their more overtly pop reputation and you could well imagine one of the Californian rock mafia doing it. In truth, they might have made a little more of it, too. Lap steel guitars might have done wonders for it, but it's a song which made Bjorn and Benny exceptionally proud and which the girls loved to sing.

By now they were searching for new directions. They started using words like 'development' and 'progression'. Different avenues had opened up to them from *Abba the Album* and Bjorn and Benny were anxious to explore further. No worries there. Their curiosity had served them well to this point and their instincts had been sound. But *Saturday Night Fever* was suddenly the overwhelming sensation of youth culture, disco was everywhere, and for the first time since 'SOS', Abba broke from their natural course and attempted to chase the fashion. Big mistake. They'd already inadvertently mastered the disco idiom with 'Dancing Queen' and in time were to deal with it in totally convincing fashion with the brilliant 'Gimme! Gimme! Gimme! (A Man After Midnight)'.

In 1978, though, they tried to be the Bee Gees and put out the worst single of their lives, 'Summernight City'. Even the Bee Gees weren't really the Bee Gees – veteran pop heroes who'd somehow stumbled into John Travolta on the dance floor, found a bit of new technology and suddenly become the hippest record merchants on the planet. There's lots of morals here about people trying to be something they're not and falling flat on their faces and Abba knew instantly they'd blown it. Their astonishing run of chart-toppers came to a clattering halt as their mystified fans came home clutching their latest booty and went marching back to the record store thinking that somehow the wrong name had been put on the label.

'Summernight City' was still a Top Ten record throughout most of Europe, but it was indefensibly obnoxious, with none of the joyous characteristics which had elevated Abba to their dizzy heights thus far. Even Benny and Bjorn themselves later expressed regret about ever recording the song, let alone releasing it as a single.

And you thought Abba wore silly clothes! Bjorn (left) with the Hootenanny Singers in 1966 when nobody batted an eye at the pink shirts and mustard suits. (Bertil Wöllner, Pressens Bild AB)

Bjorn singing with the Hootenanny Singers in more informal mode during their Kingston Trio period. (B. Mattson, Pressens Bild AB)

In the euphoric aftermath of 'Waterloo'. (London Features International)

Yes, they really *did* wear silver platform boots! Note, too, the subtle heart-shaped outbreak of flesh on Agnetha's tummy. (Redferns)

A picture of domestic bliss in a rare bout of peace and quiet for Bjorn, Agnetha and Linda. (Heilemann, Camera Press Ltd)

Agnetha at home playing the perfect housewife, though scraping saucepans somehow never seemed quite her style. (Heilemann, Camera Press Ltd)

Above: Classic Abba!
(Redferns)

Left: Abba get down
to business with Stig.
But the empire
strikes out . . .
(London Features
International)

In another life they might have been a Japanese kick-boxing team.
(Michael Ochs Archives)

Frida recognizes the guy responsible for choosing their wardrobe.
(Waring Abbott/Michael Ochs Archives)

Agnetha . . . people just wouldn't stop going on and on and on and on about her bottom. (Camera Press Ltd)

A romantic moment between Benny and Anni-Frid. Seductive lighting, a bottle of red wine . . . Benny has an uncontrollable urge to poke her in the nose. (Heilemann, Camera Press Ltd)

This is the life! Bjorn enjoys the fruits of success. (Camera Press Ltd)

Above: By the '80s Abba were a little mixed up. Here they are in their judo outfits. (London Features International)

Left: Sweden's answer to Lady Di relaxes on a trip to the States. (Michael Ochs Archives)

They thought it sounded young and groovy at a time of their lives when they found themselves thinking they were old and grouchy, but that's what emotional woes do to you.

Abba were to revisit the disco boom in some earnest on the *Voulez-Vous* album, but initially repaired the catastrophe that had been 'Summernight City' by going back to basics. A hint of Latin, an exotic story song, that fairground tinkling behind the melody line, lush chorus, a shade of Shangri-Las backing vocals, beautifully clean production. It had to be 'Chiquitita'. It emerged in early 1979 at a fragile time in their careers. The shock news of Bjorn and Agnetha's divorce was still reverberating around a disbelieving world, and they'd just appeared in New York at the biggest show of their lives – a massive concert in aid of UNICEF which also featured the Bee Gees, Rod Stewart, Donna Summer, Kris Kristofferson, Olivia Newton-John and Earth, Wind & Fire. The spotlight was focused closely on Abba, searching for cracks, their obituaries as a force in pop music already being written.

That next single had to be a killer to rescue the situation. 'Chiquitita' was that killer. Everything Abba ever did well was on the record. They also announced they were donating all royalties from 'Chiquitita' to UNICEF, a further display of solidarity sending a clear message that all was well with Abba, and life went on. It scored massively in South America, selling a million copies in Mexico alone, inspiring their first Spanish language releases; while it was warded off the top of the British charts only by Blondie's 'Heart Of Glass' and specifically the media's love affair with Debbie Harry (Agnetha in her undies). That small blip apart, 'Chiquitita' was a public announcement that everything in the garden of Abba was fine and dandy. Except, of course, really it wasn't.

The changing face of pop had deeply affected them. Bjorn and Benny were desperate to keep ahead of the game and not be seen as stuffy period pieces. They'd always prided themselves on their technological prowess and their visionary use of it, and talked long and hard of moving away from Polar and Stockholm to expose themselves to the new experiences and influences they felt were necessary to fire them into the eighties. These influences, they decided, were to be found in America. As a foursome they'd already discussed – and rejected – the idea of decamping en masse to the States for a concerted bid to conquer the American market once and for all, as many British bands found they had to do in the past. Having, they felt, sacrificed enough already of their domestic stability in the cause of international success, they weren't prepared to donate any more years chasing the aces across America.

But Bjorn and Benny felt they might be able to short-circuit the system by at least absorbing some of the modern studio techniques currently lighting up the dance floor and applying them to their next album. They spent some time at the Criteria Studios in Miami, experimenting with an American rhythm section and laying down some tracks with American producer Tom Dowd.

In the final shout they went back to Polar and Stockholm to make the album, but *Voulez-Vous* nevertheless had a different flavour . . . a harder edge, a meaner sound, a heavier rhythm, a deeper lyric, a dancier feel. Abba-ologists are still split on *Voulez-Vous*. It was the fastest-selling Abba album of them all, and did include both 'Chiquitita' and the anthemic 'I Have A Dream', but the drift to style over content smacked more of compromise than enterprise. 'Does Your Mother Know' was an appalling choice as its flagship single. It was conceived as a raw, thumping, dirty rocker to announce their arrival in the big boys' league, but instead sounded like something they might have perpetrated pre-'Waterloo' six years earlier with Agnetha and Frida relegated to hapless backing singers while Bjorn pretended to be Mick Jagger. Bjorn can never be forgiven for singing the line *'I can't take a chance on a chick like you'* and keeping a straight face. The lyric police should be round to carry out instant execution on anybody caught using the word 'chick' in a pop song. Unless, of course, it's a song about hens . . .

Worse was to follow. The next double A-side of 'Angeleyes' and 'Voulez-Vous' confirmed their embracing of the tried and the turgid. As a song 'Angeleyes' sounded like one of their Eurovision rejects and as a production sounded like it had been recorded in the garden shed; while the marginally more intriguing 'Voulez-Vous', using the Tom Dowd American backing track, suggested an ill-advised early discovery of grunge and an experiment they were perhaps well advised not to persist with for longer. Bjorn and Benny were searching, but they hadn't found. And they sure as hell wouldn't find it by blunting their most powerful weaponry and pushing Agnetha and Frida into the shadows, however much tension there sometimes was between them.

By this time, the middle of 1979, they were in the throes of their second world tour and all the inner turmoil resulting from it. There seemed no future for them, yet from the morass of mixed-up influences now swirling around them, there inexplicably emerged a solid-gold classic. 'Gimme! Gimme! Gimme! (A Man After Midnight)' was recorded as an additional track to go on a greatest hits album being released to cash in on the tour and it was a blinder. It took on disco, it took on hard rock, it took on sex, it took on credibility, it took on commerciality, it took on experimentation . . . and it sounded *great*. All of a sudden Abba were gods of the dance floor, and 'Gimme! Gimme! Gimme! (A Man After Midnight)' was, in tandem with 'Dancing Queen', the track that took Abba into the hearts of the gay scene and more than any other gave them life in the nineties. And, despite all the heavy breathing invoked by Agnetha's bum, it gave both Agnetha and Frida a genuine sexiness after all those years of contrived sex appeal and revealing costumes. This, at a time when neither had felt less sexy, having just crawled from the wreckage of their marriages. Weird, weird, weird.

Weirder still, this wreckage gave their creativity more of a fillip than any number of trips to groovy studios in America and studied analysis of disco technique can do. They defied the odds to plod on into the eighties after the world tour and, stripped of pretence and illusion, wrote the best music of their lives.

'The Winner Takes It All' introduced them to the new decade free of the cloying decorations that had turned so many against them in the previous one. No more satin jumpsuits or false glam promises. Abba finally allowed themselves to be themselves without fear of destroying any grand illusion – everyone knew the game was up. The release it injected was glorious, if galling.

'The Winner Takes It All' was and is a brilliant song – an absolute masterpiece of construction surrounding the greatest lyric Bjorn ever wrote, all the more harrowing for its inescapable connection with the group's own tattered personal lives. There was no attempt to disguise the melancholia in a brilliantly evocative video, either, a disarming portrait of a dishevelled, lonely Agnetha drowning in blue eye shadow that was too close to reality for comfort.

It preluded what was to be a formidable comeback after the dour mish-mash of *Voulez-Vous*. More than any other, the *Super Trouper* album marked Bjorn and Benny's arrival as truly *great* songwriters whose work bore comparison with any of the other great songwriters of the century. They'd mastered all the styles, they'd tasted all the bitter-sweet emotions of life and now they knew exactly how to commit them to posterity. 'Super Trouper' itself, their last Number One, was a clever and original reflection of their distaste for life on the road, while the third single off the album, 'Lay All Your Love On Me', was a vastly underrated excursion back into pure pop territory.

The whole album was outstanding. They drew on the Beach Boys once more with 'On And On And On', but they were positive and committed now; while the extraordinarily pretty 'Our Last Summer', gushingly nostalgic and sentimental but also quite beautiful, would have made an excellent single. Bjorn was also particularly pleased with 'Happy New Year', a further advance lyrically commenting on the state of the world which in a weak moment he was even moved to describe as 'political'. *Super Trouper* was also the album which included a live performance of the wondrous 'The Way Old Friends Do' (later covered by the Alexander Brothers), which Abba had used to devastating effect at the end of the show on the last tour, the four of them coming to the front of the stage to link arms around Benny's accordion and dissolve the audience into tears.

They really should have ended it there, with the big flourish, though in fairness the techno spurts which provoked their return to competitive action a couple of years later did also provide some gems, lyrically and musically. 'One Of Us' was the first sign of it, a glorious soaring melody, shades of Karen Carpenter lushness and a heart-tripping lyric. But as far as the mysterious and thoroughly confusing *The Visitors* album was concerned, 'One Of Us' flattered to deceive. Bjorn and Benny were searching again – and some of their ideas, notably on the atmospheric textures of the title track, were intriguing enough – but they seemed unsure of their direction. And if they were, their audience sure as hell were too. Their fans barely recognized them as Abba and despite the kick-start applied by 'One Of Us', *The Visitors* was universally decried as duff and many closed the book on Abba there and then. The only other single to emerge from the album was the deeply theatrical 'Head Over Heels', clever in its own way but scarcely what the doctor ordered and a resounding flop. Inexplicably they didn't release the one song from the album capable of turning things around for them, the sadly resigned 'When All Is Said And Done', a mature piece of work delicately putting the lid on Benny and Frida's marriage in an upbeat way that would have struck a chord with their audience. But the group themselves were uncertain whether they wanted to go on, and if they were uncertain, the rest of the world wasn't going to give them another chance. They'd been a thorn in the side of the hip factory for too long.

Yet Bjorn and Benny were still an explosive song-writing force with plenty of ideas still to explore and they certainly weren't ready to throw in the towel. Whether they still wanted to commit themselves to these ideas in tandem with their estranged wives was a different matter entirely. The celebrations surrounding their tenth anniversary in 1982 were just about enough to crank them back into action with some conviction. The two additional tracks they recorded for *The First Ten Years* double album compilation were both crackers, though entirely different, and giving opposing insights into the cracked experience that was Abba in the eighties.

Agnetha turned up for events looking almost dowdy, in tinted glasses and weary countenance. Frida, greying hair swept brusquely back, was described by one tabloid at the time as 'alarmingly ageing', a phrase she was to hoot at from time to time with an amusement she wouldn't have been able to find a few years earlier. Both Frida and Agnetha had solo albums to do and Bjorn and Benny were off playing chess, but their dual swansongs were both fiercely better than either was given credit for at the time.

'The Day Before You Came', in fact, was a masterpiece, quite one of the best things Abba ever recorded. A wild departure musically and lyrically from anything they'd ever done before, it was fortified by a glorious video featuring a knowing Agnetha flirting deliciously with a stranger on a train. The perfect woman looked battered but not defeated . . . and so much the better for it. A wonderful song belatedly given its due reward when revived by techno duo Blancmange a couple of years later, but it did nothing to restore Abba to public favour in '82. It was as if the world had mentally closed the book on Abba, and the compilation double album merely served to confirm it. The fact that 'The Day Before You Came' matched each of the proud parade of hits on the album seemed to carry no weight. Even more significantly it came backed by another previously unreleased corker, 'Cassandra', which dipped further into Hispanic style – 'South Of The Border' in a Swedish accent. Majestic. Better even than 'Fernando', but destined for the scrapheap as a throwaway B-side at the fag end of their career.

And then they were left with one. In another time, another place, 'Under Attack' might also have been considered a classic. Lots of studio jiggery pokery went on in the verse which perhaps confirmed radio programmers' prejudices about the emptiness of their tank, yet the performance and the chorus were slap bang on target. Played once, never forgotten, that's the motto of every pop songwriter and if the verse got in the way, the chorus fully met the criteria. So 'Under Attack' shrunk away into the sunset, too, on the back of a grungey, scowling video, all leathers and attitude, seemingly shot in a parking lot. And with it went Abba's last shot as the mightiest pop band in the universe.

Bjorn and Benny hadn't quite given up the ghost at this point and were fully prepared to go back to it after *Chess*. Several tracks, in fact, were recorded in some shape or form for the projected *Opus 10* which ultimately died of boredom before delivery. But the one song that has seen the light of day since – 'I Am The City', included on the *More Abba Gold* collection – suggests a further move into techno rhythms allied to an outstanding chorus that may not have been sufficient to have lifted them back into the front line in the caring, sharing mid-eighties, but indicated they had lost none of their unique individuality.

Abba's music stands up. Most of it does. Pretty much

all of it does. The frocks don't. The hairdos don't. The beards *certainly* don't. The arrangements and production sometimes don't. But those songs . . . those Godlike songs. Any time, any era, any place. They're up there. The best. The very *best* . . .

7

A STAR IS BJORN

'Look at me now, will I ever learn? I don't know how,
but I suddenly lose control
There's a fire within my soul'

'Mamma Mia'

J ust as Agnetha and Frida are chalk and cheese, so too
are Bjorn and Benny. The soft, lovable easygoing
nature of Benny contrasts strongly with the sharp,
organized practical Taurean mind of Bjorn Ulvaeus.

But unlike Agnetha and Frida, who found the
difference between them an impossible gulf, Bjorn and
Benny made their contrasting characters work to mutual
advantage. They were both big enough to acknowledge
their own shortcomings, recognizing how much the
other complemented their own talents. They offered
different skills, fresh ideas, new angles and, in unison,
sparked each other to greater heights. Benny needed
someone to nudge and prod and urge and inspire to prise
out his exceptional gift for composition; Bjorn's own
regimented musical vision was limited without the flare of
Benny's genius for melody.

They were both stars of different sorts before meeting,
but it's doubtful if either would have sustained any
substantial degree of commercial appeal without the
inspirational contribution of the other. It's tempting to
imagine how life would have been for them without

Abba. Benny would most likely have partied until the money ran out and maybe imagined he was burnt out too and that the group he'd hooked up with in the sixties, the Hep Stars, had represented the limit of his creativity. After all, he couldn't sing, he couldn't write a decent lyric and he couldn't get up in the mornings.

Bjorn could do all those things and he provided the impetus to stir Benny into action and challenge himself in a way he never could have done in the anarchic excesses of the Hep Stars. Bjorn had a razor-sharp mind and a rampaging ambition to match, recognizing early on the remarkable craft in Benny's musical creations, while seeing the flaws in his character that threatened to hold him back. Bjorn was honest, too, about his own talents and knew he could never be a brilliant songwriter in his own right. But the two of them together, that was different.

Bjorn and Benny have never fallen out. Over anything. There was the odd bout of 'musical differences' which crept in at various times of stress during a dodgy recording session or songwriting block, and some friction inevitably occurred during those hairy days on the road when the girls were at each other's throats hurling plates around the dressing room. But Bjorn liked Benny from the outset – *everyone* likes Benny when they meet him – but more importantly had a sacred respect for his talent, accepting the infuriating traits that accompanied it with a patient humour that both Frida and Agnetha found impossible to match. You give and you take, and Bjorn got the equation spot-on in terms of bringing the best out of Benny. Bjorn was the unofficial boss of Abba, doing the organizing, taking care of business, involving himself in every aspect of the group from ordering breakfast to working out the set list to taking charge during inter-views.

Logical, determined, controlled, intelligent, multi-lingual and – when he put his mind to something – utterly dynamic, Bjorn would have been a success in whatever field life had placed him in. In business, law, sport, fashion, politics . . . Bjorn could size up a situation and instinctively know the most productive way of approaching it for the best results. *And* he had the determination to see it through. Having committed himself to Abba, there was no way his pride would allow him to see it fail. It was seriously suggested to him at one point that he might consider a career in politics after Abba – and his persuasiveness, clarity of thought and articulacy suggest he would have made a decent fist of it too. A confirmed Anglophile, he still reads the English papers avidly and is an authority on international affairs, though he's also displayed diplomatic guile, comprehensively mastering the art of answering questions and expressing opinions without putting noses out of joint or even saying anything of note.

It wasn't always like that, though. There was a time when Bjorn, too, was a reprobate and a wastrel. Stig Anderson described him once as a 'bohemian', he was so wayward and independent, though those who know him only from the tunnel-vision discipline he applied to Abba find it difficult to believe.

He was born in Sweden's second city and its main seaport, Gothenburg, a throbbing metropolis with a harbour serving Denmark and Britain, a thriving car and textile industry, and a centre for students. It was the end of the war and life was good for the Ulvaeus family and their somewhat unruly son. He was undisciplined and temperamental and his boyhood friends and teachers would scarcely have believed they were nurturing a world-shattering talent and a man widely admired for his depth of concentration and level-headedness. His mother played and music was all around him as a kid, though it was to be some time before he displayed any real inclination to take it up seriously himself.

When Bjorn was eleven, the family moved to Vastervik, almost due east of Gothenburg, on the coast 150 miles south of Stockholm. Shortly afterwards the skiffle craze hit Sweden and Bjorn at last allowed his musical inclinations some breathing space and got himself an acoustic guitar and hooked himself up with a local skiffle group.

Nothing serious came of it, but he was established in the local music fraternity and took to playing around for fun with a selection of mates from Vastervik High School, notably Tony Roth, Hansi Schwarz and Johan Karlberg. The skiffle thing had led him to develop a deep interest in jazz and American folk music, vigorously encouraged by his school's art teacher who had a worrying penchant for 'Tom Dooley'. At Bjorn's insistence they briefly embarked on a career playing Dixieland jazz to raise money for school funds. The Dixieland jazz style directed by Bjorn was, he admitted later, an elitist pose adopted largely to impress his mates with the obscurity of his musical influences, rather than springing from any genuine passion or knowledge of Dixieland music.

Bjorn graduated from Vastervik High in 1963 anticipating a move to college to study law, but took time out to further mess around with his mates in the band. They prided themselves on their versatility and catholic musical tastes, but whether playing Satchmo or old Swedish folk

tunes, they always came out sounding like the Kingston
Trio. They were just biding their time, playing for pocket
money, but determined to make the most of it while they
could, and they took off across Europe together, busking
to pay for their travels in an old borrowed and beat-up
Volvo. They did okay, too. It was one way of spending a
holiday and they were encouraged by the response to
their Kingston Trio impressions too: they didn't get
locked up and nobody threw rotten tomatoes at them so
they figured they'd scored a resounding success.

They returned from the adventure ready to be
persuaded to be sensible and go off to college to be
properly trained for the real world. But they had one
more throw of the dice before they dispersed. While they
were away, Bjorn's mum – cowed by having to suffer all
those interminable rehearsals in her front room and
presumably deciding it was somebody else's turn to suffer
– had entered them for a national talent contest
sponsored by Swedish radio. She'd even given them a
name, the West Bay Singers – West Bay being the English
translation of Vastervik.

Their entry came to the attention of a couple of
livewire entrepreneurs, Stig Anderson and Bengt Bernhag, who were frantically in the process of setting up their
own Polar music publishing and recording company.
They had it in their minds that they needed a Swedish
language folk group as their flagship, and the talent-
spotting Bernhag's attention was drawn to the list of
entries in the contest and the fact that the West Bay
Singers were apparently performing in Swedish. Which
wasn't entirely true. Virtually all of the group's repertoire
was drawn from American folk songs and they had to dig
deep to find anything Swedish to sing, being under the

misapprehension that at least one Swedish language song was a prerequisite of the competition.

Sadly they didn't win – and neither did Anni-Frid Lyngstad who'd entered the same competition. We can't even tell you who *did* win the wretched contest, but it's safe to assume they are now leading respectable lives with a bevy of grandchildren and a drawer-full of Model Citizen awards having wisely taken their booty and promptly turned their backs on the evils of the music business.

But the West Bay Singers did reach the last twenty where they performed on national radio and they did impress the would-be moguls at Polar Music. Bengt, particularly, loved the soft-focus harmonies and the gently lilting style. They were a little crude, perhaps, but had a persuasively folkie and fashionably American style – a combination that was fast becoming the height of sixties cool. The West Bay Singers weren't exactly what Stig had in mind when he decided to set up Polar Music as a vehicle for Swedish music and Swedish musicians, but he'd already learned that instincts count far more than cold logic, and resolved that the group would represent his first independent blast at the music business.

Bjorn and the others were bowled over by this totally unexpected and bewildering turn of events. Records? Publishing? Proper concerts? The very idea left them breathless. They'd only been playing as a lark to relieve the tedium of school and never anticipated even in their most fanciful moments that anything beyond an increased ability to pull girls would result from the exercise. But here they were in an office in Stockholm talking contracts with the hugely impressive if dauntingly bluff character of

Stig Anderson and his quieter, wryly humorous sidekick Bengt Bernhag. They seemed to know all there was to know about the music industry and what they didn't know they convincingly *pretended* to know. The West Bay Singers couldn't sign quick enough.

There was more consternation from their families. There were things like university places to consider and not everybody in the wings had Bjorn's faith in the eccentric fast-talking Stig Anderson. A certain amount of familial diplomacy was required – Bjorn had been earmarked for a place at college in London to study law – but his steely qualities emerged for the first time as the Polar Music deal was struck and Bjorn Ulvaeus, Hansi Schwarz, Johan Karlberg and Tony Roth were duly signed as one of the first acts on Polar.

Stig's first move with them was typically bizarre. Having initially been attracted by the name, he decided to impose his influence at the most fundamental level of all – and change it. For no obvious reason beyond a fleeting infatuation with the strictly American trend of informal 'hootenanny' folk song evenings, Stig changed them from the West Bay Singers to the Hootenanny Singers in a faintly desperate bid for attention and supposed grooviness. It was a change that jarred with the band – but was never questioned by them – though the preposterousness of a bunch of Swedes adopting the name of a specifically American phenomenon was made even more curious by Stig's continuing initial insistence that they should be a Swedish language based group. As the limitations imposed by such a policy clearly frustrated band and management alike, this was quickly abandoned while the contradictions of the Swedish band with the American name ultimately shamed even Stig himself into releasing their records under a different name – Northern Lights – in America itself.

Their first release was 'Jag Vantar Vid Min Milla' – curiously translated as 'I'm Waiting At The Charcoal Kiln' – and the song they'd performed at the radio contest. Based on a strange old Swedish folk song, it surprised them all, hitting the Swedish charts with a bang early in 1964. They turned professional shortly afterwards, educations finally abandoned, and Bjorn became a widely respected figure in the slightly elitist Swedish folk scene for his knowledge and understanding of foreign music. His career – and Stig Anderson's Polar Music – was off and running.

The relationship between Stig and Bjorn was to be vitally important to Abba. Benny Andersson wouldn't have known a profit and loss account if it had come up and whacked him in the face – which is exactly what it *did* do when the Hep Stars ran into financial trouble. But Bjorn, hearing the horror stories of English bands being unmercifully ripped off by unscrupulous managers, took a keen interest in the Hootenanny Singers' business arrangements.

But any irritation Stig may have initially felt about the young guitarist continually looking over his shoulder was dispelled as he recognized Bjorn's genuine acumen. He found he could bounce ideas off him without feeling threatened and in time came to see him as an eager prodigy.

Stig himself was making it up as he went along. He still saw himself primarily as a musician and songwriter who was too suss to have his earnings hived off in other directions, and set up Polar as a sort of one-man co-operative. But his sympathies lay with the artists rather than the men in suits, and he saw himself as an artistic guide for the Hootenanny Singers as much as a business guru. So while Epstein wouldn't have dreamed of interfering with the Beatles' artistic output, Stig was to a large extent pulling the Hootenanny Singers' musical strings. Conversely he also involved the band in the bits that were the traditional domain of the manager – promotion, tours, sleeve design, release schedules. He found in Bjorn a crisp and focused mind and the two established a rapport that was to serve them well for the next two decades before money finally came between them.

Bjorn was the natural leader of the Hootenanny Singers, his blond good looks and charisma the one thing the band truly had going for them within the constraints of their rather limp musical style. He in turn was fascinated by Stig's tirelessness and constant enthusiasm. Stig was a larger-than-life character, opinionated and outspoken, laying down the law and never wavering in his belief that he had right on his side in any difference of opinion. He slammed the phone down mid-conversation, he'd be rude to people he'd never met, and he swore and drank more than could possibly be good for him. But his nervous energy, unnerving fidgeting and outright hyperactiveness were an overwhelming influence on a kid fresh out of Vastervik, who really didn't know much at all. Outrageously immodest, he told Bjorn he was the greatest manager in the world. Bjorn believed him . . . and continued to believe him for the next twenty years.

A lot of Stig's dominant traits rubbed off on Bjorn. He felt frustrated and irritated by the situation, believing – probably rightly – that the rest of the band were holding him back.

In time he came to encounter the same dilemma as his mentor, Stig Anderson: whether to concentrate on music or utilize his organizational skills to marshal the talents of others. For a long time Stig attempted to juggle both balls in the air, until the galloping demands of the Abba industry and the accelerating genius of the Andersson-Ulvaeus partnership finally swamped him and stranded him in an exclusively managerial role.

In a different age in different circumstances it isn't difficult to see Bjorn Ulvaeus as the business brains behind an Abba or similar. Without Benny Andersson's intuitive genius to fire his own latent musical talents, it's doubtful if he would have had much success as a songwriter. Just as he provided the catalyst for Benny's random flair, the exciting musical bonfires he helped light in his partner also provoked his own muse beyond anything he might have imagined he was capable of back in the Hootenanny days.

But the business fired up Bjorn almost as much as the music. The whole idea of the industry thrilled him, appealing to his own image of himself as an intellectual, providing the brains behind Benny's consciously laid-back attitude. He defined his own lifestyle early on – he loved fine wine and good conversation, spending hours at a time in smart restaurants with friends expounding high-brow theories on life, the universe and everything; ready, willing and able to engage in animated political debate on any country in the world. He was clever and convincing, which annoyed some people.

Bjorn was close, too, to Stig's partner Bengt Bernhag, the guy who'd zoomed in on the West Bay Singers at the Swedish Radio competition in the first place. Bengt was a wily character who'd been prominent in the Swedish music industry in various guises for more years than anybody dared recall. A funny, likeable character, he'd built a solid reputation as an imaginative promotion man who could – and had – successfully sold a succession of weird and wonderful no-hopers to the Swedish public with a gift for gimmicks and PR scams. He also got involved in A & R, discovering talent in unlikely artists with apparently little claim to it; and to complete his reputation as the ultimate Mr Fixit, he also became a respected studio engineer and producer. An amusing character with a vast depth of knowledge and experience of the business, he was the perfect foil for Stig's intimidating brashness; he'd assemble the bullets for Stig to fire.

Bengt was Bjorn's first point of contact with Polar and, anxious to suck in all the knowledge he possibly could from whatever source he could find it, Bjorn spent a lot of time with him in those early days. The agreeable Bengt was flattered to have such an avid admirer and was happy to pass on as much experience as he could about the business. Their long discussions into the night about the technical side of making records triggered in Bjorn an interest in studios and the mechanics of recording that completely engulfed him and created the grounding for his expert knob-twiddling on the Abba records. It was Bengt who took on the role of producer of the Hootenanny Singers' records and he and Bjorn were to spend a lot of time together during the next couple of years and became firm friends. Laughing at his own use of the cliché, Bengt would tell people he looked upon Bjorn as a son.

By 1970 Bengt had become seriously ill. He suffered from colitis and after major surgery was forced to wear a colostomy bag, an indignity with which he could never come to terms. He continued to work with the Hootenanny Singers for as long as he could, and produced all Polar's major groups, but after Bjorn had left the band he basically became a recluse, suffering his illness alone. When Bjorn married Agnetha in Sweden's society wedding of the year in 1971, Bengt couldn't bring himself to attend in his tragic state. Instead he drove himself out into the countryside near Stockholm and took his own life.

Bjorn heard the news shortly afterwards and was devastated. He'd learned such a lot from Bengt and owed him so much, and in turn Bengt had gleaned untold joy from Bjorn's successes and musical development. It didn't seem real. It didn't seem true. Here he was still heady from his wedding, his new bride without a care in the world, and they were telling him his great old friend had killed himself. He was filled with remorse, guilt, grief. How could he have been celebrating while Bengt was dying? He should have done more. He should have seen it coming. He shouldn't have allowed it to happen.

Benny's kindly understanding ultimately guided him through the trauma, but it was a slow healing process. Stig was keen for Bjorn to take over Bengt's role at Polar, but while he continued to spend a lot of time working in the background there, it was the wrong time and the wrong place for a full-time commitment to studio life. Here was a sensitive soul who already understood well enough the horrors and iniquities in the world, and now had a deep, deep sore of personal heartbreak to deal with on top of it. The paradox that, shortly, he was embarking on the craziest run of fame and fortune in pop history based on gleaming white teeth, false smiles, cartoon clothes and cheery tunes was something never far from his mind. He, of all of them, found it almost unbearable living in the spotlight of a make-believe world where the sun always shone and beauty lay all around.

Bjorn's innate seriousness was the single biggest irony in the blandly smiling, hypocritically cheery, perfect happy family world that Abba somehow got into their minds was their only route to lasting success. In truth, it was the major thorn in their side. It made them seem plastic, unreal and hollow – like an American sit-com full of gooey cute children, wholesome mums and despicably successful dads with immaculate complexions and a never-ending fund of witty one-liners. Life ain't like that and nobody believed Abba were for real. Ever. If Bjorn had dropped his mask and snarled and glowered the way he wanted to it would have been different. If Agnetha and Frida had dropped *their* masks and had a stand-up fist fight in public as they wanted to and should have done, it would have been sensational. Why did they get it so wrong?

Bjorn used the Hootenanny Singers as his apprentice-ship, but it was a pretty miserable, indifferent group with none of the fun and thrills that Benny found in the more lively and successful Hep Stars. But Stig saw the potential in Bjorn. In fact he saw a young Stig Anderson in Bjorn. Stig knew the Hootenanny Singers were merely a means of transport for Bjorn and actively encouraged his long-term ambitions with offers for him to come and work full-time in the Polar offices. The Hootenanny Singers, though, actually survived longer and had more hits than either of them had envisaged.

There was, after all, no shortage of diversions. Bjorn briefly bowed to outside pressure and in 1965 went off to study economics and law at the University of Stockholm while the others took odd jobs, convinced the bubble had burst. But Bjorn couldn't settle at university. He liked the idea of being a student and developing his mind, and still felt his future lay in business rather than in music and that he should stop messing around and lay the groundwork for his future life with some solid qualifications. But the group wouldn't go away. The ball had started to roll and now it was difficult to stop. The Hootenanny Singers continued to tour and record on a part-time basis until Bjorn owned up after a few months and quit college.

There was also the little matter of national service, enforceable in Sweden at the time. The prospect of joining the army hung over all the members of the Hootenanny Singers, and when they got the call-up papers they assumed it would signal the end of the group. They managed to buy themselves some time from the authorities while they embarked on a successful tour of Germany, and their records even began to sell abroad – incongruously they had a big hit in South Africa. But they couldn't put it off for ever and Tony Roth, Johan Karlberg and Bjorn Ulvaeus were eventually ordered to report to the Lifeguards Depot at Linkoping. The fourth member of the Hootenanny Singers, Hansi Schwarz, was a German national and therefore not required to serve in the Swedish military.

They were by now reasonably famous and when they arrived at Linkoping they found the military extraordinarily relaxed about the whole thing. The commander turned out to be a fan and allowed them special leave to continue to gig whenever they needed to, so against all the odds the Hootenanny Singers trawled on with their whimsical harmonies and morose songs. They'd cut the

Swedish language material right back now, realizing that English was the international language of pop and they'd be going the wrong way up a one-way street if they persisted with Swedish songs. Bjorn, the eternal pragmatist, involved himself more and more in writing the group's material, though they were to score the biggest hit of their career with an impassioned Swedish cover of Tom Jones' 'Green Green Grass Of Home'.

The Hootenanny Singers had over twenty hit singles and made nine albums in five years, before Bjorn instinctively knew it was time to take off. The group would always have a limited appeal and while he was the dominant character in the group, Bjorn still felt frustrated by having to defer to the rest of the band on certain musical matters. By 1968, Stig was encouraging him to shed the other three Hootenannies and he started recording solo singles, including a Swedish language cover of Bobby Goldsboro's 'Honey'. He also had some success with 'Froken Fredriksson', a bizarre cover of Jeannie C. Riley's country classic 'Harper Valley PTA'.

He spent more and more time working with Stig and Bengt at Polar, distancing himself from the Hootenanny Singers and laying the groundwork for what Stig was convinced would be glittering solo stardom. Bjorn wanted out from the Hootenanny Singers, well bored by this time with the dated folk style in which they specialized, and keen to push into pop and rock music. This was the style in which he found his own songwriting moving, and this was the music he was keen to pursue further. But the rest of the band had spent years refining their style and having achieved large-scale success with it were understandably reluctant to abandon it at Bjorn's whim. They had none of his self-confidence, determination and ambition, and they had no reason to have. It was a division that clearly needed to be dealt with sooner rather than later.

One night in 1966, the Hep Stars were playing a gig in Vastervik. After coming offstage they piled into the nearest bar, as they usually did, to find local group the Hootenanny Singers already there heading for tomorrow's hangovers. They swapped stories about womanizing and boozing and boozing and womanizing, slapped each other on the back and told dirty jokes in the strange tradition of male bonding.

Bjorn found himself buying pints for the big bearded guy in the Hep Stars who did all the keyboard bits and seemed somehow different to the others. While the others outgunned each other with anecdotes about the women they'd screwed and the guys they'd insulted, Benny and Bjorn solidly talked music. They spent three hours on the Beatles. Another couple on the Beach Boys. A further ninety minutes on Chuck Berry. The drinks kept coming and so did the conversation. Even the perpetually sleepy Benny began to get animated. They were, they discovered, both frustrated by the silent compromises that always had to be made within their respective group structures. They both found themselves urgently saying that their careers would be so much more satisfying if they could write *all* the group's material themselves instead of having to fit in with the dribs and drabs provided by cover versions and other members of the band. Benny was astonished to find himself nodding vigorously while Bjorn spoke of his ambition to form a group with the vision and commercial clout to not only become the biggest thing Sweden had ever seen, but also make it in the rest of Europe, Britain, America, the world!

They laughed like drains. Such ideas were preposterous, it would never happen. They hugged each other and lurched back to their respective groups. Strangers in the night.

But Bjorn and Benny's paths were to cross again several times in the future months and they had similar heart-to-hearts with similar resolutions in similar bars. On a couple of occasions they even found a piano at one end and lightheartedly started knocking out tunes on it, intriguingly discovering an almost perfect match in their styles. When neither of them was working they took to going out for a beer together and visiting each other's flats to swap tunes and ideas. They followed each other's progress around Scandinavia with keen interest and reached crisis points in their careers at similar times, though for different reasons. Benny's crisis was the taxman. Bjorn's was personal ambition.

When in 1969, guitarist Janne Frisck went AWOL from the Hep Stars, in typical Hep Star style failing to make it back from a Spanish holiday in time to take his place on a Swedish tour, Benny Andersson knew exactly who to call. Bjorn Ulvaeus couldn't get across town quick enough to become an honorary Hep Star for the duration of the tour and test his mettle in the whole daft pop firmament.

It wasn't a huge tour but it was hugely significant. After gigs they'd tour whichever town they were in searching for a bar with a piano where they could indulge their twin passions – getting smashed and making music. They were like musical Siamese twins, electrifying each other's muse and inspiring one another to push back their own musical barriers. Eventually they brought some sort of order to the attractive but rambling melodies floating from Benny; Bjorn would sit alongside him at the keyboard as he doodled aimlessly, instinctively adding his own perfectly attuned counterpoints to give Benny's meanderings some desperately needed discipline. Out on the road, in motel rooms, in each other's flats in Stockholm, the most unique and enduring songwriting partnership in pop history was casually forged. Two radically different characters coming to the end of first chapters which they had automatically assumed represented the peak of their careers, but which they now began to see were maybe merely warm-ups for the main event.

Unlike most collaborators, they were a genuine partnership, tinkering on the same set of keyboards at the same time to bang out a tune. It came pretty easily to them as well. The recurring problem they found was, having put together a neat tune, they had to graft in some words on top of it. That's the trouble with audiences – they always seem to want words to fit into the equation. A huge irritation for composers, just as news photographers will tell you that the written word gets in the way of their beautiful pictures.

Elton John had the right idea. He'd been collaborating with Bernie Taupin for a year before it occurred to either of them that they should meet and have a pint together. Elton was in London posting his tunes up to Taupin in Lincolnshire and he'd have them back by return of post full of supposedly deep and meaningful messages that nobody understood, least of all Elton. Good for Bernie, he built a career out of glorified poetry that might never have made it beyond the school magazine, to cause acute embarrassment when it was wheeled out in subsequent years.

The early Abba lyrics were abysmal. Stig Anderson – who prided himself on his tacky rhymes and eardrum-snappingly dumb imagery – had a big hand in these early lyrics and they really were stunningly putrid. *My my, at Waterloo Napoleon did surrender oh yeah/And I have met my destiny.'* What *is* all that about? You wonder how anybody could possibly go on stage in front of thousands of people knowing there are millions watching them on television all round the world and sing, *'My my, at Waterloo Napoleon did surrender oh yeah/And I have met my destiny.'* No wonder they were grinning like lunatics whenever they sang the song.

But then pop lyrics have always been nonsensical. That's the whole point. The most profound pop lyric ever written was *'Be-bop-a-lula, she's my baby, be-bop-a-lula, I don't mean maybe'* by Gene Vincent. Says it all, really. It's all you need to know. That's why some might think that Elton John wasted his money when he bought all those stamps sending his instrumentals to Bernie Taupin to stick his poems on. Did the lyrics really make any difference to sales of his songs?

Lyrics are ludicrously overrated, especially by those writing them. It's as if words somehow take on deep, symbolic significance when they are couched in pretty musical arrangements, just like stories take on a sacred reality when they are put in print. Of *course* you believe everything you read in the paper. Of *course* the lyrics of a song must be cataclysmically important if you hear them on a record.

But how many song lyrics are really that profound? Bob Dylan? The great rock poet, visionary and spokes-man for a generation, that's the great Bob Dylan. Or maybe he's just an airhead. *'How many roads must a man*

walk down, before they call him a man . . .' What's the
story there, then? Oh, I see: *'The answer, my friend, is
blowing in the wind.'* Heavy, heavy, HEAVY stuff, Bobsie.
It's a song about flatulence, right? The theory seems to be
that if nobody understands it, the words must be *really*
good. And if the words don't make any sense at all, then
they must be touching genius and us mere mortals are
simply not clever enough to understand them. Or maybe
Bob just took some dodgy acid that night and was
hallucinating.

For sure pop's lowest ebb was when it started to
imagine it meant something and had a power, influence
and importance beyond its three-minute flashes of fun,
fun, fun. Bob Dylan, the ultimate illusionist, had people
believing music could actually change things and influence public opinion to the point that it could end wars.
Saints preserve us, when Jonathan King – the finest pop
charlatan of them all – strings together a piece of utter
drivel called 'Everyone's Gone To The Moon' and has the
nation falling around on their knees in admiration
thinking he's come up with the pop equivalent of a
George Orwell novel, then we really are in trouble.

Bob Dylan never stopped a war in his life. Nor did any
of the other protest singers who emerged eagerly in his
wake, though they may have started a few in the dash to
rip their pious anthems from the speakers. Worse still, the
distasteful outburst of social consciousness during the
sixties and seventies led to all manner of bozos crawling
out from the cupboard with laughable hair and hilarious
couplets. *'Eastern world, it is exploding. Violence flaring,
bullets loading. You're old enough to kill but not for votin'.
You don't believe in war, but what's that gun you're
toting?'* 'Eve Of Destruction', written by P. F. Sloan, sung

by Barry McGuire, a former member of the New Christy Minstrels, and the man who wrote 'Greenback Dollar' for the Kingston Trio. 'Eve Of Destruction', the ultimate protest song, the symbol of a new age of youth awareness and action. Hey, you can't do that to *our* world, chum, I'm sorry, but we're just gonna have to set Barry McGuire on to ya! You could hear heads of government quivering with fear as 'Eve Of Destruction' came hurtling at them in 1965.

And yep, it was all a con. 'Eve Of Destruction' was a protest song by numbers. Flip Sloan and his chum Steve Barri were house writers at Dunhill Records, keeping the customer satisfied, writing whatever type of hit was required. The idea of staff songwriters is almost unthinkable now in a world where we've been brainwashed into believing that songwriting is all Sting and Phil Collins painfully wrenching a piece of their soul from tortured bodies dripping in sweat to share with us their inner turmoil and most deep-rooted concerns. But way back when it happened all the time. Smokey Robinson, one of the most gifted artists to set foot on this ravaged planet and responsible for two of the ultimate killer-diller drop-dead-every-time-you-hear-'em classics, 'Tears Of A Clown' and 'Tracks Of My Tears', was a jobbing staff writer at Motown. And all those other classic American songwriting teams – Holland-Dozier-Holland, who wrote most of the Supremes hits; Leiber and Stoller, who penned so many of the Elvis Presley classics; Burt Bacharach and Hal David; Goffin and King; Barry Mann, Carole Bayer Sager, Neil Diamond, yeah even *Uncle Neil Diamond* . . . they were all on the songwriting production line, churning out two, three, maybe four songs a day without thought for who might record them or in what style. Sometimes they had customized orders. A romantic number about a serving wench getting it on with a pirate in Tahiti in the eighteenth century? No problem. A sad Christmas song? Certainly, sir. A little ditty about the end of the world with a nice, chunky dance beat? You got it! Hardly the stuff of soul-tearing, but didn't all those people come up with some brilliant, brilliant songs? Yes, even Uncle Neil Diamond found one of his smoochy ballads, 'Red Red Wine', turned into a reggae classic and revived years later in the same style as an international hit for UB40. Neil Diamond wouldn't have recognized reggae if it had come up and offered him a joint when he wrote 'Red Red Wine', but it's still a great song.

Flip Sloan and Steve Barri's particular speciality was surfing and hot-rod songs, but hey, if you're paying you gets what you wants, right? And suddenly the all-American boy had got wind of Bob Dylan and didn't want to go surfing any more, he wanted to save the world. So P. F. Sloan and Steve Barri were given a new brief – save the world. They knocked up 'Eve Of Destruction' in a matter of seconds, almost embarrassing themselves by the ease of their adaptability, and Barry McGuire duly belted it out in suitably angry style in the studio. The label was so thrilled with the results that they whacked a rough mix off to a local radio station and that was the version that came out without the record even being properly completed. It caused an almighty stink, too, outraging conservatives with its revolutionary theme, being banned on various radio stations and having its lyrics analysed by an assortment of heavyweight critics. Whole debates were held on the basis of 'Eve Of Destruction' and it was held up as the benchmark of protest song in the sixties. Its potency may have been considered less lethal had it been widely known that it had been written to order by a couple of giggling guys who'd last week been waxing lyrical about the joys of surfing.

The high status of lyric writing is one of pop's most bizarre myths. The idea that a gifted melody writer needs a partner to add prose to his music is an expensive fallacy. Nobody listens to lyrics. Not first or foremost. They are merely words, appendages to be applied like a sax solo or a bass line to complement the tunesmith's craft. There's an art to it, of course . . . you have to know when to fit the appropriate words in the right spaces just as a cake decorator has to know precisely where to apply the almond icing. But the actual *meaning* of the words chosen for this task is totally irrelevant. Don't believe it? Check it out with Gene Vincent and 'Be-bop-a-lula'. In this sense at least, Marc Bolan knew his oats, recounting reams of complete gibberish in pursuit of his particular goal as king of pop. 'Ride A White Swan'. How fabulously infantile.

The pretentiousness created by this one basic mis-apprehension about pop music somehow being more profound than it has any right to be is mindboggling. It probably stems from the odious self-absorption and exploding egos of the artists themselves. You can tell just by the way he preens and changes his image every week that David Bowie somehow thinks of himself as a true artist when all anybody really wants from him is the banality of 'The Laughing Gnome'. Pop music is silly and trivial and fleeting and floating and meaningless and disposable and momentary and light and frothy and funny and worthless. *That's* what makes it so great. That's what makes it important. That's what makes it last. And *that's* what Abba understood better than most. It's why they were so great. Benny and Bjorn could barely string a sentence together to go with their early tunes and Stig could only come up with unadulterated nonsense. It was one of the great things Abba had going for them to offset the feeling that they'd been styled by a Tyrolean morris dancer.

And so, in the unlikeliest circumstances and strangely obscure surroundings, one of *the* songwriting partnerships of all time was born. Their first collaboration was 'Isn't It Easy To Say', which appeared on the *Hep Stars* album, while they also contributed two songs, 'Speleman' and 'Precis Som Alla Andra', to the *Hep Stars Pa Svenska* LP. But this was merely the hors d'oeuvre before the main course and, spending more time getting to grips with the potential of the studio, didn't they know it!

Benny Andersson was just discovering how broke he really was, and Bjorn Ulvaeus was climbing walls with the frustrations of being captive within the small-time horizons of the Hootenanny Singers. Yet the artistic potential opening up before them as each recognized the contrasting abilities of the other was monstrously exciting. Things could only get different, and different surely meant better. Exactly how much better they could get was something that nobody in their right minds could have had the remotest shot at predicting. Not even the singlemindedly ambitious Bjorn. Certainly not the laid-back Benny. And not even Stockholm's flamboyant answer to Muhammad Ali, Mr Stig Anderson. He never stopped dreaming about it, but even he didn't dare believe it was possible.

8

SUPER TROUPERS

*'All I do is eat and sleep and sing, wishing every show
was the last one'*

'Super Trouper'

Few things in the history of the western world have
been more consistently hopeless and embarrassing
than that great great institution of tack – the pop movie.

It's a misnomer from the outset. A memorial to the
breathtaking ego and conceit of the pop star who
imagines that a bunch of pubescent teenagers wetting
their knickers at the latest interesting haircut instantly
entitles them to make movies as well as crap records. This
clearly isn't the case. The disciplines involved in film and
sound are entirely different, even before we get on to the
thornier matter of whether a couple of hit singles means a
pop singer can *act*. And almost, *almost* without exception,
they can't. The grandest mystery of them all is whatever
possibly possesses them ever to imagine that they *can*.

They bounce into stardom, all bushy-tailed and bubbly,
flush with the arrogance of youth and the false sense of
importance provided by unlimited fan worship and the
fawnings of record company executives attending to their
every need, and imagine they're not only Elvis, but James
Dean too. The magic of the silver screen has thus deluded
transient popsters of three decades into embarrassing dives
into a deep end that swiftly drowns them.

There has thus been a long, ignoble parade of unmitigated donkeys in this disconcerting tradition of pop singer as movie star. The wiser among the animals at least have the grace to look embarrassed about being on screen, but too many others have bought their own publicity and ended up imagining they were truly the purveyors of something deep and meaningful. We mention no names to protect the guilty, and if David Bowie, Mick Jagger, Madonna, Kylie Minogue and Bob Geldof are beginning to shuffle nervously we can't imagine why.

It dates back to the time when Hollywood represented the *only* outlet for teenage fantasy. And rock 'n' roll, when it came, seemed inextricably linked to the screen. Bill Haley belted out 'Rock Around The Clock' over the credits of *The Blackboard Jungle* in 1955 with such spiteful gusto the whole concept of youthful rebellion alluded to in the storyline seemed to come alive. When *The Blackboard Jungle* was banned from the Venice Film Festival at the behest of the US ambassador to Italy, its cult status – and with it the march of youth awareness – began to escalate. The next year's follow-up, titled *Rock Around The Clock*, was effectively the first pop movie, cashing in on the sensation caused by *The Blackboard Jungle* and establishing the miserable benchmark for several generations of cheap, crappy movies unashamedly exploiting the commercial potential endemic in a musical revolution. A vehicle primarily for Bill Haley and the Comets with a thin storyline about the rise of a rock 'n' roll band, it also featured the Platters, Tony Martinez, Freddie Bell and Alan Freed, and ended up as one of the box office smashes of the year, its legend perpetuated by stories of bikers becoming so galvanized by the movie, they started slashing cinema seats.

Films subsequently became a natural addendum to the processes of pop fame. Here was an exciting, distant phenomenon which could almost be touched, assimilated and subsequently aped through the medium of the screen. Long before *Abba the Movie* made it possible for Abba to take a year out while the promotional wheels rolled remorselessly on around the world, the movie and rock industries got into bed together to commit some pretty deviant indulgences. New stars would think in terms of their first movie almost before their first album.

Chuck Berry came roaring into the international spotlight alongside Frankie Lymon, Johnny Burnette, Alan Freed and Tuesday Weld in *Rock, Rock, Rock* (with Connie Francis' voice dubbed in for Tuesday Weld on the singing parts). Little Richard was similarly projected across the Atlantic with his electrifying contribution to the relatively high-budget comedy *The Girl Can't Help It*, which also featured rocking performances from Gene Vincent, Eddie Cochran, Fats Domino, the Platters, Nino Tempo, Ray Anthony and Julie London (the original performance of 'Cry Me A River'). This was also the movie which introduced the ill-fated Jayne Mansfield as the new Marilyn Monroe.

Such was the accepted influence of films both as promotional tool and as an easy money-maker that the greatest rock 'n' roller of them all, Elvis Presley, was to spend most of the next decade apparently doing his level best to bury his explosive talent and appeal in a series of execrable movies. More than any of the others, Elvis couldn't act. But more than any of the others, he thought he could. He could curl his lip, he could look angry, he could get the girl and he could sing the socks off anyone else on the planet; but he was still a useless actor. His performances worsened in direct proportion to the awful roles he was expected to play. *Love Me Tender*, *Loving You*, *Jailhouse Rock* and, especially, *King Creole* offered promise, but it was downhill from there on and Elvis movies – and subsequently even Elvis himself – became something of a joke as a result.

Once Elvis had discredited the whole idea of the pop movie, others were more self-conscious about their own shortcomings. Britain's answer to Elvis, Cliff Richard, had a couple of celebrated cracks at it, starting promisingly enough with the satirical *Expresso Bongo* in 1959 and, as his own light shone ever more brightly, he starred in a couple of period marvels of tack, *The Young Ones* and *Summer Holiday*. At the time it was enough.

As with everything else they ever touched, the Beatles played a major role in redefining the concept of the pop movie. The uneasy iniquities of the Elvis/Cliff movies notwithstanding, a film was a challenge the Beatles just couldn't be seen to duck. In the true spirit of the revolution they were driving, it also had to be seen to be different from the dross that had gone before. A pop movie to exploit their unprecedented appeal and influence, but one that also challenged perceptions and created its own legend.

This was a pre-MTV, pre-video age when even television shows featuring pop stars were sparse and fans were starved of opportunities of seeing and hearing their heroes. To see them offstage talking and joking, playing out some role – however superficial and however much an extension of their own personalities – was sufficient for the complete satisfaction of all concerned. All of it provided a valuable insight into a star's inner make-up and fuelled the assumption that as a mixture of personal charisma and music had provided the main impetus of a career thus far, then it would be folly to do anything but adapt that mixture for the big screen. Normal critical criteria of plot, direction and performance were deemed utterly irrelevant in the strangely individual world of pop movies.

These weren't for movie buffs. They weren't even made for people who regularly went to movies. They were for *fans*. And fans are a breed apart, conditioned to accepting and expecting any old tosh in the name of art, making all the allowances and offering all the excuses in the world to would-be cynics.

With a mixture of the surreal, the silly, and the inspired, the Beatles did actually break the mould with *A Hard Day's Night*, directed by Dick Lester. *A Hard Day's Night* practically invented the word 'wacky', offering no pretence at anything beyond a cartoonesque vehicle for the Beatles at play, with a shrewd, underlying suggestion that their banter was 300 per cent Beatle ad-libs. This, after all, was what they were supposed to be like offstage . . . at the very cutting edge of humour, wits sharp as knives and twice as cuddly. A beautiful cameo character role for Wilfred Bramble as McCartney's grandfather set the seal on a charming romp through a zany day in the life of the Beatles, interspersed with generous musical inter-ludes. Music and personality insights – that was the deal and the Beatles fulfilled it to the letter, yet taking the medium just that teensy weensy bit left-field to create the myth of something different and inspire the use of lofty phrases like 'visionary' and 'pioneering' in the critical plaudits heaped upon them.

Abba once more took their lead from the Beatles when Stig Anderson started talking seriously of putting a movie together in 1977. Benny had already been scalded badly in a disastrous burst of movie-itis during his time with the Hep Stars and had no stomach for any sort of big screen vehicle, but the others were thrilled by the idea. Bjorn was swayed by the commercial logic of keeping the band at the very centre of public attention all round the world at a time when the real thing desperately needed to take time out, for a variety of reasons. With a movie to sell it the next Abba album would go a storm without them having to lift a finger to promote it. Agnetha was already hooked on the idea of acting as her own personal long-term future since playing Mary Magdalene on stage in *Jesus Christ Superstar* in Gothenburg before Abba were up and running; while she was also thrilled by the prospect of creating more space to enable her to stay at home. To Frida, now walking on air, a film represented another adventure in the gleeful rollercoaster her life had become. She wasn't in the business of turning her back on potentially exciting and rewarding new experiences.

Discredited or no, the concept of the dreaded pop movie held irresistible sway for Team Abba. Things were different from the sixties when the very idea of youth culture was novel, however crass, and everyone and their roadie was making a movie just to celebrate the newly invented experience of being young. Mark Wynter and Helen Shapiro made a movie, for God's sake. And there was another outburst of celluloid when they invented Liverpool. Gerry and the Pacemakers did something called *Ferry Cross the Mersey*. The Dave Clark Five made an awfully confusing movie starring Clark himself as a stunt man who does a runner in *Catch Us If You Can* (retitled *Having a Wild Weekend* in the States). And Dave Clark was only the bloody drummer!

They make films like this all the time now in the States. Cheerful wafery little efforts with minuscule storylines, but lots of nice teeth and well-scrubbed characters basically celebrating youth. The difference now is that they don't bother to stick any pop stars in them. Wise move. Matthew Broderick in *Ferris Bueller's Day Off*, Bridget Fonda in *Shag*. Knock it out, get a few hit singles off it, and forget all about it, that's the spirit. Pop as soundtrack works a whole lot better than pop as an entity in itself, for it is never more distressing than when it's self-consciously promoting itself.

But it all went downhill for pop movies after *A Hard Day's Night* when the drugs took hold and the delusions of grandeur grew ever more uncontrollable. Best – or more accurately *worst* of all – was the 1967 film *Privilege* starring Paul Jones of Manfred Mann. Singing '5-4-3-2-1' and 'Do Wah Diddy Diddy' evidently qualified Mr Jones to assume the role of Steve Shorter, a bewildered pop singer being used as a political pawn by the government and wandering listlessly around in an alien world. Looking bewildered and listless seemed to come all too easily to Paul, whose own performance was rocketed to Oscar-winning proportions by the mono-syllabic boredom projected by model Jean Shrimpton, whose own role seemed to veer between that of his girlfriend and a plank of wood.

The Stones, meanwhile, spent years trying to think up a movie idea that would somehow give them a jump on the Beatles. Jagger's ego wouldn't entertain any of the standard pop movie crassness – even when invested with the wit of a Dick Lester – and glib ideas were replaced by pretentiousness. The mythical Rolling Stones movie – indeed there were plans for a whole series of them at one point – became a standing joke, Jagger's prestigious lunches with film directors a business legend. The closest they ever got to it came when filming started for a movie in '68 called *The Rolling Stones' Rock and Roll Circus*, which involved performances in a big top by an impressive who's who of the rock hierarchy, including Jethro Tull, John Lennon, The Who, Eric Clapton, Marianne Faithfull, Taj Mahal and Yoko Ono. Halfway through it Jagger changed his mind, vetoed the whole thing and the Stones still haven't made a movie.

Jagger eventually did, of course, with a succession of excruciatingly awful roles, which comprehensively proved that, whatever his peculiar talents may be, acting certainly isn't one of them. You could perhaps excuse the impenetrable sixties art house indulgence *Performance* as a product of the excesses of the time. The makers at least had the decency to delay release of *Performance* for a couple of years. Warner Brothers were ostensibly alarmed by the degree of sex and violence involved in the film, but we suspect they were merely hoping that Jagger's credibility on screen would somehow miraculously improve, or the whole wretched thing would somehow go away if they locked it up in a drawer for a while. All well and good, but director Nick Roeg really shouldn't have dragged Randy Newman, Buffy Sainte-Marie, Ry Cooder and Lowell George into it too.

But if *Performance* was grim, what can you say about *Ned Kelly* and that horrendous shot at an Irish accent? Jagger in silly beard, daft hat and painfully fake accent comprehensively destroyed the greatest piece of folklore in Australian history. Years later Jagger was still at it, laboriously trying to demonstrate that because he could frug around a bit on stage he must have some small degree of dramatic talent. But as he so ably proved in the '92 movie *Freejack*, this patently wasn't the case.

Acting and singing, pop and movies, they rarely achieve mutual orgasm. Slade made a noble attempt at moving the goalposts, developing the sixties' idea of a thin storyline interspersing live footage into a brave drama-documentary on the rise of a rock band. Slade themselves didn't begin to pretend they could act, but accepted the basic principle that it was enough merely to be Slade to be acceptable. There was enough humour, drama and reality around them to make it almost credible as a serious piece of film, particularly because of a striking introductory cameo from Tom Conti as their manager. *Slade In Flame* was effectively the first cash-in movie made by a major teeny act which cast a shadow over the bubblegum world of pop and acknowledged the impurities as well as squeaky clean glamour. It was an idea initially developed by the seminal *That'll Be The Day*, starring David Essex and Ringo Starr, and developed into even more grotesque realities by its seedy successor, *Stardust*, again starring Essex, with Adam Faith in the Ringo Starr role as his unprincipled manager.

Bowie won some deserved acclaim for his performance in another Roeg movie, *The Man Who Fell To Earth*. Roeg shrewdly exploited Bowie's ethereal, asexual image, while a RADA training wouldn't have been lost on Sting, mixing in the dizziest thespian circles with the likes of John Gielgud, Ian McKellen and Charles Dance, and getting to sleep with Meryl Streep in *Plenty*. Sting also put in a decent showing to bring The Who's *Quadrophenia* concept album to life in a credible depiction of the running battles between mods and rockers in English seaside towns in the sixties. This followed Ken Russell's dramatic transfer to the screen of The Who's previous epic, *Tommy*, the parable of the pinball-playing deaf, dumb and blind kid developed into a dazzling rock 'n' roll party also involving the likes of Elton John, Eric Clapton and Tina Turner, with serious thespians like Oliver Reed, Ann-Margret (a veteran of duff Elvis movies) and Jack Nicholson along for the ride.

Quadrophenia, which at least had a story of sorts and the odd character you could care about, was a million times better than the big-budget pop movie of the eighties, *Absolute Beginners*. Directed by Julien Temple and based on a Colin MacInnes book, *Absolute Beginners* aimed to recreate the spirit and tensions of London youth in the fifties. David Bowie, Ray Davies, Patsy Kensit and a cast of thousands . . . and it was as bad as any of those dodgy sixties pop movies, confirming every caveat about pop stars getting involved in the cinema.

The only true way of representing the character and passion of rock stars on the big screen is through the documentary approach. The music in all its wide-angle glory, and the odd insight caught by fly-on-the-wall cameras rather than staged scenarios. That's why *In Bed With Madonna* works where all of her proper acting roles except *Desperately Seeking Susan* and *A League of Their Own* fail so miserably. The legend of Woodstock – and all the major performers at it – was perpetuated rather than chipped by Michael Wadleigh's documentary movie. Same with *Monterey*. Same with *Concert For Bangladesh*. It was easy, it was honest, and it got the job done.

When U2 accepted their duty as the biggest band in the world and finally came to confront the medium of cinema, they took no risk with their prized credibility. *Rattle And Hum* was powerful and exciting because U2 are powerful and exciting. A straight documentary of a world tour, giving little away beyond tantalizing glimpses of Bono's humour and ego and a marvellous promo for both *The Joshua Tree* album, which the tour was originally designed to promote, and the subsequent *Rattle And Hum* double album that was unleashed en route. On a later tour U2 took to playing 'Dancing Queen' on stage and in Stockholm they called Benny Andersson and Bjorn Ulvaeus up on stage to sing it with them, immediately falling to their knees crying, 'We are not worthy,' as the Abba pair approached. U2 clearly had a firm grip on both reality and their own identity when it came to making a movie, anxious not to do anything that might come back and haunt them in the future.

When it was their turn, Abba had a similar pragmatism about the venture. They knew their limitations and while there was some grand talk of developing the 'Girl With The Golden Hair' concept into a feature movie, they were desperate not to get involved in anything half-baked. They still had enough trouble trying to get people to take them seriously without actively inviting ridicule by over-stretching themselves.

If there was to be a film it had to be a film as promotional device rather than some half-assed attempt at creating characters and drama. That was the game plan and Swedish director Lasse Hallstrom, responsible for shooting most of the band's distinctive videos, was enlisted to join them on their 1977 world tour to document the great event. No risks, no lofty ambitions, just a straight commercial enterprise to make the most of their incredible following, maintain the momentum at a point when they wouldn't be around themselves, and launch them into ever more remote territories. Hallstrom's brief was a movie of straight concert footage littered with atmospheric location inserts and any complementary backstage incidentals that might come to light in the process.

But the Beatles and *A Hard Day's Night* wouldn't go away. The tour itself wasn't the glittering trail of glory they may have fondly imagined. It was a gruelling dogfight. They'd come too far, and had too much at stake for Abba the live experience to be anything less than totally immaculate in sound and thoroughly spectacular in vision. This was a tall order from the outset. Abba's success had been built on everything but live performance, exploding from Bjorn and Benny's painstaking dedication in the studio married to engineer Micke Tretow's own visionary grasp of sound and technique. The whole experience was then fed into a streamlined marketing machine that had evolved from a mixture of inspiration and luck, and the powerful weapon of video.

The strength of the melodies was everything, but Bjorn and Benny knew better than most that their songwriting was only one minimal element of what was needed to carry them through a live performance. On tour the responsibility for carrying the show would fall squarely on the shoulders of their public face – Agnetha and Frida. Both were experienced performers with their own solo track records at home, but to go out on stages all over the world in front of upwards of 10,000 people a time, their nerve and their appeal would be stringently tested. Frida, in particular, had never been a notably relaxed performer on stage, often cold and stiff in her mannerisms, seemingly regarding the audience as her enemy. But at least she recognized her shortcomings, too thrilled by the whole Abba bandwagon to argue when it was gently suggested that she and Agnetha might benefit from some professional dancing and singing lessons. Whatever it took, thought Frida, whatever it took.

Folk-parks and supper restaurants hadn't prepared Agnetha, either, for stage performance on this level, but she knew how to milk an audience and could more easily play the roles expected of her. She did get off on being adored. On that tour, though, this was one of several things on which her attitude dramatically changed. After one of the Scandinavian concerts on the tour, a Swedish critic observed with throwaway wryness that Agnetha had 'the best bum in the world'. One line in a small review in an obscure paper. But it was repeated. Again and again. Ad nauseam. Presently, in the absence of any real controversy or meat for news reporters to write about Abba, whole articles were devoted to the merits or otherwise of Agnetha's bottom. Hers became the most widely admired and hotly debated backside in the world.

The whole band was initially amused by the frankly perverted obsession with the Faltskog rear. Astonished by the unashamed depths to which the press would happily sink in the service of the public interest they treated the whole thing as a silly hoot. Agnetha herself worked up a whole series of smart-ass answers to counter the increasingly obsessive questioning about it, graduating from the statutory, 'It's very flattering,' to, 'There are worse things to be known for than having nice buttocks,' to, 'How should I know about it, I've never seen it?' The guys thought it was hilarious, but Frida's own insecurities and coldness towards Agnetha grew with every reference to the sacred bottom; while Agnetha herself gradually became irritated and angry about it all.

Years later, when Agnetha was attempting to promote

her failing solo career on dodgy television shows, smarmy presenters would dutifully ask her about the new album and the future or otherwise of Abba, then the merest glimmer of a leer would flit across their faces to betray the next question and Agnetha would tense in anticipation. 'Now Agnetha,' would say Mr Oily, 'it's said you have the finest buttocks in the world, what do you think about that?' What Agnetha ultimately thought about that was that Mr Oily needed a sharp kick up his own posterior, but ever the super-trouper she just gritted her teeth one more time and trotted out the non-committal platitudes about it being quite good fun but it really had nothing to do with her music.

Later on, when her confidence had been really shot to pieces in the early eighties, her cracked ego wouldn't even accept her physical attraction as a legitimate weapon. After the divorce Bjorn had gone on record as saying she might very well be the most beautiful woman in the world, but he just didn't find her attractive any more. She scoffed when people commented on her looks, saying it took make-up artists hours and hours to make her look so fabulous, going out of her way to deflate these deep-rooted images of her beauty. She sought solace in a succession of boyfriends, and added significant dramatic effect to the later videos for the likes of 'The Winner Takes It All', 'One Of Us' and 'The Day Before You Came' with an unglamorous dishevelled look to demonstrate the precarious emotional state those songs evoked and she felt.

On that 1977 tour, though, both she and Frida knew their responsibilities and did their very best not to let Stig and the boys down. Their choreography was basic, but rarely in sync either on that tour or indeed afterwards.

There was never any of the gloss or sheen associated with the videos – neither Agnetha nor Frida were natural movers, at best offering enthusiasm above finesse. But the simple truth of the matter was that Frida and Agnetha were never in alignment with one another. On or offstage.

The simple truth of the matter, in fact, is that Abba weren't a very good live act. And they knew it. They'd worked like they'd never worked before in rehearsals for that '77 tour in an attempt to get it right and defy their legion of critics who suspected their reluctance to tour was based on their own inhibitions about exposing themselves to mass public scrutiny without a safety net. These critics were essentially right, but Abba were determined not to give them any ammunition to prove it, and wanted to shock the world with a show of unexpected splendour that would have people eating their words all over the world. 'The Girl With The Golden Hair' was designed to play an intrinsic role in what they fondly imagined would be a worldwide reassessment and maybe a form of critical rebirth.

When you're isolated for months on end working it's easy to lose contact with the rest of the world. Time seems to stand still and you become detached from reality, concentrating exclusively on the immediate problems connected with the bass line on 'Fernando' and the girls' routine on 'Dancing Queen'. It's a slow, painful, tedious process knocking a band into shape for touring, particularly when they've never done it before. As you bicker and become tired and bored in the silence of the rehearsal room it seems the show will *never* get on the road and there's no way of estimating the likely feedback were it ever to do so. Everything seems to shrink in the enclosed walls of the rehearsal room, which after a while begin to take the form of prison walls, feeding doubts and insecurities with cancerous vigour. In such an environment it's easy to lose track of the scale of your popularity and the expectations arising from what you're doing in your little prison. People tell you things, but you're too wound up to listen. Even the long-awaited breakthrough in the States as 'Dancing Queen' flew to the top of the US charts seemed somehow unreal and meaningless in the cacophony of fraught concentration and effort required to bang a raw band into shape to take on the biggest stadiums in the world. For this tour, above all others, okay wasn't going to be enough to see them through. It had to be brilliant. Nothing less was acceptable.

When they did emerge from hiding to put their months of planning to the test they got a shock. 'Money, Money, Money' had offered the vaguest hint of a falter in their cartwheeling success. After three successive Number Ones, 'Mamma Mia', 'Fernando' and 'Dancing Queen', 'Money, Money, Money' had only reached Number Three in the British charts. Disaster! Call the unemployment office! Get some Red Cross food parcels off to Stockholm right away!

But it was a false alarm. Their first single of '77, 'Knowing Me, Knowing You', took them right back up to the top, while their next two, 'Name Of The Game' and 'Take A Chance On Me', were to do the same. Abbamania was red hot all round the world when they set foot on stage in Oslo at the outset of that tour. Crown Prince Harald and Princess Sonja of Norway were there paying their respects along with a healthy smattering of celebs to emphasize that this was not merely a pop concert, but a major event. Scalpers were out in force as the most exacting and crucial step in their already glittering careers was taken.

There was near hysteria in the hall before they came on. Just a pop group, but they meant so much to so many. The younger fans were squealing in anticipation while their parents sat quietly with resigned smiles. This was not unhealthy, this was Abba. No threat to society there. Abba represented all that was good and healthy in life – true love, combed hair, scrubbed teeth, nice tunes, quiet respectability. No parent ever complained about Abba. A few of the hipper kids on the block did but Abba's wholesomeness was infectious and acceptable to all. So the older generation smiled benignly as the cacophony of noise exploded. Mums couldn't wait for them to sing 'Fernando' (which proved you could deliver a song with an anti-war message without also calling for the decimation of society as we know it); and the dads couldn't wait to get their first live viewing of the finest buttocks in captivity.

The lights dim and suddenly there's an aggressive new noise shuddering through the arena, dominant, unfamiliar. The audience noise subsides and the sound of a helicopter becomes apparent. People look skywards, expecting to see something whirling above them, but all they see is the roof. As they search overhead the noise reaches a crescendo and spotlights focus on the stage, picking out the four characters entering the stage in glittering white. The Abba experience had begun.

There were problems. Adjustments to be made. Pacing to be improved. Routines to be streamlined. Running orders to be shifted around. But reaction throughout Europe was pretty good to those early shows and the group themselves were initially elated. It was beginning to hit them how big they actually were. They were shocked – and so were the critics who'd assumed they'd be a disaster on stage.

It was an ambitious stage show and a huge logistical undertaking. They had a twelve-piece backing band for one thing, including the team they usually used in the studio; Lasse Wellander (guitar), Rutger Gunnarsson (bass) and Ola Brunkert (drums), along with a brass section (Ulf Andersson and Lars Karlsson), a percussionist (Malando Gassama), another guitarist (Finn Sjoberg), a couple of additional keyboard players, Wojceich Ernest and Anders Elijas, plus backing singers Lena Andersson, Lena-Maria Gardenas-Lawton and Maritza Horn.

They also took with them state-of-the-art lighting and sound systems and a road crew of over forty people to work and transport it. Polar estimated that the cost of keeping the show on the road amounted to £9,000 a day. Anyone complaining about the cost of concert tickets should check out the mechanical details and staggering costs of Abba's extravagant first world tour. The reason touring has become so unpopular with bands is not only that it's an enormous headache for everyone involved, but that it's also virtually impossible to make it economic. Why take on the hassle and risk to finance and reputation when you can achieve the same results by sitting in a cosy studio for weeks on end whacking out the odd video? Or, better still, a feature film.

It's second nature to musicians to want to play live, especially when they're young and hungry. Sitting in cold transit vans bombing up and down grey motorways arguing, struggling against the stench of each other's unwashed socks, in urgent need of sleep and a nice hot dinner is perfectly acceptable when you're nineteen. The promise of fame, fortune, and unlimited supplies of adulation, respect, sex and excesses of every heart's desire make the indignities demanded seem a small but essential price to pay in the process.

Once you get there, it all seems very different. There are other pressures, greater demands. You have record company executives dangling around your neck, fawning, nudging, cajoling, bullying you to ever greater artistic endeavour, as if the creative process can be turned on and off at will like a gas cooker. The more successful you become the mightier the machine that builds around you. You *have* to take bigger and better equipment to match the ambitions of a show aimed to realize the ever more elaborate dreams of your audience. You *have* to take a huge entourage of people with you to sort it all out. People you don't even recognize when you meet them in the lift, but they're there with you, all right, at the best hotels running around feeling very important doing whatever it is that they're doing.

No major tour hits the road now without its own accountants, catering corps, PR team, tour management staff, hairdressers, valet, florist, tea-stirrer, drinks-pourer, physio, therapist and court jester. And when you're talking a real show, a Bowie/Michael Jackson/Prince type theatrical extravaganza, then it would probably be cheaper just to hire Los Angeles Coliseum for a year and transport audiences in. 'Where are we tonight, boys? Sydney, Australia? Right. That's 300,000 cans of Fosters lager behind the bar, and 200 Qantas planes landing from Sydney at noon. Make sure they're out straight away afterwards, though, so we can build the tacos stall – we're doing Mexico tomorrow!'

Abba never went through the traditional routes of

touring. Their Swedishness alone separated them from the normal processes of painful learning. Individually they all served their apprenticeships, but their experiences were radically different from the grimly exciting realities of the average American or British kid behaving abominably in the cause of some remote holy grail. Even though Benny and Bjorn may have found themselves drunk in strange bars more often than could ever have been good for them, life was never on the edge.

And when they finally achieved international breakthrough, live performance wasn't part of the equation. They were always the great exception, Abba. Two blissful couples happy to fit in with the system to ease their way to success where everybody of note since the Beatles had railed against it. Particularly since a man called Bill Grundy presented a respectable tea-time television show in England in 1976 and goaded a bunch of oiks from London called the Sex Pistols into swearing their heads off like a bunch of fishwives. Grundy was sacked and the Sex Pistols became legends overnight without lifting an instrument in anger. Punk was off and running and there was no stopping it now.

Abba were the very antithesis of punk. All their ideals, their imagery, their gloss, their glamour, their respectfulness, their musicianship, their embrace of capitalism was entirely in the face of the values espoused by those who saw punk's role in a more romantically political light. Yet punk's enemies were Yes and Genesis and Led Zeppelin and Pink Floyd and ELO, the dinosaurs who pompously emerged from their caves every couple of years to propagate the hideous stadium mentality, where stars became dots in the distance and laser shows replaced real live heroes you could touch and scream at. The guys who talked rock 'n' roll but lived in mansions in Wiltshire or – worse – were tax exiles, duping the critics and probably themselves into believing they were somehow as important as Beethoven, living on their enormous royalties and swollen egos. The guys who'd cry if they ever got their hands dirty.

Abba weren't the enemy. Abba weren't even in the game. They were just a bunch of civilians who'd somehow wandered innocently into the middle of the battlefield gliding unscathed through all the carnage, studiously avoided by the gunners firing all around them as if they were United Nations neutral observers. And thus, smiling sweetly, they waltzed through the lot of them, and in broad daylight stole all the booty.

They were regarded as a harmless irrelevance in the rock wars of 1977, and this itself gave them a unique status. While the pacifists in the grandstand took them to their hearts and gave them a standing ovation, warriors from both sides quietly but perceptibly also took to them, adopting them as some kind of perverse mascot, inverted cult heroes for daring to be themselves at a time when it was fashionable to take sides. People finally began to admit that Abba were not only popular, they were exceptionally gifted at their craft too. The people didn't often get it so right, but it wasn't just the milkman wandering the streets whistling 'Mamma Mia' and 'Dancing Queen'. At a time when compromise was deemed anathema, Abba turned it inoffensively into an art form – it was their destiny as Swedes making it in a world that had previously been exclusively American or British. The concentrated international thinking that had led them to create 'Waterloo' for Eurovision, with 'Hasta Manana' as first reserve, continued right through the material that emphasized their statelessness through those early years. They spoke for the new Euro brotherhood. It neutralized them, putting them on a different planet. Gradually, almost *reluctantly*, people began to acknowledge the air up there wasn't so bad.

Enclosed in their own world in Sweden for months on end rehearsing for the tour, Abba were amazed to find themselves suddenly the centre of some pretty heavyweight courtship. Promoters estimated there were three million applications for 10,000 tickets in Britain alone, where they played Manchester, Glasgow, Birmingham and London. It was said they could have sold out the London Royal Albert Hall a hundred times over, and outside the great old hall on the night of the concert scalpers shiftily glided around in the streets outside asking – and getting – ten times the face value of the tickets. Inside, their adoring fans had some unlikely faces – credible hard-rockers like Thin Lizzy and Led Zeppelin were out in force in a clear demonstration of the amazing crossover status now enjoyed by Abba.

At the concert itself, audience reaction was stunning. When they pay fortunes for tickets, people are determined to enjoy themselves, and Abba did put on a good show. Lots of interesting frocks, dramatic lighting, all the hits and a bit of theatre, too, with 'The Girl With The Golden Hair' segment at the end. The critics carped a bit, warbling on about the lack of warmth and passion in their performance and dredging out the old clichés about cold, clinical Euro-pop, as if this was itself a damning indictment where in fact it was their raison d'être.

Tensions mounted as the tour trudged on. If there's friction hovering at all, then the road is the place where it will leap up and confront you. Everybody's personal foibles come to the forefront, and minor irritations turn into huge career-threatening confrontations. Abba were concentrating hard enough on keeping the music right without having to deal with their endless personal disagreements too, but this was all par for the course for any band on the road. It was just that they'd never done it before in this unit and there were times when the pressure of success did begin to stifle them. They all found the travelling and the stage performance itself exhausting, while Agnetha had a regular struggle to keep illness at bay and preserve the fitness of her frail throat.

In their more reflective moments, though, they knew it was going well. Audiences greeted them with an unrelenting ecstasy that went beyond their wildest fantasies when they were romping up and down Sweden playing folk-parks and they knew they sounded good. They weren't born performers – this was the crux of their reticence about touring – but they were getting away with it, fulfilling public expectation and maybe achieving a bit more besides. The tour didn't make them money – tours rarely do unless you're a solo performer or the Rolling Stones – and it was some years before the idea of sponsorship was to be entertained. But it brought them untold invisible profits in promoting record sales and putting them on the front pages in every country they visited. Above all it offered delicious tangible proof that an unfashionable, steadfastly independent outfit from Scandinavia had exploited the system to the full and ever-so-sweetly and subtly become the biggest band in the world.

Lasse Hallstrom switched courses during the tour. The whole thing was inspirational enough to make him want to do something more than straight documentary. The guiding light of the Beatles and *A Hard Day's Night* shone above him like a beacon. He evolved a simple storyline and a rough script for a movie that could be shot around Abba without involving them in any additional pressures. Like having to act. It was the Dick Lester blueprint through and through and it was a logical creative move for Hallstrom. Tailor the Abba footage both on and off stage around a comic sub-plot, using Abba's own characters and cinema verité to give all the Abba fans what they wanted plus a little extra.

Abba the Movie was finally shot in March 1977 during the hysterical Australian leg of the tour. Australia was always destined to be dramatic. Bred on the sweet melodies of the Seekers a decade earlier, the Australians took Abba to their hearts the minute they heard 'SOS'. They had no elitist notions about Nordic gatecrashers, or the incongruity of fashion and the protocol of cool. Too remote from the rest of the pop world and too hung-up on their own cultural inferiority complex to notice or understand the complexities of pop psychology, the Australians only heard fabulous melodies and saw a couple of great-looking sheilas singing 'em. They'd never heard of Eurovision, they couldn't care less if they came from Sweden or Swindon, and they could bounce on stage in velvet pant suits or their birthday suits. They just liked the music. And maybe there *was* a small element of identification with the underdog going on there, too . . . the isolationist brotherhood linking arms and saying stuff you to the big boys.

Whatever – Abba were proportionally bigger in Australia than anywhere else in the world. It was estimated at one time that one in every two households throughout Australia had an Abba record in their collection. And, unlike the more self-conscious fan bases elsewhere, they felt no need to hide them away and, when pounced upon by some gleeful nosy bastard searching for some junk by Roxy Music, come up with some embarrassed explanation for their presence. Australians have no use for bullshit and they loved Abba. They loved Abba to bits.

When Abba hit Sydney it was massive news. Few major bands ever made it to Australia. It was too far, too uneconomic, too much hassle. Crowds flooded the airport to welcome them, photographers flocked to their hotel, and sales of the merchandise went through the roof. Abba mugs, Abba T-shirts, Abba pillows, Abba hats, Abba pens, Abba everything was shifting at a staggering rate. And Bjorn, Benny, Agnetha and Anni-Frid fulfilled all their obligations to the letter to satisfy the huge antipodean appetite. A photo-call at Sydney Opera House became a rugby scrum, they held press conferences everywhere they went, answering the same dumb questions with unfailing politeness and tolerance. They were permanently on display, decked out in their white costumes, smiling, always smiling, even as Agnetha's bronchial problems threatened to confine her to quarters. Their entourage had extended to over a hundred people now, including a dozen Australian musicians employed to play on only two numbers, and they had their very own private 727 plane to fly them around.

The war of Agnetha's bum continued in earnest as the Oz obsession with great rears exploded in animated press headlines on the topic. ('What's up? Don't they have bottoms in Australia?' commented Agnetha at one point.) The furore was fuelled by the terrifying white pants she'd been levered into which emphasized this hotly discussed part of her anatomy to a breathtaking degree. Agnetha became an eager party to the hype, turning her back on the audience, inspiring squeals of anticipation as she wiggled provocatively around stealing all the thunder while Frida sang 'Money, Money, Money'. Frida didn't appear to be hugely amused.

The Australian press – possibly even seedier and more rancid than the infamous British tabloids – constantly bombarded them with ever more ludicrous headlines. They were actors impersonating Abba; they were indulging in group sex; they wife-swapped; they were prima donnas; they spent all their money gambling; the guys had fist fights; they hated the music they were playing; they had no minds of their own and were completely dominated by Stig Anderson. Abba laughed off the stories. Most of the time.

A torrential storm hit Sydney on the day of their open-air debut in Australia, which threatened to drown the show completely. The stage was awash and the start was delayed as arguments raged over safety and audience consternation rose. Finally they bounded on stage singing 'I Am The Tiger' and the soggy audience forgave them everything. Frida went skidding on her back at one point (giving her backside its own fifteen minutes of fame) much to the delight of the assembled snappers and Abba duly enjoyed the greatest reception they'd received. Ever.

The whole Australian leg gave them a massive boost, finishing the tour on a high despite all the grief they'd encountered en route. A bomb hoax in Perth, attempted stage invasion in Melbourne, complete mayhem in Adelaide, and controversy in Canberra where Australian premier Malcolm Fraser offered them the use of a governmental plane to entice them to add an unscheduled date in the Australian capital so he could see them. The press was on to it instantly, sniffing some low politicking by the beleaguered Fraser, using Abba to try and lift his own standing in the country, and Stig Anderson steered a diplomatic course away from Canberra.

Abba felt like a real rock 'n' roll band. At last they felt no need to apologize for themselves for being Swedish, for being two couples, for being clean-cut, for wearing dumb costumes, for being bland in interviews, for singing in a foreign language. Abba were at the very pinnacle of their careers. 'Knowing Me, Knowing You' was topping the charts all over the world, Agnetha was pregnant for the second time, and Lasse Hallstrom had got himself enough material for a decent movie. The knock-on effects from the tour saw them successfully through the next eighteen months without involving them in any huge stress. *Abba the Movie* was premiered in Sydney just before Christmas, 1977, and Abbamania broke out once more in cinemas full of shrieking fans who might even have given Bill Haley a few more kiss curls. Warner Brothers won the bidding to distribute the film, which proved another wily money-spinner and marketing weapon. A glittering February premiere in London followed, with *Abba the Album* simultaneously hitting the shops and a new single, 'Take A Chance On Me', instantly rocketing to the top of the charts.

Stig Anderson – and Lasse Hallstrom – had judged the market accurately. *Abba the Movie* was light and insubstantial and was never going to have the lasting cult appeal of its main inspiration, *A Hard Day's Night*. But comedian Robert Hughes was entertaining enough as Ashley, the hapless radio presenter chasing the group across Australia in pursuit of an interview, while Hallstrom displayed a fine eye for detail in the candid peripheral shots further used to intercut the live footage. To get any more out of it he needed more collusion from Abba themselves, but any role from them beyond stage performance was largely incidental and in the end they had marginal input in the film. There were cameras everywhere all the time anyway – they simply got on with their own jobs and forgot they were also supposed to be making a movie.

It did the job. *Abba the Movie* and *Abba the Album* were further huge successes, propelling them to ever greater heights. Abba, it seemed, could do no wrong.

But what the world was unaware of – and the film and their own performances had no way of showing – was that it represented their final moment as the all-conquering, harmonious super-couples. Agnetha and Bjorn had their second child, Christian, and spent the next eighteen months arguing themselves stupid, climaxing with the famous divorce. The purity of sound, image and personality became irreparably tarnished during the year following the tour which they'd been looking forward to so much and which was supposed to rest and recharge them to such an extent that they'd come bursting back twice as good and thrice as beautiful.

Despite it all, their indomitable ambition and the huge financial stakes involved held them together and even pushed them back on the road a couple of years later, in 1979. But the resolve to maintain smiling unison had been shattered and they were to spend a miserable month grappling with American indifference, without the will to overcome it. European and Australian adulation had softened them up, while raging internal conflicts had by now shattered their ability to get down on their hands and knees and *scrap* to win new friends and admirers. Abba were stars. They could only ever be stars. They didn't know how to react to audiences who didn't accept them as stars. Many of their American shows in that '79 tour played to half-empty halls and sullen audiences who didn't know all the words. The joy had gone out of Abba during the year's break as *Abba the Movie* did the rounds, and when they went back on the road for that second world tour, their heart went out of it too. 'Dancing Queen' had topped the American charts but that seemed to count for nothing. They could have cracked America but in a way that would have made their successes in the rest of the world seem meaningless: they'd have needed to sacrifice everything and just stay on the road and swallow the crap that went with it.

There was no way they were going to do that. They were too old, too experienced, too *successful*. By this time it was as much as they could do to get Agnetha out of Sweden for a couple of weeks, let alone a three-month stretch. She'd stay at home with the kids as long as she possibly could, flying out on the last possible plane to fulfil her duties as Sweden's leading goddess/superstar. And she hated every minute of it.

Most nights the honours went to the children's choir they used on the chorus of 'I Have A Dream'. Just local kids chosen on the day of the concert and marched on stage giggling and beaming at their mums, breathless with pride. Agnetha won the sympathy vote, with her self-composed harrowingly defiant 'I'm Still Alive' showing – not for the first or last time – her willingness to use her own visible melancholia to powerful dramatic effect in an irresistible form of emotional blackmail on the audience. Bjorn and Benny were well established as the writing/

musical team and Agnetha basically stopped writing because she knew she couldn't compete. 'I'm Still Alive' was a rarity.

They were still huge and they were still adored, playing six nights at Wembley Arena which sold out in a couple of hours, and parading a spectacular backdrop and a succession of glittering costumes more blinding than anything on view first time round. The band was bigger and better with the excellent Mats Ronander joining the party on guitar and the celebs rolled out with even more force to pay homage. But the accusations of coldness that had always followed them around suddenly carried more weight. They were not so much clinical, as clinically dead. Not smiling as much now. Not so jolly any more. The smell of the greasepaint was evidently creating quite a stench in the dressing room. Everyone was older and wiser now, including the fans, who still managed to rustle up some hysteria without being quite so convincing about it, the tension up front filtering through into the stalls. It's hard to exude warmth to an audience when the atmosphere on stage is icy cold.

They didn't even make it back to Australia, scene of their greatest triumphs. It didn't make any economic sense, they argued. Why shatter yourselves spending three days there and back on an aeroplane, subjecting yourselves to all the incredible hassle and pressure that accompanies it all? And for what? A load of backslapping that somehow didn't mean anything any more and a big hole in your profits for the year, that's what.

It was a sign of the times. After they finished their dates at Wembley Arena at the end of 1979, Abba would never tour again. And whether they admitted it or not, each of them knew it.

9

BENNY AND THE JETS

'Flying high, high, like a bird in the sky
I'm an eagle that flies in the breeze'

'Eagle'

Pop stars with beards. Who needs 'em? Name one rock star you could take seriously again after being photographed sporting a beard.

Beards were that peculiar phenomenon of the hippy era and they were quite rightly seen as the symbolic antithesis of youthful energy and the true rock spirit come the punk revolution. That's why it was seen as a betrayal of ideals when Elvis Costello blew years of painstaking image-building by growing a beard in the eighties. And Sting suddenly appeared one day with a curious, wispy little tuft on the end of his chin. What was all *that* about?!? Even Phil Collins, one of the flagships of the grandiose old guard of rock grandfathers, had the decency to shave off his beard once the saboteurs of '77 had put a torch to synthesizers and reinvented three chords and an attitude.

Sure, fashions come and go and Haight Ashbury, 1967, was the only time and place in pop history it was ever fashionable to be sporting facial growth . . . and even then it had to be of Jesus proportions and complemented by tumbling hair of unending length with a silly hat for good luck. Even then you never saw Mick Jagger in a beard (apart from the hilariously inept effort he cultivated in the movie *Ned Kelly*).

But beards are for Pavarotti and Russian czars and earnest social workers. They have no place, saints preserve us, in pop music. And 1967 apart, they never have done.

So whatever possessed Benny Andersson? How could he possibly imagine he'd have *any* success as an international star with that beard? It wasn't even a *good* beard. An apologetically wispy little crop with the dreaded bald bit between the point of the chin and that curious sprouting under the lower lip. All this and a dangerously faint colouring that leads you to wonder if it's just a few stray paint splashes after a night decorating the kitchen, leading to an almost irresistible urge to grab a flannel to scrub it off.

'You haven't seen what I look like *without* a beard!' says Benny with characteristic good humour when taken to task on the burning issue in a Swedish television interview. Bjorn, himself guilty of cultivating a facial monster in later years, confirms that yes, beneath it all Benny is a no-neck wonder who looks even dafter without beard than he does with beard. So needs must and a Benny beard it's always been, though the fact remains that the Andersson beard has been as heavy a handicap to Abba's credibility as Frida's perm and Agnetha's luminous ski-pants.

It wasn't always like that. Benny – one of life's perennially indeterminate thirty somethings – was actually a teenager himself for at least nine years of his life. He had a crewcut and a suit and tie and designs on becoming a rich businessman.

Nothing fazed Benny. Born on 16 December 1946, he skated through his childhood in the outskirts of Stockholm with cheery detachment and a total disregard for schoolwork. He was the kid at the back who'd spin some impossible yarn to explain the absence of his homework which no one believed, but he had such an honest face and smiling disposition that he always got away with it. Some might say he was lazy. Teachers most certainly did. But put a piano accordion in his hand and he was transformed.

Music was in his blood. Both his dad (who ran an engineering company) and grandfather were accomplished musicians with a deep fund of Scandinavian folk tunes at their disposal. Benny was taught by them to play almost before he could walk and found himself being paraded in front of friends and relatives to do a turn on the accordion and – by the time he'd reached the ripe old age of ten – the piano. Pretty soon he found he could satisfactorily play any instrument placed in front of him and he fell in with a girl singer called Christina Gronvall, who appeared at various local youth clubs.

Benny was never driven by ambition the way Bjorn and Frida, in particular, were. He had a comfortable home, hardly wealthy but securely middle-class, with none of the hang-ups that afflicted Agnetha, or the hardships endured by Frida. Benny was an instinctive social animal, humorous, even-tempered and hugely popular. He was an avid drinker and a serious party-goer, but the only thing that ever fired his passions was music. Even in his teens he was an authority on various unlikely strands of music, but it was the Beatles – John Lennon especially – who electrified him into dreams of making a career out of music himself.

Yet still he fell into it. Benny was never motivated enough to actively engender anything himself – by virtue of his warm personality and extravagant talent, other people naturally gravitated towards him and things rapidly evolved almost in spite of the lazily charming man at the centre of it. Others suggested things and he invariably went along with them for the adventure, but his prodigious ability was always the catalyst for that development. Without doubt he was the centrepiece of Abba, the very spring from which those fabulous songs flowed and the cornerstone of Abba's appeal; and yet longstanding friends insist his languid character hasn't been remotely touched by the volcano of wealth and fame that has engulfed him since he played accordion while Christina Gronvall sang Swedish folk songs in Stockholm youth clubs all those years ago.

Christina, a striking redhead, was Benny's first love. And like everybody else, he assumed the first love would also be the last. They'd had a childhood romance at school almost since the day they'd noticed there was something different between them in the trouser department and they dated in the old-fashioned way, surreptitiously holding hands behind the bicycle sheds and scarcely looking at anyone else as they promised each other undying love. Benny and Christina were just fifteen when they announced their engagement and soon moved in together in a small flat at Valingby in the suburbs of Stockholm. Before long they were even having babies – Peter, born in August '63, and Helene, born in June '65 – but never actually got it together to marry, an oversight in Benny that Frida was also later to discover, much to her chagrin.

Benny simply wasn't cut out for a regular life with job and wife and security and sensible lifestyle. He was heavily into Christina, but he was more heavily into music, with having a good time never far behind. He had a decent stab at a conventional lifestyle, working as a janitor at his dad's firm, but he lived for pop music, playing organ every night with a small-time Stockholm covers band called Elverkerts Spelmanslag, who spent most of their time rehearsing and rarely got to play in public. Which was just as well, really, because none of them had any suitable transport to take their equipment to gigs.

One night, though, they did get a gig across town. After much consternation, they persuaded another musician, Svenne Hedlund, who'd just formed his own band, the Hep Stars, to drive them to the gig in his old Transit van. Svenne watched the gig in dismay – the band were awful, but the keyboard player was brilliant. Within weeks he'd negotiated Benny's transfer from the hopeless Elverkerts after the Hep Stars' original keyboard player, Hans Ostlund, had stormed out following one of the bouts of 'musical differences' obligatory to all young upcoming bands.

The Hep Stars were hot. They were young, good-looking (well, some of them), lively and talented – and pretty soon they were regarded as the nearest Sweden was ever likely to get to its own version of the Beatles, whom all the Hep Stars idolized and blatantly aped. Yet with Benny at the keyboards quickly having a profound influence on their musical output and Svenne Hedlund stamping his own distinctive style on the vocals, the Hep Stars rapidly established themselves at the forefront of Scandinavian pop.

It wasn't that difficult. Swedish youth, captivated by the exciting young groups with long hair and vivacious harmonies they saw tumbling out of Liverpool and all points south, were longing for a group of similarly sexy heroes they could identify with on their own doorstep.

For Sweden had a poor track record in pop music. Theirs was a musical history built largely on their own rampant folk tradition – fiddle music a speciality – with most schoolkids brought up on the old folklore tales and legends, with accompanying ballads. Wonderful, evocative ballads too, relating back to the superstitions and magical beliefs bred by a land isolated by geography and culture, and reliant on the fickle temperament of the sea for its survival. Sweden has a fascinating musical history for folklorists, musicologists, archivists and, yes, even schoolkids, but a relatively sophisticated Stockholm teenager in the sixties needed something much more tangible to fire his or her dreams.

Sweden has a fine classical tradition, too. The magnificent Royal Opera in central Stockholm is impressive evidence of its proud operatic legacy and there's a whole gamut of internationally acclaimed singers from the genre . . . Nicolai Gedda, Invar Wixell, Hakan Hagegard, Gosta Windbergh and Caterina Ligendza.

But it lagged behind the rest of Europe in terms of contemporary music. In the fifties, there had initially been little awareness of the rock revolution taking America by storm. The radio stations played a predominance of Swedish music with the consequence that record stores were selling mainly Scandinavian music. The old folk traditions had resurfaced in the upsurge of national awareness following the Second World War, and the closest Sweden generally got to international rock culture was in a procession of Swedish language cover versions of international hits by local artists. Nostalgic ballads and undemanding dance band music were the general order of the day and the staple diet of the emerging circuit of open-air parks providing summer dances and which evolved into the folk-parks where each member of Abba was to individually cut their stage teeth.

Inevitably things changed as rock 'n' roll finally hit Sweden. The original Elvis Presley and Bill Haley records started to appear in shops and even outsell their Swedish language cover versions. Sweden produced its own raw rock 'n' roll stars singing (badly) in English – notably Rock-Ragge, Rock-Boris and the celebrated Little Gerhard, who was to later play a key role in Agnetha Faltskog's genesis.

Mostly they were an incompetent embarrassment with short-lived careers and the Swedish rock scene sank into an abyss once more, to be revived at the end of the decade by the similarly primitive skiffle craze. Skiffle was the bridge between jazz bands and rock and, like punk nearly two decades later, had the dazzling attraction to would-be stars of making it perfectly possible for them to get up on stage with an even chance of success without the irritating necessity for talent. For a while seemingly every small town throughout the country had a whole battalion of terrible skiffle groups banging on washboards and yelping like Alsatians. The charm of skiffle was that anybody could do it, and mostly they did.

Mostly they'd been and gone inside a year, but skiffle did sow the seeds for a fresh generation of musicians in Sweden and laid the foundations of a rock-friendly society in which both Benny and Bjorn were taking their first steps.

Owe Thornquist, Ulf Peder Olrog and Povel Ramel developed a new Swedish style that merged contemporary rock with the old folk traditions, borrowing from many outside influences but remaining quintessentially Swedish. The Hep Stars took their lead from just such a synthesis. Benny Andersson himself entertainingly described their music as 'country and western with a German beat', which was basically his way of saying they were adapting the Americana of the Beach Boys to a setting strongly flavoured by the Swedish folk tradition. The first track Benny Andersson recorded with the Hep Stars was 'Tribute To Buddy Holly'.

The attitudes of radio stations changed, too. They had to. The pirate radio boom hadn't bypassed Sweden and there were two in particular, Radio Syd and Radio Nord – both broadcasting from ships off the Swedish coast – which caught the public imagination and showed the official stations to be remnants of the dark ages. As the government set to work to outlaw the pirates, they drastically re-jigged their own legal broadcasting networks to embrace the pop culture. One of the existing stations was completely refurbished under the name Melodirian to include a large rock input, while Swedish Radio also set up a brand new third national channel, designed to appeal largely to the youth market and containing several chart-based shows, *Tio I Topp*, *Svensktoppen* and *Kvallstoppen* being the most popular.

The twist was as popular in Sweden as it was in Britain and the States and the hair grew longer and the whole Beatlemania phenomenon was enjoyed to the hilt from afar. Everything was from afar. They watched it all. The Beatles. The Stones. Gerry and the Pacemakers. Even Freddy and the *bloody* Dreamers sold records in Sweden. And you know that if teenagers in Sweden are buying Freddy and the Dreamers records then they have to be really thirsting for groups, *any* groups, to call their own. The Swedes were *gagging* for a half-decent beat group from their own land to idolize and emulate and get the chance to squeal at in the flesh just like they could see their British counterparts doing on television. It was obvious and it was natural and it was dumb that there wasn't a Stig Anderson around then to set himself up as some kind of Sven Epstein to create one.

The Hep Stars duly became that group, though in the best traditions of rock star romance, it was the last thing on their minds when they started clattering around with their Chuck Berry and Beach Boys covers. They were intent on merging their own character to match the modern trend, unsure that anything would work or see them through anything beyond the next restaurant gig. In their more fanciful moments, Svenne Hedlund, Janne Frisck, Lennert Heglund and Christer Petterson may have quietly wondered about seeing their names in lights, but Benny Andersson never did. He was too busy daydreaming about ideas for riffs and melodies for such whimsy. Here was a guy totally preoccupied with the impossible demands of juggling a day job with his increasing preoccupation with the Hep Stars and the inevitably failing life at home with the patient but rapidly despairing Christina.

What is it about laid-back guys that inspires total fury in women? Benny wanted nothing but the freedom to indulge his one all-consuming passion – music. Beyond that you could set fire to the world around him and it wouldn't matter. Burnt dinners. A slag-heap in the front room. A houseful of Austrian weightlifters. Benny wouldn't worry. Benny wouldn't *notice*. Benny would let the world drift by him, oblivious to it all, completely unmoved and untouched by any mayhem unfolding around him. And in 1964 there was plenty.

It all washed over Benny. And it drove everyone else

crazy. It's one of the quirks of human nature that the very quality of calmness under pressure in one should drive someone else lacking that quality to the very precipice of apoplexy. The calmer they seem, the more intense the rage erupting before their very eyes.

Poor Christina. Poor Anni-Frid too. It happened precisely the same way when Benny and Frida were together all those years. This time the pressures were much more intense and their fortunes intimately entwined within the cauldron of fame. You have to be a couple of saints to keep any lasting relationship in some degree of harmony, but to do it in a goldfish bowl while being prodded by advisers, employees, journalists and hangers-on and immersed in the whole crazy damn business with its collective nosiness, jealousy and greed, is beyond reason. Frida – direct, exhibitionist and confrontational at the best of times – repeatedly snapped and hurled anything she could lay her hands on at Benny, whose sole crime had been to accept whatever horrendous situation had been foisted on them with a smile and a shrug. His one release was to go out to a bar and then in search of the nearest piano to spend the rest of the night singing Beatles songs (atrociously) rather than picking fights with passing trawlermen.

So there were fights with Christina, or there *would* have been fights if Benny had ever consented to take part in one. But he never did. And then he just wasn't around. When the heat was turned up in the kitchen Benny merely smiled and graciously conceded any point being made against him. If someone had a grievance against him, fine, Benny instantly caved in and agreed he was in the wrong and apologized profusely, whether he believed he was or not. Who cares about the finer details of an argument? It really doesn't matter who's right and who's wrong. Life's too short. So spake the Andersson philosophy.

There were fights in the Hep Cats. Lots of them. A bunch of young guys let loose on the road with a surfeit of adoring females and unlimited alcohol in every port and the dangerous arrogance provoked by the explosive cocktail of youth and fame. They fought over money, they fought over musical direction, they fought over girls, they fought over getting to the right place at the right time. All the normal things guys in bands fight over. There's just no hiding place on the road. But Benny . . . he never fought. Benny just let it all float over him, refusing to react to the torrent of tempers permanently crashing around his ears. Benny just did his thing, like Benny always did and still does.

The Hep Cats really broke big in Sweden early in 1965 when they appeared on national television playing a brazen American-style rocker called 'Cadillac'. They snarled and leapt around and generally made a ferocious racket that caused something of a sensation throughout Sweden. They weren't doing anything remotely original, and their image, style and stage moves were a crude interpretation of what they'd seen the British groups doing on television, but it hadn't been seen on a Swedish stage before. Almost overnight they had three records in the Swedish charts.

The unthinkable happened and Benny Andersson became a sex symbol. He had a chubby face and a toothy grin and, in the early days of the Hep Stars, he had a crewcut, was beardless and went on stage in a suit and tie – alongside the ostentatiously 'hard'-looking characters alongside him, Benny appeared to have been dumped there from another planet. He was not a natural stage performer and quietly concentrated on his keyboard while the others were leaping around the stage like demented rag dolls. Svenne Hedlund, the group's singer and natural leader, even broke his foot on stage on one famous occasion after an ill-conceived leap from an amp stack. If you needed any confirmation that these were wild and wacky boys intent on creating havoc wherever they turned, they titled the B-side of 'Cadillac' 'Mashed Potatoes'. Hilarious, huh?

Benny, the cuddly anti-star, became something of a cult hero and his rapidly growing influence on the band was strongly evident to all Hep Stars' followers. His first self-composed song of note was 'No Response', included on the first Stars' album, *We And Our Cadillac*. The story goes that the band needed one more track to include on the album and were quarrelling bitterly in their usual manner about what they should include to complete it, when up piped a quiet voice from the corner. 'I've written a song, actually, which might be all right.'

The rest of the band were shocked by his uncharacteristic intervention and listened respectfully while the oddball keyboard man was bullied into shyly playing it for them. The arguments were over. The Hep Stars went straight back into the studio to record 'No Response' and it was immediately obvious to everyone it was by several leaps the classiest track on the album. It was released as a single and became their biggest hit, and Benny Andersson's reputation as a songwriter par excellence was off and running.

He wrote another song, a bright poppy effort called 'Sunny Girl'. Huge hit. He had trouble with lyrics and teamed up with Svenne to put together another song, 'Wedding'. Number One. Already he had mastered the most elusive of songwriting arts, marrying simplicity and blatant commerciality to style and class. The bold organ intro to 'Wedding' also marked out his flare for arrangements.

Benny continued to write material for the group – they had another massive hit with his 'Consolation' – sometimes writing with Svenne, more often alone, and took on a more and more influential role as the Hep Stars achieved unprecedented success in their homeland. Benny loved it. He couldn't sing to save his life and he found lyric-writing a colossal headache, although in those days he was still attempting it, curiously finding it easier to write in English – which he saw as the natural language of pop music – rather than Swedish.

Benny was an unlikely pop idol. Hardly the epitome of a sexual athlete, Benny was the complete antithesis of Svenne Hedlund with his Presleyesque gyrations and cool good looks. Okay, now he'd got himself a classic Beatle haircut and was wearing groovy black shirts, but only those with several vol-au-vents short of the full buffet could possibly imagine he was good-looking. But hell, even Tiny Tim – the ugliest man in history and whose sole claim to fame was singing 'Tiptoe Thru The Tulips' in ridiculous falsetto – received volumes of explicit fan mail from young girls and even got to marry some classic American beauty live on TV. And like John and Paul, Mick 'n' Keef and, indeed, Frida and Agnetha, Benny and Svenne inspired their own fan rivalries with 'Uncle' Benny holding his own in the sex symbol stakes extraordinarily well. He enjoyed this unexpected status immensely, regarding it with unconcealed amusement and glee, but making sure he indulged himself fully in the excesses of fame.

He didn't take any of it too seriously, still not believing a lifelong career was being carved out here. He was basically having the time of his life and not imagining for a second that it would last. He firmly believed that somebody with a long stick and a hook on the end would appear on the horizon any day to reel him in and send him back to his dad's engineering works. So he made damn sure he thoroughly enjoyed it while he could. It tickled him pink that young girls were screaming at him in ecstasy and he bought himself a flash car, drank champagne, dined at the finest restaurants, entertained gorgeous women, and generally lived out a conscious parody of the rock 'n' roll cliché.

And he quietly forgot about Christina Gronvall back home in Valingby. There was an unspoken agreement among the Hep Stars that their sexiness would be seriously impaired were it to become known that Benny had a fiancée and a couple of kids waiting for him to come home in Stockholm and the fact was pointedly overlooked in their press releases and interviews. For months the Beatles had kept John's wife Cynthia and son Julian a dark and deadly secret and, once again taking their lead from the Fab Four, the Hep Stars tacitly suppressed Christina's very existence. At first Christina tried to understand, but it's an impossible demand on a girlfriend and mother, being expected to play the game, keep her mouth shut and merge into the background while watching her other half parade in high profile flaunting his rampant libido for the further titillation of a nation of gasping females.

It's difficult to believe it now we live in such emotionally liberal times (ha!) but pop was constructed on this very premise. The hidden assumption was that the

211

girl screaming at the guy wielding the guitar with his crutch hanging out actually *believes* she will marry him. That he will peer out through the lights, catch her eye, send a flunky to ask for her phone number, fall in love with her on the first date, and they'll marry the following week and live happily ever after. The flaw in that theory is then what? Having married her he couldn't possibly carry on being a pop star because the other girls would know he was no longer available and wouldn't be interested, and if he stopped being a pop star and became an electrician instead, he wouldn't be remotely interesting. Let's be fair – who wants a long-haired electrician with his crutch hanging out?

That vital ingredient of the rock myth, the groupie, might appear to have taken but one small step further in that relationship between pop star and adoring fan. The fan has more chance of being noticed if she hangs around afterwards and from there it's a small distance up the ladder to dressing room to hotel room to . . . what will probably be a night of humiliation. It turns out to be a whole new psychological ballpark and the boundary between sincere fan and professional groupie is one that can only knowingly be crossed.

So the Hep Stars knew all about groupies and the pop star theory of availability at all times. It was a theory that was happily dismantled – slowly – in the wake of the Lennon–Cynthia revelations and the revelation that girls still screamed because boys were still boys and the music itself was pretty exciting. So Jane Asher was allowed out of mothballs to be photographed on Paulie's arm and the emotional purity of pop stars was no longer considered so crucial to fan appeal. But here in Sweden in the mid-sixties the pop rules were still being made up as they went along and Benny Andersson was not allowed to have a girlfriend and two kids.

He went along with it enthusiastically enough. He was nineteen and having too much of a good time to worry unduly about the domestic situation. He never felt it was an issue that should or could have the consequences others imagined it to have. Like the others he was on a roll and he was untouchable and if nobody else believed he had someone at home, then why should he worry about it?

But it *was* a problem. As the Hep Stars hit the peak of their popularity, Benny barely spoke to Christina – their lives had diverged and there was very little common ground between them apart from the kids. One day in 1966, Benny took a deep breath and phoned Christina to break off their four-year engagement.

Christina could take only so many injuries to her pride. She'd played the dutiful, silent wife, denying a part of her life, pretending she didn't exist, and grinning through gritted teeth while the country hooted at the laddish antics of her clever boyfriend, the pop star. She was barely tolerated if she had the temerity to want to see the Hep Stars in concert, and hidden away during the show and the usual post-gig shindig like an unwanted costume from the theatre's wardrobe department. It was, she told herself, a sacrifice for the greater cause and all would be well in the end. That was her heart speaking. Her head told her not to be so dumb. She didn't cry or scream or rant when Benny made The Call and moved out. She knew it was inevitable. She knew it was coming. But one brief, cold, single phone call to turn the page on four years and a lifetime of dreams: Christina deserved more than that. And she cracked.

Christina went public on their relationship, giving a sensationalist interview to a Swedish magazine, tearing him to shreds for walking out on her and ignoring the children. She was bitter and perhaps had a right to be, but it didn't make her feel better. Some fans even discovered where she lived and phoned her up or shouted at her outside her house to keep away from Benny. There's just one thing worse than being a pop star's girlfriend – being a pop star's *ex*-girlfriend.

Benny was shocked by the episode and a little shamed by it too. He hated hurting anyone and the accusations about the kids struck home. He was stunned to be pilloried in print in this way too, having had nothing but adulation from public and press alike up to this point. It left a scar which has remained with him ever since – the easygoing, affable, laid-back Benny Andersson never trusted the press again. He'd still play the game and subjected himself to interviews and press conferences throughout the rest of the Hep Stars' life and subsequently Abba's career . . . *but he never actually said anything*.

Yet contrary to the doomy expectations of the rest of the group, Christina's shocking revelations did no lasting damage to the band. The Hep Stars' success story rolled on and on. Nobody hooked Benny in. Gold discs started being dished out like confetti, and in this corner of Scandinavia at least, the Hep Stars were outselling even the Beatles. Benny was nineteen and king of the world. Well, Sweden at least.

That's always a dangerous moment. Television pundits always say that soccer teams are at their most vulnerable immediately after they've scored a brilliant goal. They go belting up the field shrieking, 'This scoring goals is a piece of cake, eh lads, let's go get ourselves another,' and before they know it, the opposition's horrendously ugly striker has slipped through the middle and cracked a hat-trick past their goalkeeper, still busily signing autographs for the crowd.

The Hep Stars thought they were invincible. The Midas syndrome gone loopy. Money? It was flooding in, wasn't it? *Wasn't it?* Hits? Just snap your fingers and they'd be there forever and a day. Nothing could stop them now.

So they thought they'd get smart. They'd build themselves a business empire to bring in even more money and – all heart – put something back into the industry that had served them so well. They'd set up their own publishing and recording company to promote other Swedish artists and develop the Scandinavian recording industry and promote the vibrant new talent they knew was throbbing along in their wake. After all, there was bound to be a nation of young bucks out there intent on stealing their thunder, and if you can't beat 'em, join 'em – why not control it rather than take them on as competition? It would be easier that way than flogging themselves to death tramping round the country making telly appearances and playing live shows. They honestly believed they could make hit records themselves as easily as snap their fingers, so yeah . . . let's be a business empire too.

They were naïve beyond belief.

They had little proper management and virtually no worthwhile advice. They hadn't bothered with menial trivia such as paying taxes and nobody kept proper track of monies coming in and going out. They assumed they were millionaires several times over and that everything would be all right because it had been so far. They thought they could go anywhere, do anything, spend any amount of money, pursue any hair-brained idea that came into their heads.

At one point they decided to make an album in London, primarily because most of the bands they admired were British and they thought that if they recorded in England it would automatically be better and turn them into international, rather than just Scandinavian stars. So they hired a private plane to fly them to London where they set up residence in an expensive London studio, where they doodled around for a couple of weeks, seeing the sights and getting drunk before realizing they didn't actually have any material prepared for a new album and packed up and went home with nothing to show for their adventure beyond a few more dead brain-cells.

Another time they got it into their heads that New York was the place to be and, bright-eyed and bushy-tailed, they crossed the Atlantic, just to . . . *be there.* They appeared to think that their status in Sweden alone would be sufficient to stop the American music business in its tracks the moment they touched down at JFK Airport, and a whole new exciting episode would unfurl before their very eyes. They were, after all, supposedly business-men now too. But like every venture they undertook they had no plan of campaign and wandered around New York in starry-eyed wonder waiting for something to happen. It never did. They didn't play any gigs or have any promotion, and they didn't even get a release for any of their records in the States. They had a good time, though. An *expensive* good time. That was the story of their lives then.

Their greatest and most spectacular act of lunacy of them all, though, was the movie. Bands making movies were suddenly all the rage. It was a status symbol for groups, a sign of having attained a certain level of popularity and influence to make a big-screen film, no matter how hideously inept. The Hep Stars saw themselves on the same level as the Beatles, so naturally their thoughts turned to their own movie. After all, even the Dave Clark Five had made a movie. If they could get away with it . . . well, the Hep Stars certainly could. At least they had a bit of wit and character about them. They could leap around and have funny, impromptu japes with one another and hilariously surreal conversations à la Beatles with Wilfred Bramble on the train in *A Hard Day's Night*. Making movies? No worries, piece of cake. Let's go make a movie. Let's go make a movie in . . . AFRICA!

Nobody knows who initially came up with the idea or why they thought they could possibly make it happen without professional backing and direction. And nobody knows how or why they chose Africa as the location for this movie. Nobody *admits* to it, anyway. Certainly nobody has a clue why they agreed to it without investigating the finer details and studying the financial implications. Somebody said one night they should make a movie and somebody knew someone who was setting up a film company and suddenly there they were herding around Kenya or some such place like a bunch of kids on a Sunday School outing. They had a title, *Habari Safari*, and a film crew with them, but that's as far as the pre-planning went. Hey, they were high on . . . er . . . *life*. They had a charming but gobsmackingly foolish belief that it would somehow all be all right on the night. That their youthful exuberance, natural vitality and the luck of the gods would somehow see them through. It hadn't served them badly so far.

It was a few days into the trip before one of the cameramen casually enquired about the script. Script? *Script?!?* Svenne didn't think they needed a script . . . they'd just sort of roam around the place and be . . . er . . . *themselves*. The fans would love it! So yeah, they roamed around the place and acted as themselves and if they'd poured paraffin and taken a match to all the banks in Sweden they couldn't have obliterated so much money so quickly.

Not that Benny Andersson paid much attention or even cared about all this. His lyric writing had ground to a complete halt by now and he'd enlisted the help of another songwriter and guitarist, Lars Berhagen, to kick him into action again. They had a good relationship and the disciplined Lars bullied Benny into a more considered, ballady style of writing which resulted in a further shower of Hep Stars hits, but it was always a slow, lonely process for Benny, especially when you could be bumming around in Africa. 'I suppose we were a bit irresponsible,' he told the Abba fan club magazine. 'I just have to laugh at the total disorder that reigned then. No one was responsible for anything. We resolved our problems with a shrug of the shoulders and an, "It'll all work out tomorrow." '

If the Beatles were making a dog's dinner of their idealistic business empire, Apple, then the Hep Stars were making a gigantic pigswill of their Swedish equivalent, Hep House. It must have been strangely satisfying to know that there was something they could do on an even grander scale than their Beatle heroes.

They flushed away a fortune on *Habari Safari*, and gained not one usable frame of celluloid. They returned to Sweden after two weeks of the usual bickering and recriminations, somewhat chastened by the experience. They bluffed heroically about the brilliance of *Habari Safari*, but they'd shocked even themselves by the sheer volume of their waste.

Even from their rarefied vantage point in cloud cuckoo land, the Hep Stars recognized that something had to change. Men in suits were contacted to relate the bad news, but it was far worse than any of them had imagined. Accountants jumped off very high buildings rather than face the full horrific reality of the Hep House finances. The long and the short of it was that they were broke. Several times over.

But there was worse, much worse to follow. The Swedish tax people were on to their case in a big way and the bills came flying in from all directions. In tax alone they were estimated to owe over £100,000, and that was the tip of the iceberg. Hep House was bankrupt and all income from the Hep Stars' records, concerts and promotions was being channelled into paying off debts. And would be for a very long time to come. The end of the sixties had come with a jolt.

10

ONE OF US IS CRYING

'Whatever happened to our love? I wish I understood
It used to be so nice, it used to be so good'

'SOS'

The world tour through early 1977 represented a fraught final frontier in the tempestuous relationship between Bjorn and Agnetha.

Abba were at the absolute peak of their success. Already they had a track record surpassed only by the Beatles, Elvis Presley and Cliff Richard and they still hadn't set foot on a concert stage in earnest since it had all started happening. Stig Anderson's vision of world domination by pictures had become reality and Abba became the ultimate video band, their promotional films quickly becoming a kitsch art form in themselves to be slavered over by fans, gawped at by perverts, and parodied by comedians. Bands had traditionally whipped up fan frenzy on the road, but Abba could never have done it that way. Girls don't scream at girls (though Kylie Minogue was to get close to it a generation later) and boys don't go for heroines. Abba's music was based on harmonies and melodies rather than the frenzy of rhythm and sexuality. For all the girls' pouting, Abba were a peculiarly unsexy band.

Mainly, though, Abba had no real interest in performing live. They'd all done it. Benny got off now on inventing melodies and twiddling knobs in studios. Bjorn could ultimately see himself as a record company mogul, the man to out-Stig Stig. And then there was the already mixed-up Agnetha. Agnetha with the ferocious temper and her confidence forever in tatters. She'd had no shortage of ambition and she was passionate about music, but marriage and motherhood had dramatically altered her outlook. She was terrified of flying from the outset and had to be bullied into travelling anywhere – having a child exacerbated her unease about the whole thing and she was haunted by the fear of being a bad mother. She'd done her bit, she'd been a star, she'd performed on stage solidly since her early teens. All she really wanted to do now was to stay at home and bring up her kids, be a good wife and mother, and live happily ever after.

There was, though, still something of the exhibitionist in Anni-Frid. People who met her fleetingly found her cold and distant, yet she was still a party animal, a familiar sight at Stockholm's more chic clubs, always at the centre of the music community and clearly intent on living life to the full. She'd had a reasonably successful career, but hadn't achieved the level of acclaim and adulation enjoyed by the others. She had something to prove, the hardships of her upbringing still at the forefront of her mind. The exploding Abba phenomenon thrilled her the most and she wanted to be involved in every aspect of the operation. Of *course* she wanted Abba to tour, that was surely a central part of the deal. She wanted it all, and she yearned for something tangible to measure it all by. She *needed* to milk that applause.

The whole world was with Frida on that one. Questions were beginning to be asked, silly rumours circulating. That Abba didn't really exist; that the records were made by boring old session musicians and Bjorn, Benny, Agnetha and Frida were merely actors who couldn't play or sing a note, and were merely a front for the whole thing. That they *couldn't* play live to save their lives; that they'd really split up after 'Waterloo'; that they were too good to be true.

That's what happens when you don't present yourself for public scrutiny every so often. Think of Elvis after he came out of the army and all he had to show was a decade of excruciatingly bad movies. Some of the stories written about him then were monstrous. All that stuff about him being a burger junkie. Some journalists wrote that he had a fetish about guns and fired at the television when somebody came on that he didn't like. Others said he had his own mafia who never left his side and even froze out his own wife. One or two even suggested he'd got fat and was popping pills morning, noon and night just to get him out of bed and then put him back to sleep again. Weird. Even weirder that they all turned out to be true.

And look at poor old Michael Jackson. All that stuff about singing to llamas and sleeping in oxygen tents and having facelifts every five minutes, even before we got on to the allegations about paedophilia. And Jacko *did* tour with relative regularity. He just didn't give interviews. Privacy equals lunacy when you're a rock legend. It's a perverse business, all right.

The roller-coaster had reached such a pitch that Stig knew something fresh had to be pulled out of the hat to maintain its impetus. International mania couldn't be sustained by cute videos and great records alone. If you're not moving forwards, you're going backwards and Stig could never be content to settle for the status quo when there was more gold to be mined. In 1977, Abba had the world at their feet, but Stig saw only unconquered territories and homes that didn't have Abba records in the collection. There could be no further prevarication. Abba had to go on tour.

They'd got thus far as a human representation of happy families. Vigorously healthy, good-looking, talented, successful and deeply in love. The first European equivalent of the American dream and Stig dared not let anything or anybody get in the way of it. Everything in the Abba enclave was carefully guarded, protected and controlled, as if one small blight on their infallibility would irrevocably injure them. The few interviews they gave offered only bland platitudes and the air of unreality hanging over them as a result served to seal the myth of plasticity.

The truth, of course, was entirely different. Agnetha was a firebrand and Bjorn a character of formidable will and opinion. The relationship between them was never easy and its weaknesses were exposed to the full amid the massive pressures of their first world tour and the attendant hang-ups and problems it caused all of them. Everything had to be just perfect. There was no room allowed for the remotest hint of failure or imperfection at this, the height of their career, yet stage performance was by far the weakest part of their armoury. This was where they relied so heavily on the charisma and showmanship of the two girls, who both reacted badly to intense pressure. The relationship between the two of them – never good – was now subjected to microscopic attention. Only Herculean effort and sheer professionalism kept things intact on stage. It was a burden they both found insufferable and the brief respites from that spotlight resulted in an almost total breakdown of communication between them.

Worse still, though, it had a knock-on effect between Bjorn and Agnetha. They'd always been at each other's throats – this was part of the passion between them. True love, passion and caring come hand-in-hand with ferocious arguments in Agnetha's book. You don't fight with someone you don't care intensely about – that's one theory about relationships and it was one familiar to both Bjorn and Agnetha. Their squabbles, even in the early days of their relationship, frequently shocked friends and bystanders, though close associates became accustomed to the highly-charged intensity between them. At a party on one celebrated occasion, Agnetha shocked guests by flinging a smoked herring at Bjorn because she figured he wasn't paying her enough attention. The room fell silent in anticipation as all eyes turned on Bjorn, waiting with bated breath for the explosion.

Bjorn eyed Agnetha's blazing expression, checked the herring on the floor, momentarily wiped his face, and burst out laughing. The attendant eyes swivelled in turn to Agnetha to check her reaction to *that* reaction. Agnetha, too, dissolved into laughter. The audience – for the guests now began to realize that's exactly what they were – acknowledged they'd been drawn into some intimate ritual they couldn't understand, and laughed uncertainly along with them. It wasn't the first or last public display of the love-hate intensity and desire which bound Bjorn and Agnetha together.

Their whole courtship and marriage had been carried out in public, like some royal soap opera. Agnetha was a big star. She was the nation's sweetheart – a classic cliché of blonde, Scandinavian beauty, full of sweetness, romance and fragile vulnerability. Every guy in Sweden would have punched out the lights of any unscrupulous man who wronged her. Such an image scarcely took into account the ambitious venom and occasionally foul-mouthed aggression that also characterized her youth, but then public image rarely fitted private frailties.

One of the guys ready and willing to punch out the lights of any unscrupulous bastard who might hurt Agnetha was Bjorn Ulvaeus. He'd had a detached fascination with her since first hearing the striking, pained innocence of her voice on her debut hit 'I Was So In Love'. It had the overbearing sentimentality and slushiness that groovy young students like Bjorn were automatically expected to detest and always pretended they did, but secretly adored. It's the Tammy Wynette 'Stand By Your Man' factor – the unfathomable, absurdly romantic chemistry of voice and song that defies logic and turns helpless knees to jelly, leading sane creatures to psychiatrists' doors imagining there must be a serious defect in their character to give such obvious crap brain space. It was an impression that was to recur among supposedly sane students when Abba themselves were thumping out the hits years later.

In secret at the dead of night wearing an extravagant disguise Bjorn went out and bought 'I Was So In Love' . . . and proceeded to buy Agnetha's subsequent records and observe her progress on television and through magazines with mounting interest. He fantasized about the perfect woman in time-honoured fashion, visualizing the finer details of the day that they'd finally become lovers and he'd whisk her off into the sunset and they'd live together in perfect harmony for ever and ever, amen.

His distant admiration was maintained as Stig and Bengt Bernhag scooped up the Hootenanny Singers and launched them into orbit as Polar's first missile aimed at a

breathlessly expectant world. One day in the summer of
'69 the Hootenanny Singers were booked on a TV show
in Gothenburg. Preoccupied with the details of the
performance, Bjorn barely noticed anyone approaching.
A tap on the shoulder, a polite but confident voice.
'Excuse me, but . . .'

And there was the long-term object of his desires,
Agnetha Faltskog. She looked stunning and she *was*
stunning. Bold as brass, no trace of the shyness he'd
imagined, telling him she was a big Hootenanny Singers
fan, saying she thought that he personally was great and
maybe they could get together some time.

Bjorn was flattened by the approach. Agnetha made no
bones about it then or later that she wanted Bjorn and set
off to get him. Bjorn made little attempt to conceal his
own interest and it wasn't long before they could barely
keep their hands off one another. Their own respective
careers conspired to keep them apart, but Bjorn and
Agnetha – instantly besotted with one another – were
resilient and determined, going to extraordinary lengths
to spend as much time together as possible, and spending
hours on end whispering sweet nothings down the phone
to one another. They felt a bond from that first meeting in
the TV studio in Gothenburg with all the attendant
jealousies and rampant passions that went with it. Within
a couple of months they'd moved in together in a
picturesque part of Stockholm alongside the Karlsberg
Canal.

The press soon got to hear of it and built the story up
to a sensational degree, willing them to go public, and in
the first full idyllic flush of their love affair they made no
attempt to disguise it. Evidently thrilled and blooming
with excitement about the whole thing, Agnetha

admitted that yes, she was in love with Bjorn. A nation of guys decided not to punch his lights out. If someone was to claim her, then Bjorn would do – in essence it had all the hallmarks of a royal romance, which the nation could duly enjoy and analyse from the outset. Prince Charles and Princess Di had nothing on Bjorn and Agnetha . . .

They did manage to get away for a pre-nuptial holiday in Cyprus, but were back again to resume their individual careers and Sweden's love story of the year for the titillation of public and press alike. The arguments, the doubts, jealousies and insecurities were gleefully reported for a public which couldn't get enough of them and followed them into their plush new flat on the island of Lilla Essenger. They were just like any other young couple trying to build a life together. Most, though, didn't have a posse of reporters chasing after them demanding to know when they were getting married.

Ultimately the nation's sweethearts knew their duty and complied with the country's wishes. To an enthralled audience they announced the wedding of the year would take place on 6 July 1971. By now both of them were completely swept up in the flow. The romantic Agnetha was hooked on her own fairy story being hyped up everywhere, and despite her constant protestations that there would be no professional link-up with Bjorn and that she fully intended to continue her own independent career, she pursued it with palpably less enthusiasm. Everyone was distracted, but it was a significant time in view of subsequent events: the friendship and burgeoning partnership between Bjorn and Benny developed at a rate into a few casual performances on which Bjorn was sometimes joined by the adoring Agnetha.

The wedding itself further advanced the fairy tale.

Bjorn and Agnetha had bought the dream and saw it through to the point of scouring the whole country for the right setting for the royal nuptials, eventually settling on a beautiful ancient Gothic church in the tiny village of Verum in Skane in the extreme south of Sweden. It was remote – but well publicized – and over 3,000 well-wishers lined the road to cheer Agnetha on her way to the church aboard an open-top carriage led by a team of pure white horses. Over the top? Agnetha? Surely not . . .

Inside the church Benny Andersson, bless him, was sat at the organ playing 'The Wedding March' to waltz Agnetha down the aisle . . . and his own Hep Stars' hit, 'Wedding', to send her and her new husband back out to face the mass of cheering holidaymakers, bemused villagers, a thousand cameras and the panic-stricken local police force who'd never known anything like it in their lives. In the unsightly melée that occurred as the happy couple emerged into the sunlight, a police horse trod on the bride's foot and Agnetha hopped around on one foot much to the consternation of Bjorn and the suppressed amusement of the assembled masses. On another day in different circumstances she might have screamed and sworn at everybody in spitting distance, but not today. Today she was queen and today all was euphoric.

Bride suitably repaired, the cavalcade wafted back through the village to a local inn, where a lavish wedding dinner was held for the lucky guests, who included the entire Swedish musical fraternity. There was music all the way courtesy of the Hep Stars and assorted guest artists, with Bjorn hauled up on stage to perform a song written specifically for the occasion by Stig Anderson. The party went on well into the night and – in true royal tradition –

the bride and groom were coaxed out on to the inn balcony to acknowledge the cheering crowds not lucky enough to get an invitation to dinner.

The picture-book wedding was duly completed with barely a blemish and Agnetha and Bjorn scarcely believed they could ever be unhappy again. That outlook was to dramatically cloud the next morning when a call came through to Bjorn. He came off the phone ashen-faced, scarcely comprehending the news . . . his old mentor, Stig's partner Bengt Bernhag, had committed suicide. A very large balloon had burst unexpectedly in a shattering way.

It destroyed the honeymoon, such as it was. It lasted four days and Agnetha spent much of it in the unlikely role of counsellor, repeatedly assuring Bjorn that it wasn't his fault, that he couldn't have done anything, that Bengt would only want him to be happy. And then suddenly they were back amongst it all again, Bjorn bashing off to rejoin a tour with the Hootenanny Singers, who were currently topping the Swedish charts. Agnetha had work to do too. She had said on countless occasions that marriage wouldn't affect her own solo career, come hell or high water, and she was determined to maintain her own identity and musical direction, whether she was Mrs Ulvaeus or not. She probably meant it too.

One night away from Bjorn and she was ready to renounce everything. She got angry when he went away. She got even angrier when she had to go away. Their reunions were a frenzy of inquisitions, reassurances, quarrels, forgiveness and love. Theirs was a household of rare passion and colour. Careers were one thing, and singing for your supper was clearly the finest career on earth, but it all seemed somewhat meaningless and trivial now. This was different, this was *marriage* and Agnetha genuinely felt it to be sacred and untouchable.

There was always much friction between Bjorn and Agnetha. It was what fired them and fascinated them and kept them interested. They loved each other as people and adored each other for the status and respect each had. Agnetha could fly off the handle without warning – a word out of place and books, plates, jewellery, chairs, anything that came to hand would come flying at Bjorn. It was one of the things that made her so irresistible. He cherished her feistiness just as he cherished her vulnerability.

Bjorn wasn't cowed by this behaviour. He wasn't always Mr Placid himself. But he was also strong and secure and self-confident – qualities which Agnetha basically lacked and would disguise in a torrent of mental aggression and thus adored in him. Benny wouldn't have lasted five minutes with Agnetha. She needed a belligerent, competitive partner to duel with to keep her alive and excited and drive away her natural insecurity. It was when they *stopped* fighting that trouble began.

Bjorn stated in various interviews that he believed the marriage would have ended sooner had they led normal lives and not been in a group together – an unorthodox view given that the pundits of the time fondly dredged up the theory that they were yet another victim of show-business marriages. In truth they managed pretty well for the first couple of years. Sparks flew, kitchens were wrecked, the Swedish language violated, but Bjorn and Agnetha were completely wrapped up in one another. Success, after all, is the finest aphrodisiac on earth and they had plenty of it.

As Abba took root, Agnetha's initial misgivings about getting involved professionally with Bjorn were dissi-

Ain't she sweet! The seventeen-year-old Agnetha – already a Swedish national sweetheart. (Pressens Bild Ab)

The Hep Stars weren't *remotely* influenced by the Beatles! Few guessed that the chubby Benny Andersson (second from right), looking like a cross between Peter Noone and Ozzy Osbourne, was destined for greatness. (Pressens Bild Ab)

Anni-Frid Lyngstad playing happy families with Ragnar the furniture salesman and their two children, Hans and Lise-Lotte, *circa* 1967. Domestic bliss was to be short lived . . . (Göran Ärnbäck, Pressens Bild Ab)

The fairy tale is complete. A nation weeps as Sweden's most beautiful couple, Agnetha Faltskog and Bjorn Ulvaeus, marry in the picturesque village of Verum, 1971. Benny even gets to play the church organ! (Pressens Bild Ab)

Benny and Anni-Frid early on during the longest engagement in history? (Heilemann, Camera Press Ltd)

The image that haunted them for ever. The perm, the star-shaped guitar, the satin knicker-bockers, Stig's whiskers . . . Eurovision in Brighton, 1974. Abba's finest hour. Or was it their greatest disaster? (Hulton Deutsch)

Abba discover flower power, posing for the world's press in the crazy days immediately following their Eurovision success. (Hulton Deutsch)

Why would *anyone* wrap themselves in Bacofoil for a publicity shot? Desperation clearly set in during the barren years between 'Waterloo' and 'SOS'. (Heilemann, Camera Press Ltd)

The Abba girls in classic profile. Anni-Frid sings her heart out while every zoom lens in the room focuses on Agnetha's rear. (Michael Ochs Archives)

Bjorn dumped the star-shaped guitar after Eurovision. He still wore daft costumes, though . . . (Michael Ochs Archives)

Above: Abba on stage in '77 at the peak of their commercial success . . . and their rampaging wardrobe. (Heilemann, Camera Press Ltd)

Left: Practically royalty. Abba attend a royal banquet at Stockholm Castle as guests of the King of Sweden. On Benny's left are Stig Anderson and his wife Gudrun. (Hulton Deutsch)

Anni-Frid . . . and the most celebrated bum in Europe. (Barry Schultz, Camera Press Ltd

The girl with the golden hair. Anni-Frid performing as part of the 'fantasy' sequence originally touted as a concept album and stage show in its own right. (Barry Schultz, Camera Press Ltd)

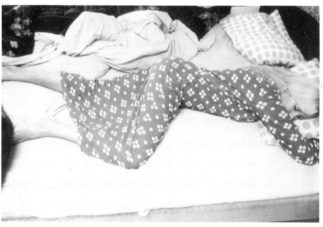

Sometimes it just all got a bit too much for poor Agnetha . . . (Heilemann, Camera Press Ltd)

Power to the four-wheel drive. Agnetha wouldn't fly anywhere you could reach on a nice coach. (Camera Press Ltd)

Above: All she ever really wanted was to be a good mother and go shopping a lot. Agnetha caught unawares in London after it had all begun to go sour. (Colin Davey, Hulton Deutsch)

Left: The man who believed . . . and made it all possible. Stig Anderson, songwriter, entrepreneur and businessman. Just don't mention oil . . . (Bengt Malmquist, Polar Music International)

pated. At first it was loose enough to be merely fun – a darn sight more fun than roaming around Sweden on her own playing concerts, at any rate – and the Frida factor scarcely seemed an issue.

When Abba became more serious, Agnetha was too joyful about being pregnant to consider any negative ramifications of their association. When Abba appeared in Stockholm in their bid for the Swedish nomination for the 1973 Eurovision Song Contest, Agnetha was almost nine months pregnant and – dressed in multi-coloured smock and white trousers – sweating in case a premature birth scuppered their chances. It didn't, but Abba lost anyway – controversially – with some people claiming the sight of a pregnant woman on stage had wrecked the group's chances. Listening to the dross they had to compete against, nobody could think of any other reason why they'd lost. After all, pregnancy and pop are uncomfortable bedfellows, the whole, enticing basis of pop being built on the idea of the star being fanciable and available and even in the heady, liberated age of 1973, it was hard for such a heavily pregnant woman to be considered on either ground.

Stig and the rest of the band were outraged by the indignity and unfairness of the defeat, but Agnetha couldn't give a toss. Baby Linda Ulvaeus was born less than a fortnight after the defeat of 'Ring Ring' and with the press once more on the track of a new chapter in the country's favourite soap, she felt fulfilled and content with life exactly as it was. She got off on the fame as much as anyone and had a particular pride in the music, keen for success to follow, but it didn't burn within her as keenly as it did for Bjorn or Frida. Had she known the extent to which it would ultimately consume and alter her life,

Agnetha would undoubtedly have run a mile from Abba.

She was a small-town girl with traditional values. Marriage, babies, cosy homes and true love . . . these were her aspirations now and they were values that had never seemed more real. She had a streak of arrogance and uncouthness about her and at first she seemed dominated by ambition, loving the adulation of audiences and the power and importance given to her by a press thirsty for news of her every move. But having a baby was the greatest thing that had ever happened to her . . . and everything else paled into insignificance.

When she gave birth to Linda she imagined that the failure of 'Ring Ring' to win the Swedish vote for Eurovision would signal the collapse of all their dreams of international fame and fortune, and she was content to confine herself to Sweden in future, where she had nothing to prove and could be selective about her work.

As we now well know, 'Ring Ring' represented not the end of something, as she'd imagined, but the launching pad for a new beginning. That Stockholm defeat was sufficiently humiliating for the rest of them to provide the fuel for a more concerted attempt the following year and the avalanche of fame that resulted. And it brought with it almighty problems for Agnetha, anxious to be with Bjorn and play her role, but facing intolerable demands on her time and emotions: it was hard to handle being the world's finest bottom *and* the greatest mum on earth at the same time.

Nobody *made* her do it, of course, and she too was caught up in the excitement of it all. She was also quick to realize that Bjorn was absolutely committed to Abba and if she didn't go along with it then the marriage would be a barren pretence of snatched phone calls, fleeting visits home, postcards and nasty rumours from afar. There were really no choices and she was a voluntary participant in the preposterous vision of two perfect couples that Stig was rapidly evolving in his mind and his marketing strategy.

Bjorn and Agnetha didn't involve themselves in the side-effects of fame – the partying and the whole celebrity stakes – and for two years they held it together amid the explosiveness of Bjorn's will and Agnetha's temper. Away from the pressures of Abba, the pair were blissfully content, ski-ing, riding and yachting for pleasure and thoroughly enjoying the fruits of family life with Linda. But, of course, the more successful Abba became, the more it encroached on this idyllic domesticity . . . and the more Bjorn became enraptured by the mechanics of writing and recording, the more alienated and confused Agnetha became within the group.

The cumulative stresses of the tour and the subsequent birth of the new Ulvaeus baby, Christian, in December 1977 confirmed for Agnetha that her place should remain firmly at home. If the world tour represented a peak of sorts it also changed everything. Until now they'd felt totally in control of their own destinies, but now they'd stepped beyond the edge of their own horizons without a safety net. Their characters and their relationships were tested to the full. The broadbacked Frida, the sanguine Benny and the disciplined Bjorn swam . . . but a panic-stricken Agnetha fled back to her water-wings.

Bjorn and Agnetha stopped arguing after that tour. They stopped arguing and they stopped communicating. Their passion had been fully spent amid the draining stresses of travel, hotel rooms, calls home, and the mounting guilt of part-time parenthood. The resentments between Agnetha and Frida and resulting recriminations spilled over into both personal relationships. Agnetha snapped at Frida for always being late. Frida roared back at Agnetha for being so uptight. Bjorn and Benny stepped in to calm them down, and had their own heads bitten off in the blaze of irritation and anxiety that accumulated the further they went around the world.

Frida's view of Agnetha as someone who found it impossible to relax or enjoy herself struck a chord with the other two. Bjorn, particularly, found himself increasingly intolerant of Agnetha's foibles and phobias, joining Frida's attacks, clearly exasperated by her capitulation to pressure. The group were in unknown territory and it *was* scary, but they were in it together for the duration and Bjorn was tired of being father protector and making excuses for her frailty. Out there on the road on the other side of the world Abba discovered that the great adventure was just no fun any more.

Afterwards, tempers subsided and with them Bjorn's fascination with Agnetha. As she rested in preparation for the birth, Bjorn was back in the studio with Benny working on what would become *Abba the Album*, while also involving himself in the production and some of the business arrangements surrounding the release of *Abba the Movie*, which had been filmed during the fraught Australian leg of the tour. There were holidays and business meetings and production schedules and endless hours in the studio and Bjorn and Agnetha drifted where a year or so earlier they would have been at each other's throats firing groundless accusations about infidelity and lack of caring, which were always guaranteed to blow away the cobwebs and keep them on their toes.

Now work and indifference got in the way and they allowed it to happen. Bjorn became contemptuous of Agnetha, continually criticizing and ridiculing her, shattering further her already shaky self-esteem. He threw himself deeper and deeper into *Abba the Album*, finding himself with no desire to dash home as he had before and, preoccupied with her own worries and concerns about the house and kids, Agnetha did nothing to entice him. They resorted to cold, distant sniping and backbiting, which grew the more painful for their inability to stop themselves destroying the extraordinary love they'd always taken for granted and assumed would never fade. But the unthinkable was happening and they were powerless to do anything about it. Sweden's golden couple had gone rusty.

Not that anyone realized it at the time. These were, after all, super troupers of rare professionalism. They continued to play their allotted roles, showing off new baby Christian and fulfilling Swedish expectations as the country's two most glamorous people now apparently became the perfect family. Except now they didn't just belong to Sweden any more. They were the property of the world, and the world didn't necessarily buy the story any more.

They did try to sort out the problems and there were various attempts to relight the flame. They talked endlessly about it all, they even tried counselling and marriage guidance, resorting to a psychiatrist to help them dig out the dross in their lives and discuss frankly the complex problems surrounding the conflicts of their personal and professional lives. That brought its own problems as rumours spread that Agnetha was having an affair with her therapist. Things fell completely apart during the summer of '78, the band's relative inactivity stripping away the last vestiges of a union that may or may not have been salvaged by the drastic intensity of another barrage of work. A tour may perhaps have thrown them at each other's mercy when they needed it most . . . but more likely it would have ended with them killing one another.

As it was, 1978 was a miserable year. *Abba the Movie* was howled at from Malmo to Malibu and *Abba the Album* had a similarly violent welcome from an increasingly cynical international press, though it still managed to sell in mountain-loads and produced in 'Take A Chance On Me' one of their greatest records ever.

Mostly Agnetha was too wrapped up in parenthood to notice or care. Bjorn fell drastically out of love with her and was too drained of emotion to consider continuing the sham. Their marriage had been too intense to survive indifference and the forthright, clearheaded Bjorn resolved to do the right thing. Talking, counselling, therapy . . . it all proved to be as hopelessly draining as the marriage itself. As journalists – still hot on the trail of the AGNETHA HAS AFFAIR WITH PSYCHIATRIST story – sniffed the breakdown of the Ulvaeus marriage, Bjorn issued a short statement to the effect that he and Agnetha were seeking a divorce, adding with more optimism than belief that Abba would continue unaffected by this minor hiccup. It was, they said, an 'amicable' split. There has never been an amicable split in the history of love and marriage.

'We just couldn't live together any longer and we are filing for divorce,' they announced simply. 'When you talk about everything and still don't get through to each other then you must take the consequences. We just grew apart.'

Agnetha was devastated. Stig wasn't too thrilled either as he saw the carefully nurtured and preserved image of human and professional perfection shattering before his eyes. He really shouldn't have worried. Abba finally shed the remnants of Eurovision froth with the collapse of Bjorn and Agnetha's marriage and, publicly acknowledging for the first time that they were human after all, wrote the most meaningful music of their lives. Freed of the constraints of teeth and smiles, their music took a broodier turn for the better, with Bjorn turning in significantly mature lyrics and Benny developing a much broader base to the music.

It is absolutely true that the best, most meaningful music results from personal misery. The basis of Phil Collins' whole solo career was built on the agonies of splitting with his first wife, as documented so graphically on his breakthrough album, *Face Value*. After that he had to resort to covers of Motown and old Mindbenders hits for his million-sellers as he found true love and happiness with his second wife, before going back in desperation to dredge up the past on his '93 album, *Both Sides*, for some serious self-examination and another whopping great hit.

The death of James Taylor's girlfriend, Jackson Browne's wife, Eric Clapton's son, Mike Rutherford's dad, David Bowie's brother, Kate Bush's mother . . . these are the extreme examples. Awful, personal tragedies resulting in angry, confused, guilt-ridden, therapeutic songs that make irresistible listening. They make you uncomfortable, like you're eavesdropping on someone's grief, but witnessing personal torment evokes a powerful response in the casual observer, as well as providing valuable insights into what are usually well-guarded psyches. The songs that touch you most are always those written from the very pit of human emotion and the pain of love and its catalogue of deceit and disappointment is the one songwriters always come back to. It's the exception that proves the rule in the great 'All lyrics are crap' debate. Because its audience can always identify with its traumas in one form or another, love is the staple diet of pop songwriting, whether it's the Shangri-Las mixing melodrama with teenage rebellion in the ultimate pop death disc 'Leader Of The Pack' or Bob Dylan snarling and spitting his way through the angriest, most bitterly recriminating ballad of love turned to hate in pop history, 'Positively Fourth Street'.

Late in the day, with the breakdown of the Agnetha–Bjorn marriage, Abba cottoned on and instantly made the leap from wonderful pop band to outstanding, timeless songwriters too. And when the Benny–Frida relationship also ended in tears, then they *really* started to cook and moved swiftly into the realms of greatness.

Ironically Benny and Anni-Frid decided to get married just a couple of months before Bjorn and Agnetha announced their split. It's tempting to conclude that the two events are related, and that Benny and Frida elected to formalize their longstanding relationship as a career move for the sake of image to offset the damage to their public status they knew would result from the Ulvaeus parting. It wasn't beyond Stig's intellect to suggest such a thing, and there are clear precedents of the British royal family timing announcements of national joy about engagements, pregnancies and weddings to divert attention from some monstrous mismanagement of the economy by Her Majesty's government.

But it wasn't Benny's way, and Frida had long been resigned to her role as lover and not wife. It irked her, sure it irked her . . . another case of playing the also-ran and supporting act to Agnetha's glamorous lead. There were constant jokes about the spoils won by the blonde vision she shared the spotlight with who seemingly had everything – the brains, the looks, the *husband* – while she was the plain one who couldn't even persuade her boyfriend to marry her. It was never like that with them, but the jibes still hurt.

Benny and Frida had met one night in 1968 in a bar in Malmo, where they'd both been appearing with their respective groups. A vague air of recognition from both sides, a couple of drinks, some casual conversation, and that was it. No instant lust. No inkling that the meeting was to change both their lives. A friendly chat, a joke or two about mutual friends and the inanities of life on the road, and that was it, they were on their way to another suitcase, another hall.

Shortly afterwards they both found themselves on the panel of some stupid pop quiz programme on a radio station in Stockholm and ended up going for dinner together, a shared interest in the good life immediately coming to the fore. Again there was no bolt of lightning between them, just the slow burn that is the traditional way of things with Benny, which gradually whipped up more pace as their paths continued to cross and their mutual love of partying and dining out cemented a firm relationship. There was none of the electrifying frenzy that surrounded Bjorn and Agnetha whenever they were together, but Benny clearly found Frida to be a class apart from all the women he'd had before and she in turn admired his relaxed friendliness, easy nature and charismatic self-confidence.

Anni-Frid's own career and self-esteem were in some

disarray when she met Benny. Her records weren't selling as well as she'd anticipated and her propensity towards romantic ballads and jazz standards earmarked her for late-night clubs, supper bars and cabaret venues rather than the more enticing pop market. She was respected as a singer – technically her range and feel for notes puts her streets ahead of Agnetha – but she wasn't a natural stage performer, with little confidence, charisma or audience rapport to lift her profile. She wasn't cute, dainty or explosive, like Agnetha, and she knew it because she was told it often enough. Cold, stiff, awkward, plain, uneasy, distant, aloof . . . these were words applied to both her personality and stage performance that came back to haunt her time and again. Nobody was going to leap up from the audience to punch out the lights of the man who whisked Anni-Frid off her feet. It was a salutary experience to discover that talent alone wasn't going to be enough to take her where she wanted to go, and in her testier moments she ranted bitterly about the upstarts emerging with half of her ability being hailed as the next big thing and given big budget backings by managers and record companies which knew no better. Happens all the time. Pop appeal is about sex, not talent, and with any luck always will be.

There were many occasions when Frida felt alone and friendless in an alien world and wanted to throw it all up and go home to Ragnar and the kids. Start again. Say it was all a terrible mistake. She wasn't cut out to be a singer. A wife and mother, that's what she ought to be, and whatever gave her the absurd notion that she could be a star? Ragnar would welcome her back with open arms and no recriminations, she knew he would. But Frida *was* blessed with resilience and determination and, while she toyed with the idea of giving it all up and going home, there was a ferocious ambition within her that kept her going.

Nobody made a big fuss in the papers when it transpired that she and Benny were an item, and nobody seriously expected it to last. There was some snotty backbiting about the family she'd left behind in Eskilstuna and the odd jibe about Benny being a marriage-breaker and it hurt, but it wasn't the first or last time she'd have to close her eyes to ignorance and narrowmindedness. Anni-Frid always had to do things the hard way.

They moved in together into a small flat in Stockholm in 1970, causing another minor scandal, having officially announced their engagement a few months earlier. The public invested them with none of the warmth and goodwill with which they followed the unfolding adventures of Bjorn and Agnetha. The unkempt Benny Andersson was considered an undisciplined, irresponsible character and Anni-Frid was the outsider, the scarlet woman who'd abandoned her devoted husband and children. Utter nonsense, all of it, but that's journalists for you. And then soon the respective relationships of Bjorn–Agnetha and Benny–Frida were being compared and played against each other like a newspaper battle between cowboys and Indians.

Frida was the driving force in the partnership, necessarily taking a grip on the disorganization that's always been integral to Benny's character. In return he gave her respect and admiration for her abilities rather than her achievements and rode through her prickliness and resentments with his accustomed charm and humour, accepting her tantrums with a grace and unflappability she'd never encountered before. The consequence was that she calmed down and learned to trust a little more, and he started getting to appointments on time. It was a good deal all round.

They planned to get married, but somehow never got around to it. Benny could never get it together to make the necessary arrangements and Frida was initially happy just to see how things worked out, one failed marriage and a troubled past behind her already. She was a cautious romantic, seldom believing anything anybody ever told her about *anything*, especially not Benny Andersson, in whom she recognized an unreliably free spirit.

But they worked it out. He survived her unpredictable mood swings and she put up with his laid-back attitude and indecision. It worked pretty well. They came to trust and rely on one another totally, believing – probably rightly – they'd both be half as effective personally and professionally without the other.

When it finally came, Frida adored the fame and applause every bit as much as she'd thought she would. Each cheer, every record sold, all the column inches in the papers she saw as just reward for the crap she'd endured beforehand. It didn't prevent her occasional dips into depression; or the illogical bouts of jealousy about Agnetha that had Bjorn and Benny meticulously making certain that each had an equal share of the spotlight; and it didn't stop her throwing crockery at Benny when his vagueness threatened to send everyone around them completely comatose; but it did give her immense satisfaction and an unshakable belief that she and Benny would last for ever.

So they didn't get the marriage together and events rapidly overtook them as the Bjorn–Agnetha Show swept them away. Anything that followed in the immediate aftermath would inevitably be seen as second-rate and

Frida already had enough hang-ups about the glamour queen next to her without inviting that comparison too. Once the Abba bandwagon was off and rolling at full tilt then there just wasn't the time to even think about it. That's what Benny said, at least.

It became a standing joke within the group as they awaited the regulation question from interviewers about Benny's reluctance to name the day. His constant side-stepping of the issue was greeted with hoots of amuse-ment from Agnetha and Bjorn, though Frida didn't always see the joke. Once in America during a TV interview on the *Dinah Shore Show*, Benny was harangued mercilessly by Shore about why he'd never asked Frida to marry him. Shore virtually insisted that he propose there and then, ensuring maximum ratings for the show. But she had a formidable adversary in Benny, who refused to rise to the bait and with barely a flicker of detached amusement in his expression didn't deviate from his stock answer about not having the time, but it would happen one day. In the end it stopped being an issue, and nobody could ever see them getting married, just as they could never see them splitting up.

But people were wrong on both counts. Their relation-ship survived fame, criticism, ridicule, petty jealousies and all the absurd penalties of living within the goldfish bowl of constant public attention. They even survived the traumas of the infamous world tour and the pressure-cooker life it involved. The more famous they became the better Frida seemed to like it, and while Benny was always anxious to get back into the studio, he became a contented tourist. Just make sure there was a piano in every hotel they were booked into and he was sorted.

While Bjorn and Agnetha smarted and analysed and

ripped each other apart with mind games in their hotel room, Benny and Frida made the very best of it, socializing, getting themselves out and about as much as they could, partying the nights away in an unnervingly raucous manner. They had spats, but they were usually forgotten as briskly as they arose and, whatever else, at least they knew that the other wasn't screwing around. *Didn't* they?

In an appropriate lull in Abba's activity, Benny duly kept his word and married Anni-Frid. On 6 October 1978 Benny Andersson and Anni-Frid Lyngstad were married in almost total secrecy in Stockholm. No open carriage taking the bride to a Gothic church, no cheering crowds lining the streets, no massed ranks of press and cameramen. Just a couple of close friends as guests and a church warden and the couple's housekeeper as witnesses. The contrast between the private nature of the event and the carnival that had been the Ulvaeus wedding seven years earlier was deliberately marked. They'd lived together for nine years and they'd been chewed up by the publicity mill more times than they cared to think about. They weren't dewy-eyed kids in the first flush of love and Frida particularly had suffered too much adverse publicity to want this day soiled by the attentions of the press. They were also well aware of the struggle Bjorn and Agnetha were having holding their marriage together and didn't want a song and dance about their own celebrations, as if to rub their noses in it.

So they married quietly and unexpectedly, simply issuing the news through a short press release at a safe distance afterwards. Not that they could ever win. Getting married without telling anyone? Come on, chaps, play the game! The press weren't best pleased to discover this one had slipped through the net, but Benny and Frida knew the score with the other two and they weren't playing the game any more.

Agnetha and Bjorn's courtship, marriage, split and divorce were played out in the full public gaze, in a dislocated synchronicity with Abba's own fortunes. The Benny–Frida thing was conducted in the shadow of the others' relationship in more ways than one and there was no telling that it was ever on shaky ground. Familiarity breeds contempt and, involving herself in the whole Abba enterprise much more than Agnetha ever did, Frida was always at Benny's elbow. Benny, distracted and immersed in his own musings, began to react more than he used to and the relationship started to become as volatile as the Ulvaeus marriage had been.

It was a shock, though, when Benny fell into the arms of Mona Noerklit, a sophisticated and accomplished TV presenter, successful and well-liked throughout Sweden. Nobody had any explanations, least of all Benny. It just happened. Abba had already torn up all the rules that had defined them in the first place and Bjorn had emerged from the arduous and painful split with Agnetha and was widely rumoured to have had a brief fling with Liz Mitchell of Boney M before falling head over heels in love with advertising copywriter Lena Kallersjo, whom he later married and who – as was frequently pointed out – looked a dead ringer for Agnetha. Agnetha, meanwhile, was a picture of misery, a trail of boyfriends in her wake. It was as if somebody had lobbed a nail bomb into the whole Abba dream so carefully polished for so many years and the whole myth had exploded around their ears. Even Benny was fazed by this. Even Frida freaked. And their marriage creaked . . . and collapsed.

Benny wasn't about to live out any more lies. It was all too suffocating, too weird to contemplate handling an affair on top of everything else. And the bottom line was that he was hooked on Mona and wanted to be with her, full stop. He went home, told Frida about the new love of his life, and moved out. Just like that. They divorced in February 1981.

Frida was heartbroken. One more blow to knock her flying when she thought she'd got a grip on this human survival business. She was hurt, bitter, angry, destructive, self-destructive and mystified. She sobbed and threw things and hated Benny and hated herself and didn't imagine she'd ever have the courage to set foot outside her door again. And when she did she imagined everyone was pointing at her screaming, 'Failure! Useless! Worthless! Unattractive! Unwanted!'

She survived. They all survived. And they continued. That was the most amazing aspect of the whole thing. Out came the polite little press release about the 'amicable' marriage breakdown and the hopeful line about Abba continuing as if nothing had happened, almost questioning why anybody on earth should ever imagine they'd consider splitting the band.

If anything proves the incredible resolve which drove Abba to such heights of popularity, it was their decision to continue when everything was falling apart. How *could* Agnetha contemplate staying in Abba after that world tour when the most intense love she'd ever known in her life became hideously transformed into contempt and scorn? How could Frida have even *thought* of staying in a band with Benny after he'd confessed to falling in love with Mona? How could Frida and Agnetha have suffered each other for so long?

It wasn't easy. But then it couldn't have been easy to have built the whole candyfloss edifice that was Abba.

They really did want it that bad and at the end of the seventies there were still enough insecurities hanging around for them to *still* want it that bad. Even Agnetha, for all her genuine hatred of planes and travelling and hotel rooms and being away from home and Frida and, by then, Bjorn . . . yes, even Agnetha was talked into another throw of the dice after the marriage breakdown. She still wanted it, and she still went on another world tour, even though it was even more petrifyingly fraught than the first and almost turned her into a gibbering wreck.

And Frida. She didn't forgive. She *couldn't* have forgiven. You'd need to be a saint to have forgiven Benny for running off with another woman after everything they'd gone through together and, whatever else, Frida was no saint. But she still wanted it. In fact she still wanted it more than anyone and plunged right back into the dream, fatally flawed though it now was, with a commitment and enthusiasm that must have amazed Bjorn and Benny, who were themselves distinctly lukewarm about the whole thing by the time they embarked on that second tour in 1979.

Once Bjorn and Agnetha had decided to be sensible and adult about the whole thing and treat each other with respect and make sure the kids didn't suffer and all the rest of it, then it was easier for everyone to swallow the idea of Abba surviving a second marriage break-up. And the organization was the most powerful force in keeping the whole thing churning over. Stig wouldn't hear of his beloved Abba dissolving, not now, not ever. By the time Bjorn and Agnetha split, Abba was a multi-million dollar enterprise with business interests all around the world. How could a few personal grievances be allowed to spoil that?

So not once, but twice, running repairs were made and the whole thing was kicked back into action with (bleeding) hearts worn firmly on sleeves. The old stories of close friendships were still being trotted out to justify increasingly frozen smiles. Both parties said their working relationships had improved now they were free of all that ugly emotional bonding, which basically meant they kept themselves to themselves and weren't having stand-up rows all the time. Now they just got on with it as cordially as they could, smothering the anger and tears in their supreme professionalism and enduring dedication to the cause.

Their most lethal ingredient now was the distraught, hapless figure of Agnetha. The pure golden girl of Scandinavian song was suddenly, *electrifyingly*, a tragic heroine experiencing the same unnerving fall from grace that had characterized people like Judy Garland, Edith Piaf and Marianne Faithfull. Her slightly shrill voice would often appear to waver in its register alongside the more comfortable, mellifluous harmonies of Anni-Frid, but now that wobble in her voice assumed a spine-tingling desperation.

It *may* have been purely coincidence and it's hard to imagine that Bjorn and Benny could have been that harshly calculating about it, but the construction of their finest song, 'The Winner Takes It All', the perfect desolation in Agnetha's singing, and the galling starkness of the accompanying video, created one of the single most harrowing images in popular music.

Swimming in a mess of blue eye-shadow, hair a tousled

mess, Agnetha approaches the camera looking like she hasn't slept for a week and hasn't eaten all year. She stares with haunted eyes and sings with plaintive, injured pride, *'I don't wanna talk about things we've gone through . . . though it's hurting me . . . now it's history . . .'*

How could she sing that song? How could Bjorn have written it for her?

Because now we all knew. And she knew that we knew. Such painful beauty, such a bleeding heart, such raw emotion, such *theatre*.

We wanted to reach out and grab Agnetha off that video screen and cuddle and cuddle her and make it all right. Maybe that's exactly what she wanted too.

11

I HAVE A DREAM

*'And my destination makes it worth the while
Pushing through the darkness still another mile'*

'I Have A Dream'

By the end of 1969 Benny and Bjorn were through with being stars. They'd done the whole bit. They'd been screamed at by nubile girls, they'd been on all the main TV shows, they'd been on the covers of the teenage magazines, they'd partied all night. That, they'd resolved, was that.

They weren't teenagers any more, they'd achieved everything on offer in Sweden and they didn't fancy recycling themselves. And, thrilled by the inspiration each took from the other, they instinctively felt their destinies lay in their new partnership. They couldn't quite see why, where or how it would work, but Ulvaeus and Andersson realized from the outset that they were a team.

After Bjorn had guested with the Hep Stars on their folk-parks tour in 1969, there was no way he was going to settle back with the Hootenanny Singers. He was already becoming deeply embroiled in the Polar dynasty with Stig Anderson and Bengt Bernhag and believed more and more that his natural forte was as a catalyst for others, pulling the strings behind the scenes. Meeting and hitting it off with Benny Andersson stopped him momentarily in his tracks – he knew this guy with the brilliant though undisciplined musical brain would somehow have to come into the equation.

So Bjorn gradually prised himself out of the Hootenannies, though he still played a major production role on their records – with Benny also helping out – and the group was to continue sporadically in Sweden for many years, frequently covering Benny and Bjorn songs in the ensuing decade.

Benny quit the Hep Stars for good at the end of that '69 tour. The financial nightmare that faced them in the wake of their tax mess was too horrific for either Benny or the band's singer Svenne Hedlund to deal with. They knew they'd have to tour constantly for several years before they even began to put a smile on the taxman's face and put any money in their own pockets and it was a prospect they couldn't face. After their pioneering runaway success as Sweden's first supergroup, it was an ignominious conclusion, though one that maintained the constant · parallels with the Beatles, themselves now undergoing the traumas of Apple and the Allen Klein years. The other Hep Stars did resurface eventually as the Rubber Band, but with their two driving creative forces gone, they met little success.

Discovering they could happily work together without hassle or financial shackles within the peaceful confines of the studio with the unlimited potential it offered, Bjorn and Benny began to see themselves as a songwriting-production team in the Motown tradition. They'd be Polar's in-house team, writing and producing to order, keeping office hours, maintaining perfect discipline in their work, and treating the whole thing as an unemotional exercise, a job pure and simple. Their vision was extraordinarily naïve. Benny Andersson couldn't be disciplined if he'd been chained to a bed by Miss Whiplash. Looking like he'd crawled through the Black Forest, chainsmoking, Scotch in hand, slumped over a piano at three o'clock in the morning, that was the scenario in which you were to find the genius of Benny Andersson, not going to the office on the bus, bright-eyed and bushy-tailed, knocking out half a dozen hit singles and catching the 5.30 p.m. rush-hour bus home again.

It was a nice thought, though, and Bjorn was unfailing in his insistence to Stig and Bengt that from now on they should be considered a team and any future commissions for Polar would have to involve Benny as well. No problem. Stig liked Benny well enough, fully recognizing his talent, and promptly formed their own company, Union Songs, as an outlet for this new arm of the family.

They made some progress too. They wrote and produced for a succession of Swedish artists – Brita Borg, Arne Lambert, Lena Andersson, Jarl Kullo, Ted Gardestad, and Svenne Hedlund. Around this time Bjorn also had some success as a solo act, specializing in eccentric covers.

And when they weren't in the studio recording stuff with other artists, they were in the studio themselves, playing around with ideas, making demos. Benny was having a ball, but seeing how well they worked together and *knowing* what they could achieve was driving Bjorn mad. It was always Stig's dream to break a Swedish act internationally; Bjorn started to believe more and more that somehow it could and should be he and Benny. They put out their own records as a duo: 'She's My Kind Of Girl' became a huge hit in Japan, selling a startling half-million copies. Fluke, really, but it showed they were on the right track.

They followed it with other singles, notably 'Lycka' ('Happiness') and, a bit later, 'Det Kan Ingen Doktor Hjalpa' ('It Can't Be Remedied By A Doctor'), 'Tank Om Jorden Vore Ung' ('If Only We Had The Time') and 'En Karusell' (Merry-Go-Round'), all significantly featuring their girlfriends Agnetha Faltskog and Anni-Frid Lyngstad on backing vocals, though they weren't then credited. They even released a duo album, *Lycka*, in 1970, which prominently featured the girls and included one track co-written by Agnetha. The pieces were falling into place.

Their first live performance as a four-piece occurred in the relative obscurity of a restaurant in Gothenburg at the end of '70. Bjorn and Benny were booked to appear there and, almost at whim, the girls joined them, basically just for the hell of it. They announced themselves as Festfolk (Party People) in acknowledgement of Benny and Frida's legendary social lives and conceived a cosy cabaret act of cover versions which they fondly imagined would appeal to the diners. They were wrong. The group enjoyed themselves immensely, but the audience clearly didn't, greeting the act bouncing around before them with sullen indifference. No worries. They'd only done it for a hoot, not as the first day of the rest of their lives. It hadn't worked, but there you go, chalk it down to experience. They had their own careers, didn't they?

The summer of '71 had a profound effect on all their lives. There was Bjorn and Agnetha's wedding, Stig's partner Bengt Bernhag's tragic suicide, and – straddling both events – a Swedish folk-park tour involving Benny and Bjorn, with Agnetha along for the ride. Benny's singing was always reminiscent of a tortured frog, while Bjorn wasn't exactly Elvis Presley, so the glamour, variety and vocal expertise offered by Agnetha was warmly received. The team clearly worked and, with the benefit of hindsight, it's astonishing that it took another three years for the Abba line-up to blossom fully, especially given that the girls were now making regular appearances on the Benny–Bjorn records.

Stig wasn't entirely convinced that the idea of a two-boy two-girl line-up would work, and was against giving Agnetha and Anni-Frid equal billing on the records. It was the old theory of sex appeal. Girls bought the records and girls didn't want their idols to have girlfriends. They certainly didn't want to know that they were talented girlfriends and have their faces rubbed in the fact by seeing them up there on stage and given equal billing on the records. The idea of a happy, loving foursome seemed too kitsch by far even for the commercially minded Stig, never one to miss a gimmick or a selling point.

He had, in any case, developed enormous faith in the Bjorn/Benny partnership, but Bjorn and Benny believed their future lay not on the stage but in the studio, while Agnetha was hugely proud of her solo career and had no inclination towards sacrificing it for the sake of playing second fiddle to the boys. 'I don't,' she said tartly, 'want to become known as Mrs Bjorn Ulvaeus.'

So off she went, playing Mary Magdalene in a stage show of *Jesus Christ Superstar* at Scandinavium in Gothenburg in 1971. Unlikely casting for the Swedish public persona of Agnetha, fairytale wedding and all, and it took her several steps beyond the slushy love songs that had been her forte before now. Her version of 'I Don't Know How To Love Him' became a huge stage hit, her own songwriting matured as a result of the experience – her 'Our Earth Is Wonderful' was greeted with acclaim befitting a messiah and hailed as a classic (mostly by Bjorn) – and the rejuvenated Faltskog had her sights set firmly on a future in stage musicals. No Mary Magdalene, though, for Lyngstad, still the poor cousin in the foursome, still struggling to find herself in a mix of cabaret smooch and soft jazz.

They had another crack as a four-piece at another cabaret gig in Gothenburg almost a year to the day after their first, and with no more serious intent than before. Once again they got a resounding thumbs down from the audience, though Bjorn's analytical mind began to pinpoint the problems and, with them, the true possibilities within the framework of the four. He was realistic enough to know there would always be limitations for them as a duo and if they were to maintain some sort of professional life as performers they needed the lightness, variety and charisma the girls could offer. He saw the fact that there'd been virtually no precedent for a successful two-girl two-boy band in Sweden or anywhere else as a positive not a negative. Where they'd gone wrong on the two occasions they'd attempted the line-up was not in the concept but in the lack of belief they had in pursuing the idea. They'd freely adapted and compromised themselves into a sugary sweet act bristling with cover versions tailored specifically for a stereotypical cabaret audience. The result pleased no one.

Bjorn became more and more convinced the act could work *on its own terms*. He felt that if they backed their own beliefs and concentrated on their own songs and allowed their own personalities to come to the fore rather than some woolly idea of what people wanted, they'd at least achieve some satisfaction out of the link, if not necessarily great success. It made sense. Agnetha and

Anni-Frid were on hand most of the time, singing on their records and in the audience at most of their gigs and, feeling that their own duo work wasn't getting off the ground, Bjorn floated the idea of having a crack at formally converting their personal relationship into a professional one and going out as a four-piece. The others took some convincing – and Stig wasn't initially keen.

There were contractual problems, too. Bjorn and Agnetha, who by now couldn't be seen together without either trying to eat or throw things at one another, had written a song together called 'This Is The Way Love Starts'. A sort of 'Ballad of John and Yoko' without the aggro, it depicted in gushing detail the story of their love affair. If they were Sweden's favourite living soap opera, then they might as well exploit it, and despite Agnetha's protestations about individuality and differentiating personal and professional, the pair were so besotted they couldn't wait to get the record out. Big problem. Agnetha was signed to CBS and Bjorn to Polar, and Stig refused Bjorn permission to record for another label, even for a one-off. The record did eventually come out, but not without some low muttering and high disgruntlement in a certain lovenest in Stockholm. Ultimately it reached Number Two in the Swedish charts.

However, a trip to Japan in 1972 on the back of the hit Benny and Bjorn had had there with 'She's My Kind Of Girl' solidified their plans to work together as a four-piece group. Bjorn and Benny had become celebrities in Japan without even setting foot there and jumped at the invitation to submit an entry – and perform it – at the World Song Festival in Tokyo. It was an idyllic trip. Two ecstatic young couples, wildly in love, being treated like royalty, fêted and admired by people in an alien culture.

The Japanese took to them right away and have provided a thriving market for Abba ever since. Stig's insistent promise to break Bjorn and Benny abroad kept echoing through Bjorn's mind. He saw the way the Japanese hungrily grabbed any western culture they could find, saw for himself the way 'She's My Kind Of Girl' had gripped the imagination of the nation, and saw that 'international' didn't just mean America and England. Bjorn and Benny came up with a brand new song, 'Santa Rosa', specifically for the event which was given a rapturous reception by the Japanese audience. The success of the trip, both musically and personally, convinced them the way ahead was for all of them to work together on a regular basis. They returned from Tokyo refreshed and thrilled, wondering if Stig would buy it.

Back home in Stockholm they went straight into the studio to put this new resolve into action. They recorded a new song, 'People Need Love', which thrust Agnetha and Anni-Frid right at the front of the mix with no trace of the guys at all and insisted to a still unconvinced Stig that the girls got equal billing on the sleeve. Stig blew his top. He'd been staking everything on building Bjorn and Benny into an international force and here they were proposing to fritter away all that work and dilute that appeal into a combination with their girlfriends which, for the life of him, Stig couldn't begin to see working.

There were fierce arguments between them, but Bjorn and Benny stuck to their guns. They couldn't see how you could possibly sell a record under the names of two guys when all you could hear was the sound of two girls. Bjorn's determination is almost as legendary as Stig's intransigence and it was Stig who eventually gave ground to his favourite protégé, fully believing the preposterous idea would be proved duff and they could then resume their career as a duo. So 'People Need Love' was duly released and attributed to Bjorn, Benny, Agnetha and Frida . . . and became an instant smash all over Scandinavia. Stig is quick to eat his words when there's profit at the end of it, and conceded that what had sold the record had been the novelty value of the close harmonies between Agnetha and Anni-Frid and, suddenly seeing this might even be the breakthrough he'd been seeking, set off on his travels to try and sell it around the rest of the world. He didn't, though he did make his first small dent in America, where the record came out on Hugh Heffner's Playboy label and received a small amount of airplay as a result, scraping into the lower reaches of the charts. Stig was still being awkward about the agreed accreditation, though. The record went out in America under the name Bjorn and Benny with Svenska Flicka.

The follow-up, 'He Is Your Brother' (with 'Santa Rosa' on the B-side), didn't get an American release, but was another hit at home – again under the unwieldy name of Benny, Bjorn, Agnetha and Frida – underlining their status as a fully fledged group. Stig, now resigned to the group idea, began to set his sights on Eurovision as the short-cut to his dream of international glory. He was aware of the contempt in which Eurovision was held in serious rock circles, particularly in Sweden, but felt a little ridicule at home was a small risk given the potential rewards that could accrue from even a good placing in the contest, let alone a win. What sort of argument was credibility and self-respect against a worldwide television audience of 50 million?

In 1972, Stig had entered an Ulvaeus–Andersson song, 'Better To Have Loved', for Eurovision. Performed by the winsome Lena Andersson (no relation) it came in third in the Stockholm heat, went on to top the Swedish charts, and sold Stig completely on the idea of Eurovision. The following year the Swedish Broadcasting Company came back to invite them to submit another entry and this, Stig decided, would be the big one. If Benny, Bjorn, Agnetha and Frida were ever going to get off the ground then now was the time for it to happen.

He commanded that all energies be directed into coming up with a song to take on the world. Just like that. 'Okay Benny, just knock out a song that'll take on the world, will you? And after you've done that, be a luv and make us a cuppa, okay?'

As Benny had already found to his own cost when he convinced himself he could be a nine-to-five writer, writing a song to take on the world ain't as easy as it seems. Utter simplicity is the most effective songwriting technique . . . and by far the hardest. But Stig was promising everyone he met – taxi drivers, postmen, complete strangers in the street – that his babies were going to clean up at Eurovision this year and the boys knew better than to disappoint him. Stig is the sort of character who will march up to you and inform you that in precisely ten minutes there will be tempest and storm, and you find yourself rushing out to buy every raincoat and umbrella in town. It's only when you realize that it's a sweltering summer's day in Sydney that you question his judgement.

That's the beauty of self-confidence. Say something loudly and brashly enough and you will be believed. Any doubt in your voice and you're rumbled and your argument is lost. But saying it loud and saying it proud instantly sting the insecurities that lie dormant in everyone and they will invariably meekly kow-tow to somebody who *sounds* as if they know what they're talking about. The theory is that few people like to argue with someone they don't know very well, and fewer still take on somebody who sounds aggressive about it. If they feel *that* passionately about it then they must be right. It's the art of management and Stig Anderson did it better than most.

All the great rock managers – well, all the *famous* rock managers anyway, understood the psychology totally. Don Arden, the self-styled 'Al Capone of pop', once apparently stormed into Robert Stigwood's office after hearing (erroneously) that he was trying to sign the Small Faces, smashed his desk and held him head-first over his fourth-storey balcony. And Malcolm McLaren, mastermind of the great rock 'n' roll swindle, shocked even the Sex Pistols with his insatiable appetite for outrage and excess. Allen Klein, 'the man who broke the Beatles', could shout louder, inspire more terror and earn more money than is reasonable for one human being. Tam Paton was the man who sold the unsellable, the Bay City Rollers, and was sent to prison for three years on charges of indecency with young boys.

Tony Stratton Smith backed mavericks and eccentrics, conducted business meetings from his bath, was often either drunk or at the races, and was rumoured to be a British spy. The extraordinary Larry Parnes presided over the Kinks' stage fights and once burst in uninvited on a private Muhammad Ali training session with the Troggs in tow for a photo-opportunity. The delightfully reckless playboy Simon Napier-Bell guided Marc Bolan's early career, boasting he could 'find a group on Tuesday, sign them on Wednesday and get them a record deal on

Thursday', and took Wham! on a pioneering tour of China.

The sinister Colonel Tom Parker, the granddaddy of all rock managers, had a fearsome reputation but was rarely seen – and that was just by Elvis Presley, the guy he managed throughout his career. Al Grossman *bullied* Janis Joplin, Jimi Hendrix and Bob Dylan into household name status and once told his staff: 'This place is about money, not music.' The tyrannical Bill Graham, lord and master of the summer of love, virtually *invented* hippies and Haight Ashbury.

Stig Anderson earned his place in this hallowed hall of fame just by the sheer conviction of his ranting belief that Bjorn, Benny, Agnetha and Frida were to take the world by storm in 1973. It was unconsciously played, but it was the nicest form of blackmail ever perpetrated. Stig's eternal bragging predictions about the unlimited success at his fingertips was ultimately a public declaration of his belief in the abilities of his charges. If somebody believes in you to such a degree that they scream it from the rooftops by day and by night, placing their own reputation firmly on the line in the process, then you are going to be flattered. Big time. You are also going to feel incredibly loyal and you are going to feel extremely responsible and determined to reward that belief by doing your very best to the limit of your ability. Benny and Bjorn were fired up to produce something pretty mighty damn special for Eurovision '73 in a way they'd never been in their lives before.

Hyped to the hilt by Stig, they were totally, irrevocably convinced they'd win Eurovision in '73. Not just the Swedish heat, but the whole bloody thing. And then they'd be rich and famous beyond their wildest dreams and live happily ever after in a castle in Switzerland. One small problem stood before them, however – first they had to come up with a world-beating tune. Something *international* was required. An easily translated lyric. An instantly memorable chorus. A bright, flashy tune.

In the dark depths of the middle of the night, Bjorn and Benny poured hard liquor down each other's throats and slugged out melody lines as if their lives depended on it. Every note was dragged out screaming from them and thrown into an overcrowded hellhole with other notes to punch and scratch and clamber to the surface in the hope of getting random selection for a place in the chorus line. Some notes would be chosen, grinning and leaping to attention to perform their bit in the big arena, only to offend their masters and be tossed aside without warning and stamped on beneath an avalanche of cigarette ends and Swedish oaths.

Once accused of finding it unfairly easy to write songs, Bob Dylan rounded angrily on his interviewer and said, 'Beneath every note I write there is a pool of sweat.' That's how it was with Bjorn and Benny. That's how it's always been with them. And despite all the evidence to the contrary, it got harder as they went along. They became more skilled, more practised in the art of selecting the correct notes from that ugly, howling pond before them, more streamlined in the way they discarded whatever didn't work. It was just that the bits which didn't work increasingly outweighed the bits that did and the more they exhausted certain themes the harder it became. If you study the overall output now you can see the breadth of the styles they covered, reggae, country, disco, heavy metal, rock, folk, MOR, military, rock 'n' roll . . . they were all there. This was Benny and Bjorn at the dead of night desperately clawing out new uncharted musical territories to stimulate themselves in order to stimulate their audiences. They wrote some godawful crap along the way, but when they got it right they were sensational.

It took an awful long, painful while, but finally they thought they were sensational that night in the Stockholm Archipelago when they finally chiselled out 'Ring Ring'. Eurovision here we come. Look out world, the Swedes are on their way. By this time they also had Micke Tretow on board. Tretow had just completed a course in electrical engineering when he heard of a vacancy for a junior tape technician at Metronome Studios. His astonishing appetite for work, his fund of ideas and his obvious technical flair earned him a flourishing reputation well beyond his years and experience. He found himself mixing Agnetha and Frida's solo albums, and endeared himself to Bjorn with the imaginative contribution and cool professionalism he brought to the Hootenanny Singers' recording sessions.

Bengt Bernhag's illness and subsequent death gave him the opportunity to expand his ideas at Polar, where he worked flat out, spending hours alone in the studio working on tapes, trying out ideas, learning his craft. Bjorn and Benny liked his attitude and were themselves visionary enough to encourage ideas that older musicians found difficult to accept. Micke produced the Bjorn–Benny *Lycka* album – a relative flop, but it cemented a working relationship between the three of them that was to bring them all incredible rewards.

Micke was eventually employed full-time as in-house studio engineer with Polar, engineering and producing a variety of acts and eventually going on to play a crucial role in the distinctive Abba sound throughout their entire career. He became a knob-twiddler supreme, experimenting with tape speed, overdubbing instrumental tracks and creating a definitive Abba studio sound that became the hallmark of their work irrespective of the grand array of musical styles Bjorn and Benny dipped into when they wrote the music. On 'Ring Ring', the first time Micke was given full licence to express his ideas and experiment, he began to define the Abba sound. All involved were thrilled to their boots with the results.

They would win Eurovision in 1973. Nobody doubted it. Nobody *questioned* it. They just couldn't grasp the idea of being beaten. Not by . . . *somebody else.*

As the day of judgement arrived, every sigh or twitch on the heavily pregnant Agnetha's face was monitored anxiously, with an accompanying rush of male support anxious to rest cushions on backs and bring soothing mugs of tea. They had worked out a contingency plan should Agnetha go into labour as the band started playing their tune. Agnetha sang lead on 'Ring Ring', but they'd rehearsed it over and over with Anni-Frid taking solo lead. Well, you can't be too sure, can you?

It was a weird time for all of them, but Agnetha was in an understandable turmoil of emotions. It's harrowing enough to be on the verge of dropping your first-born any second without the additional trauma of going on stage knowing that the difference between a good and bad performance could have a profound effect on the rest of your life. Everyone fussed around Agnetha like mother hens and, while in a daze of indefinable anxiety, Agnetha perversely enjoyed it, stoically protesting that all would be well, don't worry about a thing.

She was right on one count. Baby Linda behaved

herself and remained firmly in womb for the duration that night in Stockholm. Unfortunately the judges were less accommodating. Bjorn's heart sank the moment he saw them. They looked too straight and sensible by far, the types who wouldn't recognize a decent song if it crept up and bit their wotsits off. The type of judges who, in an earlier life, savaged the young Elvis Presley as a monstrous affront to society. The types who were intent on voting for nice girls in cute frocks singing pretty tunes. They wanted to be soothed and charmed and unchallenged. They looked like they wanted their mugs of cocoa and their pet poodles to bring them their slippers and maybe an early night tonight, dearest?

Bjorn, Benny, Agnetha and Frida they couldn't cope with. Shaggy hair shaking all over the place, flared trousers you could be lost inside for months. Belting around the stage like complete maniacs. They didn't even have a proper name for the group. And *one of them was pregnant*! Not on really, is it?

They sank backstage in shattered bewilderment. They should have won it. They knew it. *Everybody* knew it. Tears were shed. Agnetha was suddenly very tired, deciding she didn't want to sing any more anyway. Ashen-faced, Anni-Frid was facing the awful prospect of reviving a solo career that had never been too enthralling in the first place. Bjorn couldn't understand it; bemused and bitter, the whole thing was a mysterious affront to his sense of logic and fair play. Even Benny was deathly quiet, sourly muttering about the injustice of it all, watching his dreamy optimism flush down the toilet.

It was the lowest point of Stig's career. It went beyond depression. Beyond rage. Beyond futility. His anger and frustration were burning red before his eyes and it seemed like they would never pass. But even then, even in the darkest depths of his emptiness and misery, Stig was thinking of the future. He was already plotting to come back next year . . .

12

WATERLOO

'We just have to face it, this time we're through'

'Knowing Me, Knowing You'

The lunatic has always stalked celebrity. It's the one great intangible terror of fame . . . the fear that dare not speak its name.

Once you take logic, reason and motive out of the equation, then everyone's a target, any time, any place. There's no rationale for madness, no opportunity for defence. There's no way to legislate against the gruesome lure which fame has for twisted minds and social cripples, apparently drawn to acts of violence on the rich and famous, as if in some kind of inverted bid for reflected glory. The possibility of random strikes without motive forever lurks beneath the consciousness of those foisted into the public eye, fuelled by the instances – rare and isolated but nevertheless inescapably imprinted in historical legend – when the hits have been made. Think of the kidnapped Lindbergh baby, who was murdered; Paul Getty's grandson, who lost an ear; Patty Hearst, who ended up toting a gun for her kidnappers and serving a jail term.

Nobody ever screamed at by a howling mob hasn't also fretted about the dark side of that coin. It can be a thin line between the helpless adoring admirer and the obsessive fanatic, who sends you letters every day, followed by roses, then turns up backstage, on your doorstep, demanding more and more of you. At what point does devoted fan turn into dangerous psychopath? And if you're the star when does your natural gratitude at an effusive display of support turn to polite warnings to back off, and ultimately anger and aggressive rejection. Is *this* the point that the fan becomes psycho or is it earlier? Or maybe the obsessional will nurture their passionate infatuations privately, suddenly exploding in shattering and very public violence. Who knows? Not I, Mr Wolf, not I . . . nor anybody. Which is precisely why it's all so terrifying for anybody who's ever been the object of insistent fan worship.

The shattering reality of the lone nutter preying on a hero was numbingly planted at the forefront of every singer's consciousness when Mark Chapman started pumping bullets into John Lennon's chest on 8 December 1980. For Bjorn and Benny, schooled on the Lennon legend, it was hard to accept. From his boyhood love of music to early Hepstardom, Benny had regarded Lennon as his spiritual guiding light. Bjorn's inspirations had been primarily American – and American folk and blues musicians at that – but Benny's personal god was always John – his rasping vocals, his detached arrogance, his surreal humour, his earthily melodic songwriting, his ability to cut through all the crap. It was John, always John, for Benny. The night of Lennon's death Benny could be found in a club in Stockholm, drunk on sorrow, at a piano playing Lennon songs. He went on for hours, playing everything he knew, seemingly oblivious of the people who'd gathered round him to listen and sing along not knowing whether to laugh or cry. It was Benny paying his own personal tribute in the only way he knew how, playing well into the night almost in some kind of therapy session. It seemed to Benny, as it must have seemed to a lot of people, that this was the end of something. Innocence? Youth? Idealism? It was certainly something more than a bunch of good songs.

The spectre of crazed fandom hung heavily over Abba at the height of their success. They could – and did – walk around Stockholm largely unmolested by the trappings of fame. An occasional autograph, the odd giggling snatch of conversation, a few waves from a safe distance, but the Swedish, with their natural reserve, largely respected Abba's privacy and tended to let them be. It was one reason they were keen to stay in Sweden, crippling tax and all, because they were bombarded with none of the hysteria they encountered in America, Britain and – especially – Australia. At home they could just about hang on to their sanity. They were often irked by the lack of respect and recognition they got at home, but it cut both ways – they could get on with their lives and they felt safe.

There again, the Swedish prime minister Olaf Palme felt safe, too, when he was suddenly gunned down in the street walking home from a cinema in Stockholm in 1986. And just forty-eight hours before Mark Chapman met his quarry in such cataclysmic fashion, John Lennon was giving an interview to Andy Peebles from BBC Radio 1, saying how much he liked New York because he could live there without being hassled or feeling threatened.

Agnetha, desperate to be the perfect mother, constantly worried about the effect her celebrity and absenteeism were having on the children, Linda and Christian. When they were small the kids came with them whenever humanly possible, but she worried about this too, wondering what might be the long-term effects of disorientation and extensive travel. Don't children need to be brought up in a secure and settled environment with two loving parents at home seeing to all their needs?

Once the children were born, Abba was always an emotional compromise for Agnetha and it scarred her deeply. There was no doubt that she wanted to be a good mother to the kids much more than she wanted to be a big star, and as soon as the incredible depth of Abba's fame began to sink in, Agnetha was like a dog being taken for a walk on a lead, being dragged reluctantly along as she tried to dig her heels in, anxious to get back to the bone buried in the garden. The family nannies were superb, but Agnetha lived in fear of going home after a tour to find Linda asking who she was; or suddenly getting the call from home about some dreadful outbreak of illness; or the children becoming mentally unstable through the neglect of absentee parents. And on the darkest nights of all, she'd contemplate the unthinkable . . . the sinister consequences of her and Bjorn's fame. One night a Lindbergh kidnapping with a ransom note. Or worse. Just because you're paranoid it doesn't mean to say they're not after you.

The nightmare exploded in the early eighties: an anonymous letter, a short, sharp threat aimed firmly at Agnetha's weakest spot – the children. There had, for a while, been people hanging around. Nobody special. Just fans. A couple of Germans, in particular, would hang around outside her door for days. They weren't sinister, they just wanted to say hi and express their admiration, but they unsettled Agnetha. There was something about her that attracted the loner – and in fact continued to attract people to hang around her for long periods of time in a strange sort of silent vigil, as if attempting to absorb the vibe of beauteous superstardom she still exuded.

And it got worse before it got better. After the split with Bjorn her very obvious abject depression attracted its own bizarre mixture of people offering broad shoulders to cry on and complete nutters who sensed a kindred spirit and offered their own desperate misery as a means of allaying her own. Seemingly overnight the fresh-faced picture of Scandinavian health and beauty had been replaced by a weary woman with the world's woes on her shoulders. She was still beautiful, but now it was a tragic kind of beauty. She looked injured and vulnerable in a way that attracted a stampede of marriage proposals; a succession of father figures who wanted to kiss her and make it all right; and an unexpected cult status among lesbians convinced of her latent homosexuality.

The early eighties were an awful time for Agnetha. She'd hated the first Abba world tour in 1977. It had provoked too many neuroses, caused too many arguments and jealousies with Anni-Frid, too much friction with Bjorn. And despite the brave public pronouncements of an 'amicable split', she'd been torn apart by the divorce. It was the worst thing that had ever happened to her – a long, painful, tortuous chapter in her life complicated by the expectancy of everybody around them that they'd all carry on working together as if nothing had happened. A mere snag in the stocking of life.

'I was very down after the separation,' she addressed one interviewer-cum-therapist. 'I was petrified at the thought of being on my own. Bjorn always took care of everything and all of a sudden I had to learn to stand on my own two feet.' Journalist anxiously glances at her two feet. 'Our winters are very dark in Sweden and that kind of gloomy weather can feed depression as well. I'm a very nervous person and I'm very reserved and shy by nature despite my image.'

Agnetha tried heroically to bear her burden with pride and dignity and not betray Abba's image of immaculate deception. She came out all teeth and smiles in the tried and trusted manner, but it became such a sham that it ultimately defeated even the considerable actress within her. Once the initial raw pain of the separation had subsided she harboured no personal bitterness towards Bjorn who, she figured, was suffering at least some of her loss and sense of failure too, and was still fighting her corner to some degree. She felt that he, at least, understood her and once the break had been made – drawn out though it was – she bore him none of the animosity that was spiralling between her and the other two. They were, after all, still their children's parents and the children were paramount to both of them, so there was a quiet dignity in the distance they put between one another.

With this in mind she allowed herself to be talked into going on the world tour of 1979 and instantly regretted it. She had to be shovelled on to the plane and plied with drinks to get her through the flight and then tumbled off at the other end in a haze of alcohol, shock and nervous exhaustion. Instantly she felt like a stranger in the whole entourage. The last tour had been awkward and painful, full of backbiting and recriminations. There was none of that anger this time round . . . just *nothing*.

She felt conversations falter when she came within earshot. She didn't speak without being spoken to. She had virtually no contact with the others offstage and, while superficially cordial, relations between her and the others had all but broken down. Messages came through via third persons about where she should be at what time and she felt like a gatecrasher at her own party. Her own misery on that tour was compounded by the fun the others seemed to be having whenever she saw them. Especially Bjorn.

Her attitude hardened the more she saw that Bjorn was making a considerably better fist of the split than her. Recording a TV special in Switzerland, Bjorn had become friendly with Liz Mitchell from Boney M, disappearing with her at a party one night to fuel rumours of an affair which quickly got back to Agnetha. She was to be even more shocked when, within a week of their divorce, Bjorn was skipping around like a new-born lamb having fallen into the arms of Lena Kallersjo. It was a high-profile affair which Agnetha interpreted as one final humiliating and very public declaration that Bjorn had completely over-come, unscathed, the ravages of their divorce. Lena, an advertising executive who, gossip writers never failed to mention, looked a dead ringer for the former Mrs Ulvaeus, had taken her place with a vengeance. It hurt. Wounds she'd hoped were healing suddenly bled profu-sely again . . . and they bled yet again when Lena became pregnant and Bjorn married her in January 1981 – barely two years after he had split with Agnetha. Her depression started all over again. Not that Agnetha herself lived the life of a nun after the split, but her relationships didn't stick the way Bjorn and Lena's had.

But the kidnap threats were the worst thing to happen to Bjorn and Agnetha. They tried to put them out of their minds and convince themselves they were just crank calls, part and parcel of their chosen occupation. Ignore them, said their friends. Real kidnappers don't warn you in advance they're going to kidnap your kids, they just *DO IT*. But how do you tell a mother to forget it? Especially a cautious worrier like Agnetha.

'When that sort of thing becomes reality it's awful,' Bjorn told the *Daily Mail*. 'You can say, "Oh, it wouldn't happen to me, it happens to Italians, it won't happen to me." But suddenly it dawns on you there might be some crazy bastard out there. The kids are the dearest you have and it's awful. Then again, if you look at it statistically there aren't many kidnappings. The chances of it happening to you are very, very small. I used to say that to myself.'

It was small comfort for Agnetha. And the threats were insistent enough for the police to take them seriously. Nobody was ever caught or charged with making the threats and, cranks or not, Agnetha was taking no chances. A police guard was placed on her house and Agnetha became a semi-recluse, terrified of allowing the kids out of her sight lest they be snatched in her absence.

Her enthusiasm for the whole Abba experience was pitched into terminal decline by the threat of the madman in the shadows. Her horror of flying, her dislike of Frida, her endless homesickness, her recurring stage fright, the tedious hours spent in make-up to be turned into some kind of alien princess fantasy figure, the painful embarrassment of posing for smiley pictures alongside an ex-husband who was now sleeping in someone else's bed . . . all might have been overcome. All *had* been overcome with differing degrees of personal sacrifice along the way, but the fear of losing her children flattened Abba dead on the spot for Agnetha.

There was simply no way she would be prised out on the road again after that '79 tour. Too many agonizing memories. One day she was on a luxury light plane which was caught in a terrible storm and thrown off course somewhere over Washington, DC. The pilot lost radio contact and lost his bearings as the plane shuddered and circled, desperately seeking somewhere to land. Agnetha was convinced she was going to die. She was beyond hysteria, resigned to her fate, cursing the things she hadn't said and done. The ordeal went on for ninety minutes as the pilot established that the small airport where he was due to land had been rendered useless by the storm. Now he was virtually out of fuel and beyond help. Agnetha had her eyes screwed tightly shut for the duration, unable to utter even a prayer, awaiting the end.

But the pilot pulled off a minor miracle and got them down. A quivering Agnetha emerged with her nerve-ends in tatters, her fear of flying fully vindicated, swearing she'd never set foot on an aeroplane again. Ultimately she did. But rarely. Trains, boats, bicycles, jogging, fine. But she needed a platoon of hypnotists, several shots of something stupefyingly alcoholic, and a dozen underlined assurances that her journey was absolutely necessary.

Later, she promoted her solo album *Wrap Your Arms Around Me* managing to avoid getting airborne completely, risking seasickness and the rigours of the North Sea to come to Britain. However, there was to be a quirky near-tragic pay-off to her horrors about travelling on her return. On a coach driving back towards Stockholm through the south of Sweden, Agnetha walked along the aisle to speak to someone at the front when the coach jerked suddenly across the road as the driver lost control and screamed at everyone to sit down.

Seconds later Agnetha was flung through a window as the coach careered off the road, turned over twice and wound up in a ditch. Agnetha survived again, this time with cuts and bruises and a further huge acknowledgement of her own mortality. Small wonder in the circumstances that in subsequent years Agnetha decided just to stay at home and not mix with the rest of the world at all if she could possibly help it.

It was obvious at the end of that '79 tour that it would take an enormous amount of enticing to coax Agnetha back in the studio with Abba, let alone back on the road. Not that the others had any inclination towards touring again at the end of it. Benny saw touring as valuable time wasted away from his beloved studio while Bjorn never much liked appearing on stage and saw only the business logic behind it. Even Frida had become exhausted and disenchanted by the whole tedious routine of travel/ soundcheck/gig/hotel. Once her marriage to Benny had collapsed her famous love of partying died with it.

In short, nobody wanted to tour with Abba again and none of them expected to. However, none of them – except perhaps Agnetha – expected Abba to end. 'It won't last for ever . . . we'll stop when it's no fun any more . . . there are other things we want to do . . . there's more to life than Abba . . .' Stock answers, snatches of interviews along the way began to suggest the idea of an end to Abba eventually, but even at the end of that tour, with their personal relationships in rags and financial headaches hovering, they didn't anticipate for a second that this might actually be the end. They just needed an enormously long break to recharge their batteries, mend a few badly damaged bridges, and reinvent themselves.

It happened with groups all the time. Fleetwood Mac. Classic prototype. Abba thought they had inter-relationship problems, but they were a gentle game of dominoes compared to the explosions forever going off in the Fleetwood Mac camp. This was the group who, legend has it, spent most of the seventies coked out of their skulls, living in different continents but coming together occasionally to rip each other to shreds, swap partners and screw each other's brains out. And they *still* put out platinum albums every so often. Abba had problems? They didn't know they'd been *born*.

Stig certainly wouldn't hear of them splitting. Ever. Frida kept an open mind. Bjorn and Benny were desperate to do other things, stretch themselves into alternative areas, and test exactly how good they really were before they even contemplated a return to Abba. They were exhausted but an absolute split didn't appear on the cards . . . even during the laboured recording sessions that produced the uncharacteristic darkness of *The Visitors*, an album that unnerved even their most loyal subjects.

The Visitors was so mysteriously dour that it had amateur analysts beside themselves with excitement studying the lyrics, searching for clues about what was widely believed to be an album of hidden meanings. It's a great pop sport, invented when Bob Dylan was coming out with songs of endless verses with long unintelligible words and bewilderingly surreal story lines. Songwriters from Lennon onwards perfected the art, throwing in obscure references that were nine times out of ten meaningless but sounded like they were profound.

Who was McCartney's fool on the hill? What about Lennon's eggman and walrus? Or Don McLean's father, son and holy ghost in 'American Pie'? And Dylan had a whole catalogue of the things. And was McCartney really dead because he was crossing Abbey Road in bare feet? Who exactly was fooling who here?

So finally in the twilight of their collective career, devoid of sense of purpose, creativity or enthusiasm, Abba were credited with serious intelligence. They'd craved this acclaim for so long but had always been denied it at the height of their success and genius. Pop's perverse that way. *The Visitors* wasn't a hugely successful album, not by their standards, badly failing to match the commercial peaks of *Super Trouper*. But it made them interesting. Because the game was up and they weren't bothering to play it any more. No more smiley smiley sleeves here. Just mysterious red lighting, a study of sorts, and four sullen, pointedly separate souls keeping their distance and looking heavy.

The music and sleeve were both heavy with psychological overtones. Many thought they must have just read too many H. G. Wells books and that *The Visitors* was a reference to alien beings. Others took it a step further and felt the visitors/aliens imagery was an oblique reference to themselves as transient travellers in a world that was forever to misunderstand and misinterpret them.

Some took it to be their concept album. The serious in-depth songwriting which Benny and Bjorn had long wanted to do but which they still didn't dare come clean about and foist on a public that only ever wanted them to fulfil the unreal fantasies of chocolate cake happiness. *The Visitors*, it was decided, was their *Hotel California*.

In the end it just turned out to be the resigned parting shot of a group that had used itself all up. 'When All Is Said And Done', an obvious and heartbreakingly brave postscript to the end of Benny and Frida's long relationship, was by far the best track on the album and one of the best things they'd ever done. It also served as an accurate reflection of their feelings towards each other and towards

Abba . . . and therefore of the album's overall message. It was a signal of defeat and disillusionment that ran through the rest of the album, too. 'One Of Us', 'Soldiers', 'Like An Angel Passing Through My Room', 'Slipping Through My Fingers' . . . there was precious little joy here. Depressing? Absolutely. Negative? Just a bit. Painful? Sure thing. Honest? *Totally*.

The Visitors wasn't Abba on acid dipping into sci-fi. It wasn't even Bjorn and Benny flexing their muscles into a heavy, conceptual state of mind. And it certainly wasn't just another pop album. *The Visitors* was the album of a band dying on its feet.

There was no summit meeting. No show of hands. No official decision. No announcement. But Abba were shot to pieces. They didn't want to play any more. They didn't decide to split, they just couldn't face continuing. Not for the time being.

The public seemed to concur. 'One Of Us' was a Top Three record, but the next single taken off *The Visitors*, 'Head Over Heels', barely dented the British Top Thirty. After eighteen consecutive Top Ten records, 'Head Over Heels' was the worst-selling single since 'I Do, I Do, I Do, I Do, I Do' seven years earlier. Success had lifted them beyond the stigma of Eurovision, cushioned them against the spitting anarchy of punk, and protected them from the constant barbs of critics and fashion. But finally they'd been done by their own indifference, declining to promote their records at this advanced stage of jaded exhaustion, allowing their bruises to tell their story.

The secret of Abba's durability is the timelessness of class. Despite the flares, the stacked heels and the perms, fashion and time were irrelevant to Abba. The proof of that has been in their appeal to new generations. They had their best run of success through '77/'78, flying directly in the savage face of punk at a time when tunes and melodies were considered less acceptable than a holiday in Beirut.

But now they'd lost all heart for the battle. There were no more singles released from *The Visitors* and their lives went careering in opposite directions. Their marriages had long gone. 'I couldn't live without Benny,' Frida told a journalist one day. Bad move. Three weeks later he'd run off with TV star Mona Noerklit. Now, just as *The Visitors* was signalling the group's laboured death throes, Mona and Benny were celebrating the birth of a son, Ludwig. This, exactly one week after the birth of Bjorn and Lena's first child together, Emma.

From dominating their lives for the past decade, Abba was now the last thing on any of their minds. Frida had long nurtured dreams of solo stardom, the bitterness of her pre-Abba rejections still an irritating grievance. She would have no better chance to achieve it in the grandest of manners, while proving to Benny and to everyone else how strong and independent she was. She was anxious to show she didn't need him or them. She got rid of all her Abba-associated business interests and shipped out to London to concentrate on a new beginning with a solo career.

It proved to be a shrewd move. It saved her the millions the others lost in the financial chaos that strangled the Abba business empire in the wake of the disastrous entry into the oil market and the snowballing losses it provoked in allied companies. Frida had extricated herself from the decline of Abba's fortunes at exactly the right time.

It also preserved her sanity. The solo album she moved herself to London to make, *Something's Going On*, was more important to Frida than merely an escape from Abba. Frida held out for a long time to have her album produced by Phil Collins. His *Face Value* album had come out the previous year and Frida loved it more than any album she'd ever heard in her life before. She played it every day for months, sucking in every nuance of the arrangements, studying and identifying every word of the lyric. *Face Value* depicted in graphic detail the pain of Collins' divorce, but Frida thought he could have been describing her own personal situation. Frida wanted to make her own *Face Value* to get all traces of bitterness out of her system and to try to understand it all better. And she insisted that Collins had to produce it. She was adamant about it. No Phil Collins, no solo album, she stated defiantly.

She got her way. Phil Collins duly produced *Something's Going On*, pitched in with one song of his own, 'You Know What I Mean', and duetted with Frida on one track, 'Here We'll Stay'. It could scarcely have been more different to Abba. There was also material by Russ Ballard, Rod Argent, Bryan Ferry, Stephen Bishop, Giorgio Moroder and Tomas Ledin, once an Abba backing singer and the one and only link with Abba she used on the album.

The whole thing was a therapeutic, confidence-building exercise for Frida. It allowed her to free her mind from the long history of quarrels and pressures that had been steadily dragging her down over a long period of time, and become absorbed in something fresh. It was rejuvenating. Away from it all in London working on her own record, the wounds of Abba were forgotten. *Something's Going On* was no commercial success, but it was a healing exercise and a happy experience for Frida. She got on well with the affable Collins and was tremendously excited and ferociously proud of the very different style she was tackling on the record.

It didn't capture the public's imagination. Now, approaching middle age, with her hair cropped and styled in the manner of a hard-nosed successful businesswoman having abandoned all pretence at sexiness, her solo foray was regarded as an indulgence. The fans might have accepted a solo album from Agnetha, and they might have gone for an Agnetha–Frida duo album – which was seriously considered at one point, except that they couldn't have shared a studio for long enough without killing one another. Most people considered that Agnetha and Frida were Abba anyway, so few would have seen the point in that.

Here and now in the summer of '82 a Frida solo album seemed pointless. Few people considered that Abba might be at an end. They'd just made a dodgy album and the hits had faltered, but hell, Abba were here for the duration, they'd be back for sure with a new album and hits-a-plenty. They'd survived two marriage break-ups, they could surely live through a commercial hiccup.

Frida was circumspect with her answers when asked about Abba. She confirmed their general dislike of touring, but offered nothing to suggest they wouldn't be coming together again. The truth was that Frida herself didn't really believe Abba wouldn't happen again. The immediate pain of the split with Benny, the arguments with Agnetha, the business headaches, and the nerve-ends frayed by touring had dissipated. Having put distance between them, her own relations with Bjorn and Benny were cordial again and as it became obvious that her own solo career wasn't about to lift her into a brand new sphere of popularity, she reacquainted herself with the possibility of getting Abba off and rolling again.

Nobody in Abba's back-up team imagined they wouldn't be back once the batteries had been recharged. In the meantime Stig was ready to exploit the tenth anniversary of the group to the full. He released a greatest hits double album complete with smiley gatefold sleeve and Frida decked out like a Christmas tree, with some kind of orchid bizarrely tucked into her cleavage. There was even a new single – and a cracker at that, another Agnetha blue eye-shadow special, 'The Day Before You Came', criminally ignored in the rush to play all the golden oldie tracks, but one of the greatest Abba songs of them all.

The First Ten Years album was a huge success, topping the album charts all over the world, and pulling the group members back together after a long separation for some limited promotion and various receptions in their honour. Hardly a comeback, but enough to let people know they were still around, still operational. Frida seemed happy to be back in the family and even Agnetha appeared calm and convivial. They talked tentatively of a new album. Bjorn and Benny were even inspired enough to knock out a couple of new songs in readiness for the event.

But they were to be deflected. Bjorn and Benny had long harboured ambitions of writing a musical. They'd flirted with it for long enough, frustrated by the limitations of the pop format and the lack of respect and recognition it accorded them. Attitudes towards them were switching dramatically in Sweden on the back of the greatest hits album and the warm feelings of nostalgia it was creating, but the Ulvaeus–Andersson partnership yearned for more. They wanted to test themselves in the broader world. The heavier aspects of *Super Trouper* and *The Visitors* weren't so much cryptic messages of inner turmoil as Bjorn and Benny stretching themselves, trying to prove they could move beyond the familiar vacuousness of pop which now bored them rigid. They desperately sought new stimulus and inspiration. Their songwriting sessions now consisted of many jaded hours fighting off tedium as they chiselled out a song, and then tossing away their work in an irritated outburst of dismay and disappointment. They didn't know what, but they needed something else.

Tim Rice was looking for a new adventure having filled every theatre in London's West End with his musical collaborations with Andrew Lloyd Webber. Lloyd Webber was now off working with other people and Rice wanted to stretch his muscles too. Well versed in the value of using exotic foreign political situations with legendary characters (Eva Peron, Jesus Christ), Rice had it in mind to write a musical about the East/West cold war. But not some boring old study of Russian politics; a human story about two lovers thrown together at a . . . *chess* match! Tim's major problem in all this was that he can't write tunes. He's got lyrics coming out of his ears, but tunes . . . tunes is hard. Bjorn and Benny had the reverse problem, and Tim knew it. He'd always been a huge Abba fan. He'd been one of the few people who recognized the genius in their melodies and arrangements and put a hopeful call in to them to float the idea of a musical together. He didn't hold out too much hope. They were so busy and successful and probably wouldn't want to get involved.

He was wrong. Bjorn and Benny were tickled pink by the idea. They were flattered beyond comprehension that someone with such clout in an area of entertainment they coveted would be calling them. They went out to dinner together in Stockholm and the wheels for *Chess* were instantly set in motion. Bjorn and Benny were suddenly alive again, ignited into action by this third partner. Any lingering thoughts of a new Abba album were put on hold once more.

There's a paradox about the respective status of a song like 'Waterloo', using a nineteenth-century war in Belgium between the French and the English as its root, and a whole collection of songs surrounding a chess match in Iceland. The former is considered trivial and silly, while the latter is a serious work of art. Why? Because there are a whole armful of songs about the chess match instead of just three minutes about Waterloo? Or is it simply the elitist notion of theatre being superior to pop, seducing audiences, critics and Ulvaeus–Andersson themselves into believing that the *Chess* project was somehow wholly more meaningful.

Abba were laughed out of court when they leapt up and down in satin flares singing 'Waterloo', but give 'em a chess board and Tim Rice as a partner and they suddenly get accorded in-depth profiles in the posh papers and television specials. But is the stage musical really that substantially more worthy than pure pop for its own sake? It's all songs. But just sticking them together on a stage with a pile of flashy costumes and a daft story-line seems to invest them with a new significance and importance and somehow elevates their authors into the grown-ups' world.

But surely the concept of the stage musical is no more ridiculous than the original Napoleonic theme of 'Waterloo' and Eurovision '74. Rodgers and Hammerstein, considered among the greatest songwriters of the century, have a veritable mineshaft of wonderful musicals on their CV. But look at 'em. *The Sound of Music*. A bunch of kids yodelling up and down a couple of mountains in Austria with . . . *a nun*?!? Come on, the very concept of a load of nuns standing around gossiping in the back yard of an abbey, slagging off the new girl and suddenly launching into *song* is a seriously weird notion. Seriously weird. And that's before we get into the realms of big bad Nazis chasing them across the countryside.

Most musicals are similarly unreal, totally bonkers. *Seven Brides For Seven Brothers*. *Paint Your Wagon*. *Sweet Charity*. *Annie Get Your Gun*. A musical about some sharp-shooter in the wild west? Who could possibly want to go and see that? All of it utter fantasy. Which is precisely why people did go and see *Annie Get Your Gun*. In their droves. But theatre, cinema, pop music – it's all fantasy. And when that fantasy is used to say something about real life and encroach on truth, then the fantasy becomes all the more potent.

This was the crux of the technique used by Andrew Lloyd Webber and Tim Rice to staggering commercial effect in their musicals. Their first hit, *Jesus Christ Superstar*, brilliantly – and controversially – hit on the idea of portraying Jesus as the world's first celebrity, the adored pop star of his day. Crazy, but shrewdly logical. Crucially, they used the rock medium to break the idea to a shocked public. When Rice and Lloyd Webber constructed *Jesus Christ Superstar* they were complete nonentities with no composing track record at all and there was not even the remotest possibility of anyone financing it for the London West End stage . . . or any other stage, come to that. They didn't even bother trying.

But they did utilize the trend of the day towards rock concept albums and *Jesus Christ Superstar* was presented to an initially sceptical, indifferent public in the form of the grandest concept album of them all, with a cast of singers who bought the flattery of being considered as something other than airhead rockers

Its rise was a slow process, too. But eventually the album became a hit, the Jesus as Elvis theory grew on the public, and entrepreneurs began to see the enormous potential of applying the principles of the stage musical – long derided as the exclusive domain of parents and the hopelessly romantic by the younger generation – to modern currency. It was, when all was said and done, a cracking story.

Jesus Christ Superstar duly became the trail-blazing pioneer of the new stage musical, dragging in its wake other quasi-religious rock musicals like *Godspell* (starring David Essex, bless him) and their own long-discarded first assault on the genre, *Joseph And The Amazing Technicolour Dreamcoat*. The musical had been reborn and, having already turned Jesus into a media star, the scope for Lloyd Webber and Rice for future productions was unlimited. A musical about the wife of an Argentinian dictator? Why not? So after Jesus as Elvis, we had Eva Peron as Marilyn Monroe. And the partnership persisted in their original policy of using the recorded matter as the first column in the march of a new meisterwerk. A few careers were made on the back of it too. Little-known actress Julie Covington was suddenly elevated to reluctant heroine status as she took 'Don't Cry For Me Argentina' into the Top Ten. Strange, strange song which made the imagery of 'Waterloo' positively mundane, but a gilt-edged hit from the first chorus. A woman singing an emotional love song to not just one lover, but a whole damn *nation* of lovers. *Evita* was destined to be a surefire colossal hit musical from the moment that 'Don't Cry For Me Argentina' by Julie Covington got its first airplay.

Benny Andersson and Bjorn Ulvaeus watched it all in awe. Their own rise had vaguely coincided with the emergence of Rice and Lloyd Webber as a songwriting phenomenon and they were full of envy. Long denied real respect themselves, they saw the Lloyd Webber/Rice musicals as something to shoot at. They talked long and hard of composing their own full-length musical and even had one or two half-hearted shots at imitating the genre within Abba. In their hearts they knew they'd have to step outside Abba to do it – the public just wouldn't accept any wide diversions from the pop single mentality they'd couched themselves in. But they made one or two small steps in a conceptual direction, most notably with their 'The Girl With The Golden Hair' theatrical segment showcased on their 1977 tour.

Bjorn and Benny were excited about 'The Girl With The Golden Hair'. For the first time they had a vision of a future beyond Abba and planned to develop 'Golden Hair' into a full-length musical in its own right. In 1977 it was merely a somewhat crude 'mini-musical' featuring Agnetha and Frida in identical blonde wigs, acting as clockwork dolls, representing split personalities of the same character while a sinister grave-looking actor arrived on stage to make the links. In truth it was hardly a world-shatteringly original storyline, concerning the destruction of a beautiful young girl's innocence and vitality in the pursuit of fame and glory and the shady characters determined to use her en route. Not quite the colourful epic proportions of *Jesus Christ Superstar* and *Evita* and wholly inappropriate, even as a taster, at the climax of an Abba concert in front of a bemused audience who were just there to sing along with 'Fernando' and witness first hand Agnetha's miraculous bum.

There was talk of turning it into a film, but in the end the 'Girl With The Golden Hair' concept drifted. Meetings were held, the dreams of a complete stage musical persisted for a while and then ultimately disintegrated as the Abba machine cranked into action again.

'The Girl With The Golden Hair' appeared in its truncated form on *Abba the Album*, with just three tracks, 'I'm A Marionette', 'I Wonder' and 'Thank You For The Music' surviving intact. Once again the segment largely confused more than it impressed with its emphasis on arrangement and dramatic effect, though 'Thank You For The Music' did eventually become one of their most familiar tracks if not one of their biggest hits.

Bjorn and Benny's ambition remained unfulfilled, however, and the nagging desire to see their work presented on a stage with all the accompanying status it provides continued to gnaw at them. Once Rice had put in his call, the die was cast, though it was to be an inordinately long time, marked by frenetic Abba activity and personal upheavals, before the wheels of *Chess* were put into any sort of motion.

Rice presented Bjorn and Benny with three different ideas for a musical. The one they went for was *Chess*. 'I always wanted something about east and west,' said Rice, 'but I wanted to write about real people affected by the cold war. There were all these stories about the chess matches involving people like Bobby Fischer and Boris Spassky and that seemed to me to be a good starting point for it.'

Once they got into *Chess* all thoughts of an Abba reunion were put on ice. Here was Rice with his glittering track record and fund of ideas providing strands of thought and storylines which genuinely revitalized them. There were compromises to be made as Bjorn and Benny – accustomed to using their own stringent standards as their only quality control – had to bow to the greater experience of a third party. But they found it stimulating rather than frustrating and the initially distant dreams of a stage musical gradually formed into a viable and cohesive reality. Rice presented the basic scenario of the plot and Benny and Bjorn would come back to him with a song and guide lyric. Rice would then construct a streamlined lyric and it would go back to Bjorn and Benny for further polishing, and then back to Tim for more rewrites. It was a long, arduous process but it worked for both parties.

Chess, the soundtrack album, was released ten-and-a-half years after Abba came to international attention with 'Waterloo'. They used the usual Abba mechanics, recording the project at Polar and using regular Abba backing musicians like Rutger Gunnarson on bass, Lasse Wellander on guitar and Per Lindvall on drums, with their great faithful Micke Tretow engineering it. The lead singers were largely Rice cohorts – Elaine Paige, Barbara Dickson and Murray Head – all immensely impressed by the supreme professionalism of Ulvaeus and Andersson in the studio. They stuck to Rice's tradition of putting out an album ahead of the stage show to test the water, a policy that Bjorn and Benny, still learning the trade of musicals, heartily concurred with. In the event it yielded a couple of singles that sold three million apiece, 'One Night In Bangkok' (by Murray Head) and 'I Know Him So Well' (by Barbara Dickson and Elaine Paige). The show eventually hit the London stage in 1986 and had a long, successful run in Tim Rice's accustomed manner. For Bjorn and Benny, it represented a giant step. Now they knew they were *proper* songwriters.

Chess didn't necessarily signal the end of Abba. Bjorn and Benny always denied Abba was finished and after the relative painlessness of the tenth anniversary celebrations and compilation album, they kept an open mind on a comeback album, though the thought of embarking on any more tours still put the fear of God into them.

But with *Chess* safely born, and both Frida and Agnetha putting out solo albums – and finding the waters choppy – there was a real feeling that they could bury their differences long enough to put together a brand new Abba album. It was what everyone wanted – the fans, the record company, and Stig Anderson especially. Frida resigned herself to the fact that her pull with the group was stronger than it would ever be on her own, told friends that she wouldn't be making any more solo albums, that time had healed the wounds and Abba would be returning twice as good as they had been before.

Bjorn and Benny started work on the songs for the projected new album, which even had a working title of *Opus 10*, and confirmation seemed to come when the four members of Abba reunited for a Swedish TV show paying tribute to Stig Anderson. They even *performed* – sort of – giving an apparently impromptu rendition of a nursery-rhyme type effort called 'Tived – Shambo', purported to be one of the first songs Stig had ever written, over three decades earlier. It was sufficient evidence for everyone to assume that all was well in Abbaland and the Stig show was merely a lighthearted prelude to a serious return to action. It turned out to be the last appearance they ever made together.

Opus 10 was never recorded. After the excitement of *Chess* and all the fun of the openings and seeing the new horizons appearing before their eyes, Bjorn and Benny couldn't muster the energy or enthusiasm to get Abba rolling again. When they got together to discuss Abba they found themselves instead talking animatedly about their next stage musical. They found their lives had veered radically apart. Their individual lifestyles in the eighties conspired to greatly complicate the logistics of pulling anything together and they no longer had enough appetite for the battle to overcome these complications. Frida, having given Stig and *Chess* the full benefit of her support, had now moved to Zurich. Bjorn, the Anglophile, decided he'd finally act on a long-held desire to live in the English countryside and moved Lena and his new family to an estate in Henley. And Agnetha, involved in a series of unhappy relationships and screwed up more than anyone by the business, wasn't talking to anybody without being spoken to first. They were taking much-needed time out with even the constantly inspirational songwriting partnership of Bjorn and Benny displaying signs of wear and tear and in urgent need of a rest. The two largely stopped writing together during Bjorn's exile in England, though they remained firm friends.

Stig was desperate for Abba to record again, but ultimately none of them cared enough to hold it together. They didn't need the money and they didn't need the grief.

Abba never officially split. They just sadly disappeared into the sunset. There were no more aces to play.

13

IT'S A RICH MAN'S WORLD

'If I got me a wealthy man
I wouldn't have to work at all, I'd fool around
and have a ball'

'Money, Money, Money'

S tig was cute. Right from the outset, he played the game with a rare astuteness. It may have been pure fluke, it may have been brazen bluff or it may have been the shrewdest, most meticulously-planned business assault in the history of pop music.

He guided Abba to international fame and wealth with an exhaustive, single-minded devotion that left business colleagues gasping for breath and wondering at his sheer, unwavering depth of belief and commitment. Okay, so they'd won the Eurovision Song Contest. So what? It didn't mean anything. 'Waterloo' might get played as a quaint goldie oldie in years to come, and those Napoleon costumes would be just about the only things they would be remembered for in the new, improved eighties, wouldn't they?

Like Abi and Esther Ofarim. Anyone remember Abi and Esther Ofarim? They never won the Eurovision Song Contest, yet they should have done. They were classic Eurovision fodder. Image, mentality, weird frocks and clean white teeth, roaring out of the blocks spelling International Superstars On Their Way with a capital C-R-A-P. Yeah, Esther and Abi were the lovable eccentrics who were spiritually in Brighton showing Livvy Newton-John, Gigliola Cinquetti and Mouth & McNeal a clean pair of heels even if their hit – their one hit – 'Cinderella Rockefella' came over like, oh, a demented Elton John and Kiki Dee on acid. Too bizarre, too camp even to win the oddball vote at Eurovision. Whatever happened to Esther and Abi? Who remembers them now? And what do you remember? Frilly white cuffs and macho jackboots, right?

Few imagined we'd be hearing too much of Abba once 'Waterloo' had been blown out of the water. Not even in Sweden – *especially* not in Sweden – where international success was looked upon as a treasonable offence and they were mercilessly beaten with birches in every paper or magazine in the country. Foreign visitors to Sweden were shocked and amazed to set foot off the plane at Arlanda to find themselves suddenly accosted by hordes of weeping Swedes kissing their feet, pleading forgiveness on behalf of the nation for breeding such creatures as Abba.

But Stig believed, and for him it all seemed so predestined. His career before Abba and Eurovision seemed like a rigorous apprenticeship. There were other artists, other success stories, other songwriters, other collaborations, but Bjorn and Benny . . . they were the catalyst to trigger Stig into a single-minded quest for world acceptance that was unprecedented in Scandinavia or anywhere else.

Stig planned Eurovision like a general deploying his armies. Every step, every ploy, every manoeuvre was meticulously researched and planned: the Abba stickers that had taken over Brighton on that fateful day in 1974 like power-crazy triffids; the DJs on every major radio station in Europe who suddenly found themselves clutching a copy of 'Waterloo' and staring at it like it was the meaning of life itself; the papers up and down the land who found themselves writing complete drivel about the group with the two couples whose names might just have escaped them, but the blonde girl's glamour didn't.

Yeah, Stig put £20 on Abba to win Eurovision, and you bet he collected his £400 winnings the next day too. But he never, ever, ever saw it as an end in itself. This, he told Benny and Bjorn firmly, was not the pinnacle of their careers, it was merely the beginning. And it was at this point that Stig's extraordinary business acumen came into its own. Stig painstakingly went all over Europe setting deals with different companies to release Abba records. France, Spain, Switzerland, Germany, Italy, Hungary, Australia, the USA, Canada, Japan, Fiji, the Cayman Islands, Mars, Jupiter. If Stig thought there was a market there then that was it, he packed his toothbrush and he was on his way, contract in hand. He went behind the Iron Curtain, he went to places where Eurovision was entirely unknown, he went to territories where record players hadn't even been invented.

It was a painstaking process and people thought he was mad. This just wasn't the way managers were expected to behave. You didn't do this sort of thing. You negotiated a deal with a major company in Britain, or the US or wherever and basically sorted out an agreement with them to license the record for release through their own labels in the rest of the world. Simpler and easier for all concerned, really.

But Stig had no intention of doing it like this. With the same logic that drove him to found Sweden Music, he was determined to control *everything*. Each territory, every release, all the promotional campaigns in all the countries in all the world. It was horrendously arduous. And for what? Everyone knew Abba were one-hit wonders.

It was a long, long eighteen months between Brighton and 'Waterloo' and Abba's reacquaintance with the Top Ten with 'SOS'.

The trail had apparently gone cold extraordinarily quickly. Apparently. In fact, none of this worried Stig unduly. He got shirty with the Swedish press for constantly deriding them, but he could handle flops – he'd had enough of them. He'd learned long ago that thick skin and rock-like self belief were essential pre-requisites of this business. Besides, Stig had vision. Vision and planning. They covered all the bases: image, style, looks, professionalism, but mostly *music* – they were the perfect pop band. They were exactly what the world needed. It was just gonna take a bit of time for the world to realize this . . .

So, far from sitting around sulking and licking his wounds in the supposedly barren period between 'Waterloo' in March '74 and 'SOS' in September '75, Stig was systematically laying the foundations for the time when the world was indeed ready to sit up and take notice and adopt Abba into their hearts as all right-minded, thinking people surely would. He was haring round the world setting up individual licences for releases in every territory known to man or beast.

Abba, too, were packed off to do battle in the field. They toured across Europe in concentrated bursts and where finances and simple practicalities precluded a proper live performance, they made lightning promotional visits. They even flew to the States, appearing wide-eyed on the *Mike Douglas Show*, a hugely popular syndicated daytime talk show which they gurgled their way through with charming naïvety. They also released the *Waterloo* album, with mixed fortunes.

It was a rigorous campaign and it was gruelling for all concerned. Even then Agnetha's worries and insecurities came hurtling to the fore and the initial excitement of their assault on the world gave way to the frustrations, irritations and petty bouts of paranoia brought on by the wearing lifestyle. Pretty soon Agnetha was regularly chafing to be getting home to concern herself with what she saw as her more serious role in life as a wife and mother. All this and the dreaded second album syndrome. Even for cheerfully addictive workaholics like Bjorn and Benny, the age-old terror for newly-appointed rock gods of trying to write and produce new material to match that first blockbuster – in this case 'Waterloo' – with something equally fresh, innovative and commercial, while still horsing around the world promoting the last one was a bit of a headache. That's why rock stars go tumbling into drugs and debt and terrible sex scandals. All that sudden fame and paper wealth. All that ego. All that acclaim. All that libido. And they want you to write new hit songs too? It's a weird old game, the record industry, that's for sure.

Abba didn't get into this syndrome. Clean-cut was, after all, their calling card. They weren't kids on the first rush of success and they never touched drugs, though egos were always an underlying problem and the guys, at least, weren't averse to heading for the jungle juice with real passion after a hard day's night. Work, work, work was their vice all right. The year following Eurovision pushed them all to the limit, though. Questions were asked within the inner sanctum of Abba about whether all this promotional work was truly necessary.

But it paid off. Even those turkeys, the singles that bombed in the recognized civilized world, actually started to show their faces in charts in Austria and Turkey and Japan and Poland and Albania and Greenland. And already in Australia all they had to do was sneeze and they were soaring up the charts, even though they'd never been there. Even the dreadful, no-hoper turkey treat to end them all, the wretched 'Ring Ring', was nestling defiantly at the top of the charts in Holland, Belgium and South Africa.

Stig's philosophy was instantly proved inspirational. By personally involving Polar in direct licensing of Abba records to individual countries rather than giving one major company worldwide rights, he was ensuring not only much greater financial gain from each deal, but more commitment from those countries to break Abba and sell the records. It was a policy that ultimately made them millions and established Stig's reputation as a wily entrepreneurial wizard.

'Work hard, do your best, don't forget *anything*, and don't take it too seriously.' These were the guidelines on life adhered to by Stikkan Anderson, and which he often quoted in later years to the legions of admiring fledgling managers who came knocking at his door in search of the holy grail. Other managers had orgasms just at the thought of the profits Stig was creaming in at Polar. He had CBS in Britain, Warners in America, and the other majors in the rest of the world all eating out of his hand, kow-towing to this one little guy from Hova: chain-smoking, hard-drinking, fast-talking, entertainingly irascible – and turning the face of the record industry on its head with his perfect little pop band from Sweden.

The truth of the matter was that Stig loved it. He adored doing business. He got off on it to such a degree that he knew he must be doing it right. He'd always considered himself first and foremost a lyricist, but as things rapidly developed, the business took a grip on him and there was no turning back. Anyway, who needs lyricists? They're ten a penny. Bjorn and Benny found they could cope in the artistic department perfectly well without him.

Stig was also notoriously canny, running a watertight ship. There were no excesses, no extravagances. There was to be no Apple-esque frittering of time, money or surplus energies in this set-up. Even at the very height of Polar's trading as one of the most profitable companies in the world, when they were gleefully quoted as being second only to Volvo as Sweden's second-biggest exporters, they only employed a relatively minimal staff of fifty.

Early on they saw the economic sense of buying their own recording studios. They converted an old cinema in Stockholm into one of the finest studios in the world, in which Bjorn and Benny happily camped for weeks on end whenever they were in the country. Why pay money to someone else when you can do it yourself?

In consequence the Polar organization had a familial intensity about it. People worked their socks off in that company and Stig's own single-minded perfectionism and unbridled passion and energy made him an exacting boss. Yet he inspired the most ferocious loyalties that largely hold good even today. He looked upon Polar as an insular clan, expecting, demanding and usually getting wholehearted commitment to the cause from all those around him, offering exactly the same deal himself in exchange. An almost touching, peculiarly Swedish code grew up around the Polar clan. And Bjorn, Benny, Agnetha and Anni-Frid were the chief clanspersons. That was understood. Stig loved them all with a father's fervour . . . which was why he found it so bitterly hard to come to terms with what he saw as their ultimate betrayal when they fell out and ended up in court years later.

That outcome was unthinkable through the late seventies as they carried all before them. Once 'SOS' had signalled their revival with a vengeance in 1975 and Bjorn and Benny seemed merely to have to turn on the tap for another dozen chart-toppers to come pouring out, the Polar profits rocketed. The members of Abba each took a wage from Polar but were also partners in the company and watched the millions flood in from all corners of the world with delight and amazement. Stig owned 100 per cent of Sweden Music and 50 per cent of Polar Music International, including the studio, but Benny and Bjorn, particularly, were earning massive royalties on their songs.

Stig did manage other artists, different musicians – there was a Polar roster of fifteen acts at one stage – but most of them were friends or had somehow been touched by the Abba satellite. Stig's son Lasse Anderson worked in the Abba studio. His daughter Marie (who later married singer Tomas Ledin, once an Abba backing vocalist) worked as promotions manager at Polar. Even his young son Anders worked part-time for the Abba fan club, while Stig's wife Gudrun – once a weaving teacher – was a director of the whole empire.

The problem was Sweden. If you're living in God's chosen country, then you must expect to pay prime rates for the privilege. The standard of living is exceptionally high, greater even than the United States: Sweden is a prototype of the perfect European country. It has one of the most extensive social welfare programmes on earth, and is renowned for its picturesqueness, cleanliness and comfort.

However. Somebody has to pay the piper and a few nights on the beer in Stockholm will clean you out, no problem. Welfare services take care of 70 per cent of the national budget and Sweden has the highest tax rate in the world.

As wave after wave of success accumulated for Abba, Stig watched the money disappearing in tax and wept. They were paying the top rate of 85 per cent tax, which meant they were virtually running the country's welfare system on their own. They talked of becoming tax exiles, but rejected the idea. Why should they? This was their home. They loved Sweden, despite the flak they were getting for being famous, well-groomed and successful at a time it was right-on to be scruffy, angry and starving. There was to be a time when they moved away, but this wasn't it. Internationally they were synonymous with the country; their studio, their headquarters, their friends and family, their *inspiration* was all there and they had no real desire to leave, big, bad taxman knocking at their door or not.

The problems of money management weren't entirely new to Benny at least. The disaster the Hep Stars had made of their finances was a cautionary lesson for him and he could sniff the danger of Abba falling foul of the same traps amid the euphoria of their international break-through. But it didn't have to be that way, and Stig Anderson made damn sure that it wasn't. They took advice and the advice was invest the money. Instead of meekly relinquishing it as income tax, they were urged to offload it into business ventures. After all we're not talking small change here. Anderson's astute business sense had already hooked in untold wealth. In 1977 Abba were estimated to have earned over five million pounds. In 1978 it was nearer six million. The net worth of the group around that time was reckoned to be in the region of fourteen million.

And so they started speculating. With – initially at least – spectacular results. The idea was that their earnings would now be channelled into different companies, making them liable to 33 per cent capital gains tax on any share sales, which was a much better option than paying 85 per cent income tax on earnings as private individuals.

'The music business is much too small for the kind of money we were handling,' said Stig. 'We wanted to spread the risks.'

Successful financial and leasing operations were set up to provide this tax shelter and the company was later floated on the stock exchange. Initially these extraneous business enterprises were concentrated on property, real estate offering a traditionally sound investment for speculators. Abba became substantial minority shareholders in Badhus, a quoted company which bought Sturebad public baths and sauna, one of Stockholm's oldest, most picturesque, most celebrated landmarks.

Even more significantly, they bought a large minority holding in Monark, the country's biggest bicycle manufacturer. This was a particularly inspired investment. By buying into Monark, Abba became part of the very fabric of Swedish daily life – and their timing couldn't have been more impeccable. Their move coincided with the dramatic rise of the environmental lobby, which itself emerged on the back of an oil crisis. The result? Sale of bikes in Sweden suddenly rocketed. Monark in its turn bought up Harlekin, the four members of Abba's own company, set up to collect the royalties from their record sales and generating profits of up to twenty million Swedish krona a year. They also bought interests in everything from gardening product companies to packaging firms to clothing manufacturers to valuable art collections. Every one a winner. For sure they had the Midas touch.

Like J. R. Ewing before them, oil was their downfall. Abba were effectively the first western band to shift big units behind the Iron Curtain. It had started as a glorious accident right in the early post-'Waterloo' days. An ambassadorial visit to Sweden by some Polish dignitary was reported in the Polish press, along with a brief mention of the strange western phenomenon called Abba occurring at the time, and a reference to the fan club address.

Next thing Stockholm citizens knew they were being confronted by the strange sight of postmen lurching along the roads, staggering under the weight of colossal sacks of fan mail from Poland. 'Hallo Abba people,' they wrote. 'We are fans in Poland. We want records and things. Please send. Please me marry the blonde one.'

Western music was actively discouraged all through Eastern Europe at the time – even wholesome, melodic varieties like Abba's. It was a major league migraine to sort out a visa to pop your head round the Iron Curtain for an afternoon way back then, let alone go there flogging Abba records off the back of a lorry. The cold war was still several degrees below freezing, dividing east and west, and there was more chance of Agnetha winning Miss World than the Berlin Wall falling down.

But where there's a market, there's a way. Stig couldn't bear the thought of all those people dying to buy Abba albums and being unable to do so, and set his considerable enterprise at work in solving the problem that had defeated major acts for generations – how to ship albums behind the Iron Curtain when those countries had rigorous restrictions on foreign currency going out of the state.

The answer, clearly, was to be paid in something other than currency. Eastern Europe was beginning to open up to western influences despite itself and the bandwagon that began to roll in Poland rapidly swept through the other Iron Curtain countries and into Russia itself. It wasn't entirely discouraged by the authorities either. There was nothing deeply sinister or corrupting, after all, in Abba's lyrics or arrangements and Stig's vision of a truly international pop group appealing with equal persuasiveness across the entire world began to be realized.

Abba the Album sold an unprecedented million copies in Poland in 1977, exhausting the country's entire allocation of foreign currency. In Russia they were allowed to press only 200,000 copies of the album, though demand within the USSR indicated they could have sold 40 million. For somebody with Stig's love of dosh this was enough to make him cry. Something clearly needed to be done to make more Abba records available in these countries, with an alternative means of payment. That's how they devised a barter system that subsequently became adopted by other leading acts as a viable means of breaking into previously inaccessible territories.

The method of payment was almost immaterial compared to the greater good of spreading the word to more corners of the world. It was a key factor in Abba's phenomenal sales figures – the mere availability of their work in places western music had rarely strayed before instantly expanded their potential markets, and they were markets that had been gagging for years to get hold of this stuff – almost *any* stuff from the west, in fact.

So Stig took on board some pretty strange commodities in lieu of cash. The further they got into Eastern Europe, the stranger the form of payments. Art treasures, toys, musical instruments, rare coins, sports equipment, shirts, even Polish potatoes, at one point. Whatever . . . this was private enterprise at its most provocative, and the business heads at Polar usually found an outlet for their swag. Several of their dips into new industries came as a result of this unorthodox manner of payments.

But in 1977 Abba set up a deal that was ultimately to cost them dear and lead them into one industry too far. They worked out a system whereby Iron Curtain record sales were partly paid for with Romanian oil, which they imported through a link with another Swedish company already trading behind the Iron Curtain, and which they could then buy and sell on the Rotterdam spot market.

It was an attractive initiative. Abba were already the richest pop band in history and while the oil industry was notoriously unpredictable they had little compunction about getting involved. An air of invincibility had surely cloaked them now, rendering them impenetrable by the quirky market forces that can make rich men paupers overnight in this game. The very idea of oil clearly tickled Stig Anderson, fast fancying himself as Scandinavia's answer to Aristotle Onassis. He knew no fear.

They did it right. They took professional advice, pulled in some experts and formed a new company, Pol Oil, to control the operation and rake in the millions. That was the theory anyway. In truth it became the biggest mistake and the first serious wrong step of their business careers. It literally cost them a fortune, and caused them almost as much embarrassment as those dreaded Napoleonic pant suits.

Speculating in oil is a dodgy business which frequently catches even experienced campaigners with their pants down. The market is like a giant Ferris wheel spinning massively out of control at a thousand miles an hour and suddenly going up in flames just as you start to enjoy the ride. You pays your money and you hope and pray and hang on for dear life. It's a thrilling, heady gamble – just as long as you've got a head for heights.

Abba – through Pol Oil – got involved at a boom time for the industry. The financial world was full of rags to riches stories, chancers becoming instant tycoons, and fortunes being acquired virtually overnight. It all looked very, very good for Abba. Except that by the time they got Pol Oil off and running and they started pitching the serious money into the new company, oil prices had levelled out. They went headlong into a major deal just at the precise moment the bottom fell out of the market and the whole thing collapsed around their ears.

They invested in 55,000 tonnes of Egyptian crude oil at the end of 1979. Pol Oil bought the oil at $40 a barrel, which was higher than the normal going price. As a small exporter, Egypt geared its prices to spot market levels rather than official oil selling prices, which – luck would have it – were substantially lower than spot prices at the time.

Shortly afterwards spot market prices collapsed. Egypt radically cut the cost of its oil and the value of the Abba oil tumbled drastically. Pol Oil frantically sought a buyer but there were no takers, and the longer they failed to offload it, the more money they were losing. Their $40 barrels were touted around for $34 and they ultimately blew in the region of $2 million on the cargo. All this and massive charges for storing the wretched oil in tanks in Rotterdam. Storage tanks are difficult to find at the best of times and the hire costs for the privilege of keeping something that was daily losing them huge amounts of money was another major financial burden. The whole enterprise became the mother of all nightmares and they abandoned their interest in the oil industry at the first available opportunity.

The oil debacle, though, preluded a whole series of financial skirmishes that dogged them in the later years of their Abba careers. They set up an investment company, Kuben, as the planned centre of operations for their increasing involvement in the Swedish manufacturing industry.

This was well into the game. Both Abba marriages had foundered by this time and the whole future of the musical entity looked in jeopardy. In 1982 Frida, on her way to London to launch her solo career, flogged off her entire stake in the operation. Smart girl.

Pretty soon the others must have wished to God they'd done the same. The losses sustained by Pol Oil seriously put the skids under Kuben as it became apparent that they were badly overreaching themselves with their constant speculation, paid for with borrowed money. In 1982 they were estimated to have spent $39 million buying up company shareholdings, but by the end of that year the company's equity accounted for only 2 per cent of the balance sheet. They were quite simply spending money they didn't have, borrowing more and more money as they speculated ever more heavily in an attempt to get it back. When the three bells didn't come up on the one-arm bandit they were in deep, deep trouble. Their property and financial enterprises continued to flourish, but mostly everything else was a disaster area. They sank deeper and deeper into the whirlpool of ever-decreasing returns, borrowing dangerously to stave off financial collapse and gambling desperately on risky investments. At some point the merry-go-round was gonna slither to a halt and then it was own-up time.

Kuben planned to buy up Monark, the successful bicycle company, to get it out of trouble. The scheme was to borrow the money for the deal – and then fund the loans from Monark's own finances. It collapsed when Kuben failed to secure the necessary 90 per cent of Monark shares. The oil disaster had seemingly triggered a collapse of the house of cards at HQ and there was some bitter bloodletting in the process.

Early in 1983 the whole business arm of the Abba industry fell apart. Amid some ugly infighting and personal recriminations within the 'family', the management of Kuben was replaced, though Stig Anderson himself remained on the Kuben board, which was fighting for its life. Eventually, they got 90 per cent of the Monark shares – expensively – and Stig frantically tried to patch together a rescue programme for the company.

But he was too late. The Stockholm Stock Exchange Council suspended dealing in its shares, declaring itself 'alarmed' at the lack of financial information provided by the company, and the game was up.

Abba – minus Frida – were left with just one viable option: they had to sell out. Another investment company, Aritmos, based in the south of Sweden with interests in the leisure and food industries, bought a controlling 53 per cent stake in Kuben, and with it Monark and all the other manufacturing industries Abba had so keenly involved themselves in during the late seventies. It represented another major loss of face and loss of capital. At the time Abba had acquired the Kuben shares they were worth 50 kronor each. At the time Kuben share dealings were suspended they were trading at 230 kronor each. They sold them to Aritmos at 25 kronor per share. They'd lost the main arm of their business wing . . . and another small fortune.

They held on to a small number of shares 'for old time's sake', but the painful business effectively ended their evidently reckless forays into industry. 'We hope,' said Bjorn ruefully, 'to get away from the connection that's always been made between Abba as a pop group and other operations.' In future, said Stig, Abba would be concentrating solely on showbusiness.

A wise move, but the nightmare came back to haunt them. The Swedish Inland Revenue came to take a close interest in their business dealings and ultimately alleged they'd evaded tax payments in the region of £4.6 million relating to their business affairs.

They were particularly interested in Polar Music's disposal of Pol Oil, instituting a civil case against them for payment of the tax allegedly owed, and claiming they'd concealed nearly £4 million in getting rid of the oil trading company. Stig was also alleged to have evaded £800,000-worth of taxes in a complex deal involving their property company, Stockholm Badhus.

The problems went on and on amid threats that Abba would face criminal charges and could possibly end up in prison. Abba in prison? The very thought sends a chill down your spine, doesn't it?

The proceedings were settled out of court and they didn't end up in prison, but they did wind up with a further humiliating battering to their pride and yet another full-blooded assault on their wallets. Their reign as tycoons had very definitely ended, though they didn't bail out to go and live in cardboard city right away. Abba were still reckoned to be worth £4 million.

But the whole sorry decline of their business empire had taken its toll. It symbolized the end of an era, the collapse of a dream, the final amen to a golden age. The stuffing had been knocked out of them . . . and so had any thoughts they may have had of putting the show back on the road.

Abba as a working entity was truly dead and gone.

Stig Anderson, though, didn't retire quietly. Gratified by the riches the industry had given him and anxious to retain an involvement, in 1989 Stig endowed the annual Polar Music Prize 'for significant achievements' in musical life. He has succeeded in keeping his name at the forefront of European music and the Polar Prize is now one of the world's richest and most prestigious awards.

It occupies much of Stig's time these days – the ceremony itself is a massive event, staged in collaboration with the Royal Swedish Academy of Music, attracting musicians from all over the world, and attended by the King of Sweden. Each prize donated by Polar is worth more than a million kronor, emphasizing not only Stig's commitment to the industry and his status within it, but his fabulous wealth too. The prize is designed to acknowledge all areas of music and prizewinners have already included a vast range of artists from Paul McCartney to Dizzy Gillespie to Polish classical composer Witold Lutoslawski.

Stig Anderson remains larger than life.

14

WHEN ALL IS SAID AND DONE

'Nothing more to say, no more ace to play'

'The Winner Takes It All'

A gay club in London, 1994. The night is throbbing with excitement. The camper they come the more they enthral and the juke box keeps on crashing out the hits.

All the old favourites. 'Relax' by Frankie Goes To Hollywood. 'Searchin' (I Gotta Find A Man)' by Hazell Dean. 'You Think You're A Man' by Divine. 'Better The Devil You Know' by Kylie. 'I Want That Man' by Debbie Harry. 'Don't Leave Me This Way' by The Communards. 'Big Spender' by Shirley Bassey. 'Delilah' by Tom Jones. 'Stand By Your Man' by Tammy Wynette. 'I Will Survive' by Gloria Gaynor. Each greeted with a crescendo of excited shrieks and a dance floor full of thrusting leather, every line sung loud and proud, a personal statement.

But these are merely the simmering warm-ups for the main event. And when it comes the place goes loudly berserk. Whistles. Catcalls. Roars of approval as the revellers swarm on the floor, beaming. 'Dancing Queen' by Abba. Undisputed monarch of the gay disco.

The public rehabilitation of Abba began, as so many phenomena have done, in the gay clubs. The camp appeal inherent in the outrageous costumes and the fading glamour of Agnetha and Frida became more and more apparent as the eighties wore on. The insistent melodies and up-front imagery that the gay fraternity found so appealing blended well with the bright techno-pop they had adopted like a badge.

The groups that had replaced Abba in terms of public affection and commercial success were Culture Club and the Human League and Wham! and Depeche Mode and Frankie Goes to Hollywood. They were worlds apart in style and inspiration yet were paradoxically natural successors. The early output of Wham! was as crass in its own way as the early Abba material, *and* they started out with two prominent girl singers, Pepsi and Shirlie, deflecting the spotlight and underlining George and Andrew's exploding sexuality. If Wham! were the definitive pop act of the eighties, then the others weren't far behind. Culture Club, with Boy George, all make-up and unthreatening excess, were out-and-out tunesmiths, owing more to Abba than they or anybody else acknowledged in polite company. The first Culture Club smash, 'Do You Really Want To Hurt Me?', was smooch personified and would probably have been rejected by Abba themselves as an overdose of schmaltz. But Abba had to be careful about that sort of thing in a world that perceived them as unhip and silly. Culture Club were young and funny and cheeky and wore make-up and went to all the right London clubs. Culture Club could get away with it and did. A different era, different attitudes.

With Boy George's love life ('I prefer a cup of tea to sex') and studiously controversial thoughts on society a permanent joyful puzzle to culture vultures in the eighties, gay attitudes pervaded pop music more influentially than at any other time in contemporary history. Pop music had flirted with it in the seventies when Abba were starting out and David Bowie and Marc Bolan flaunted their bisexuality as a marketing ploy and Queen, Sweet and Slade wore make-up. But during the mid-eighties gay values were right up front in your face. There was still an element of the cartoon about Boy George and Frankie, but there was real sexual politics going down in the hidden agenda.

A lot of things started to make sense for a lot of people as history was rewritten and Abba were no longer the depth of uncool, but the height of glorious kitsch. On tour years earlier Bjorn had been disconcerted to find persistent groups of adoring German boys hanging round him in silent worship, but there had otherwise been little evidence of Abba's lofty eminence in gay circles. But now it could be told. Agnetha and Frida's gradual emergence as the tragic heroines of pop further consolidated gay solidarity with an act they already had firm sympathy with.

Blancmange were one of the first to testify at the Abba retrial and support its not-guilty verdict. They were a duo from Blackpool or some place with an inordinate amount of cred in the new synth age and here they were rescuing one of Abba's greatest, but most criminally neglected songs, 'The Day Before You Came', from the scrapheap. For that Blancmange should be knighted, or similar. They turned 'The Day Before You Came' around, doing what Abba themselves had failed to do, and took the song into the British Top Thirty. It was a great version. And it preluded a rediscovery of all things Abba – and with it the whole avalanche of seventies fashions. After Blancmange the covers came thick and fast. Some artists felt the need to protect themselves against the hangover of ridicule still associated with Abba in certain isolated circles of pop society, mostly those bereft of brain cells, but the general interpretations concentrated on the sheer musical excellence of Bjorn and Benny's songs.

The whole psychology of cover versions is itself intriguing. Mostly people who record covers do so because they're not smart enough to write their own hits and to take on a song that's already proved its hit credentials to an earlier generation is largely a short-cut to success and a cop-out of the creative process. There are, of course, a few honourable and notable exceptions here. The greatest cover version of all time was Joe Cocker's 'With A Little Help From My Friends', totally dismantling and then re-energizing an already famous song and giving it such radical new meaning that it completely outstripped the original. The Beatles' versions of their own songs were always considered sacredly definitive until Joe Cocker came along to tear up the rule book. By the time Wet Wet Wet got around to 'With A Little Help From My Friends' a couple of decades later, it was to all intents and purposes a Joe Cocker song and the blue-eyed boys of Scotland appeared to have sanitized it beyond recognition, though in truth they were merely restoring the values the Beatles had originally placed on it.

Mostly, though, there have been more bad cover versions than good. Recording bad covers of good songs should be a hanging offence. There is simply no excuse for taking a great record and recording a new version of it, unless you are going to do something entirely different with it and improve it. Joe Cocker apart, it's virtually impossible. A few Christmases ago, at the end of the 1980s, the hearthrob of the day, Rick Astley, decided he'd corner the lucrative Christmas market and perform a textbook weepie version of the old Nat King Cole standard, 'When I Fall In Love'. Fabulous idea, Rick. It had Number One for Christmas plastered all over it. Until Capitol got wind of it and quickly rushed out the infinitely superior Nat King Cole original. The result? Nat King Cole got a posthumous Top Five Christmas record and poor old Rick Astley's commercial credibility took a bit of a battering from which he barely recovered.

The best cover version of all, though, is the one that unearths a great song that *should* have been a hit and breathes new thought and life into it to the point that people actively seek out the original. Paul Young's 'Wherever I Lay My Hat' is a classic example. An obscure, obnoxiously macho Marvin Gaye B-side suddenly transformed into a spellbinding classic of heartbreak and self-pity.

'Tainted Love'. A ten-a-penny disco record by Gloria Jones, Marc Bolan's girlfriend. It was she who was driving the car in the middle of the night that time when it flew off the road in West London and wrapped itself around a tree, killing Marc instantly. They still lay flowers on that tree for Marc. Gloria survived but is largely forgotten. But not by Marc Almond and David Ball of Soft Cell. They took Gloria's disco thud of 'Tainted Love', stripped it down and dressed it up in synth-techno tinsel, and turned it into one of the greatest records of the eighties.

Such works of secondary inspiration are sadly rare, but Blancmange moved some way into it with 'The Day Before You Came'. At the very least they encouraged others to investigate the treasure chest, and the whole incredible Abba after-life took off from that point. Few covered Abba songs in their lifetime, but there have been plenty since the group's death.

Check a few of them out. 'Money, Money, Money' by the Nolans. 'Thank You For The Music' by Vera Lynn. 'Arrival' by Mike Oldfield. 'Take A Chance On Me' by the Brighouse and Rastrick Brass Band. 'Name Of The Game' by Any Trouble. 'Dancing Queen' by Brotherhood of Man. 'Waterloo' by Dr & The Medics. 'The Winner Takes It All' by Mireille Matthieu. 'Hasta Manana' by Army of Lovers. Elvis Costello also had a deep fascination with Abba, about which he was happy to expound for hours on end to anyone interested, and was perfectly capable of playing all their hits on an acoustic guitar in the privacy of his own home. Along with most of the male population in the civilized world, he had a particular fondness for Agnetha, dedicating his *Imperial Bedroom* to her, and even submitted a song, 'Shatter Proof', for possible inclusion on her *Eyes Of A Woman* album. Agnetha sadly decided against recording it.

The prime ringer-dinger mother of all Abba covers came much later, however, in the summer of '92 when veteran techno duo Erasure went public on their Abba fetish. Their *Abba-esque* was one of those crazy, crazy notions that might – in another era with another group – have buried their careers so far beneath the ground it would have taken a team of miners to haul them out. But Erasure weren't given to bowing to convention. Vince Clarke, hailed as a teenage keyboard wizard, wrote a bunch of songs for Depeche Mode and then bailed out just as they were starting to earn the prizes for all those soul-destroying trips up and down English motorways playing dives and colleges full of hostile students.

He then eschewed all thought of pursuing fashion and obvious commercial enterprise, recruiting a plain, over-weight unknown from Essex to do the singing for him while he plonked around to his heart's delight on a variety of keyboards. Alison Moyet could scarcely have been less well cast as a pop singer at a time when glam was making a determined charge as the new romantics chased the last remnants of punkdom from the building. But that voice . . . That voice was something else. Releasing records under the name of Yazoo, Clarke and Moyet had a series of catchy, original, memorable hits before the introverted maestro and the feisty fireball of a singer he'd nurtured began to fall out, finally discovering what had been evident to everyone else from the beginning, that they had nothing in common.

Alison Moyet went on to resounding solo commercial success as an unlikely queen of the CD generation, while Vince Clarke continued his own highly individual path, tinkering with keyboards and daft ideas and maintaining an astonishingly consistent chart track record. His fascination with oddballs led him to form Erasure with another unknown, Andy Bell, a former choirboy with a rampant capacity to shock. It was always an incongruous partnership. The shy, studious, hetero Clarke, and the gregarious, flamboyant Bell, camper than a row of tents. Their catalogue of success since getting together in 1985 was a choice advertisement for the power of musical quality to overcome all, but their ability to shock without causing offence provided an edge and sense of daring largely absent from the pop musicians thrown up by the synth revolution.

So Erasure didn't blink an eyelid when they took on Abba. There was nothing contrived about it, they weren't doing it out of any sense of perversity, or even any laudable ideal of elevating the songs of Ulvaeus/Andersson to their rightful place in pop history. But steeped in that whole gay disco lifestyle, Andy Bell regarded Abba as gods, while the muso Clarke had a staunch admiration for the genius of the songwriting. For a long time they'd wanted to pay their own tribute without any thought of what it might or might not do to their credibility or commerciality. They'd actually planned to record an entire album of Abba songs, but ultimately trimmed it down to just four – 'Lay All Your Love On Me', 'SOS', 'Take A Chance On Me' and 'Voulez-Vous', all performed in frantic trademark hi-NRG. A labour of lust, *Abba-esque* rocketed to the top of the British charts within a week of its release.

Its success all over Europe was stunning. For the world were voting not just for Erasure, but for Abba too. It was a decade since they'd sung a song in earnest and Abba fever was breaking out all over again. There was an enthralled new generation and a rapidly back-pedalling old one, finally coming clean and celebrating a rarely-matched catalogue of songs without fear of scorn. Abba were cool. Official.

Once released from the constrictions of elitist conditioning, the pro-Abba lobby was unleashed in furious overdrive. The cover band phenomenon, which had been initiated in Australia as a joke by Bjorn Again, exploded on an international scale that could never have been predicted. Gavin Edwards (Bjorn Volveus), Peter Smith (Benny Anderwear), Annette Jones (Agnetha Falstart) and Tracy Adams (Frida Longstokin) never expected a full-time career to come out of it when they started presenting themselves doing Abba impersonations as a popular party piece. Various club and pub bookings followed, inspiring unexpectedly enthusiastic reactions from audiences bellowing along with every chorus. They were astonished by the way Bjorn Again captured people's hearts, but assumed it was a purely Australian thing. Abba were, after all, deified in Australia more than anywhere else on the planet. Top league bands visiting Australia were few and far between. Thus starved of the real thing, Australians leapt upon the idea of copycat bands, expressing their appreciation of the music through the agency of whoever took it into their heads to dress up and sound like their heroes.

Same principle as all the Elvis copyists, some of whom make a lucrative living touring in the States just by being Elvis. Well, it's not as if you're ever gonna get the chance to compare it with the real thing, is it? Elvis copyists are all over the place. Elvis is perfect because a) he's dead, b) he's the easiest person to impersonate in the history of music – perfect that curled lip, grab a white flared suit and you're halfway there, c) there's an enormous fund of material to choose from, d) there's loads of different eras and styles to suit any age, shape or size of impersonator, e) there's an army of drongos out there who will always be agog to go out and lavish money on anything that tries to foster the fantasy of an Elvis alive and well, however croaky of voice. In Britain alone, there's a celebrated Indian Elvis, who could be the real thing . . . except for the turban and the colour of his skin. In London there's even a celebrated Chinese restaurant where, between the second course and the coffee, the patron will suddenly don guitar and rhinestones and start belting out 'Return To Sender' in the accustomed manner. Very badly, but that's hardly the point.

The publicity attracted by Bjorn Again inspired the formation of many other Australian bands using their own heroes to garner some small vicarious chunk of the glory, the best of them – like the Australian Doors and Elton Jack – following Bjorn Again's trail to Europe. The phenomenon was really starting to take off in a big way around the time Erasure were thinking about recording *Abba-esque*. Bjorn Again were now touring major halls throughout Europe and had received a tumultuous ovation at the Reading Rock Festival, luring Abba obsessions out of ever-darker closets, while the Bootleg Beatles, the Strolling Bones, the Scottish Sex Pistols and the Royal Family (Queen) were all doing roaring business. Other Abba tribute bands quickly joined the bandwagon with varying degrees of success – ReBjorn and Super Trouper from Australia, Voulez Vous from Liverpool, Arrival from Germany, Dancing Queens from New Zealand. All seemingly going about their business with the tacit approval of the originals, their sense of humour as intact as their business brains: it stands to reason that the more these tribute bands spread themselves, keeping alive the music, the greater the legend of the original will swell, record sales and royalties swelling with it.

When Bjorn Again first emerged internationally and appeared on national television in Sweden, Bjorn Ulvaeus sent them a telegram of encouragement: 'The best of luck,' he said. 'It was always my belief that someone who looks like me ought to have a successful career!'

It didn't, however, prevent the original Abba suing Bjorn Again for breach of copyright when they started using the Abba logo with the back-to-front B they copyrighted long ago. Ulvaeus also subsequently went to see Bjorn Again live and went backstage afterwards to personally congratulate them on the accuracy of their impersonations. Arriving backstage he encountered Bjorn

Again, still in full role mode, greeting their guests in pseudo-Scandinavian accents. 'Hi, I am beink ferry plist to mit yew,' they beamed in sing-song unison, only to freeze in horror as they realized exactly who they were addressing. Bjorn, who'd already found the inter-song introductions uncomfortably patronizing, didn't flinch in telling them as much. 'You make us sound a bit dumb Swede,' he said. 'Otherwise it's great.'

There's no reason why Abba, or anyone else, should take offence at bands paying genuine tribute in this way. Had Bjorn Again been around a decade or so earlier, Abba might have used their clones to tour for them, thus removing the most difficult aspect of their work while maintaining the level of profile and promotion necessary to keep them at the top of the heap. It would have been the perfect solution for them – as it was, Abba were once accused, in a catalogue of ridiculous news stories circulating in Australia, of being imposters, a glamorous sham implanted as the public face of Abba because the real thing were boring middle-aged studio musicians who had to be locked away from the public because they were too ugly. Abba laughed bitterly at that. They were suffering all the agonies of touring and the unacceptable exposure it demanded to be accused of being a *sham*?

After all, the copycat band offers no threat to the real thing. It's not as if they're suddenly going to be making hit records. That's the problem. When you base your entire act on someone else's creativity you can then hardly go into the studio and recreate exactly their recorded output too. It's the ultimate frustration of the tribute band. There will always be a ceiling on your achievement. Unless you're smart.

When Erasure hit the top of the charts with *Abba-*

esque, Bjorn Again were off the blocks at a pace, whacking out their own ingenious answer, *Erasure-ish*. A bunch of Erasure songs performed in the style of Abba by four Australians. That's sharp. It got them into the charts, too, and the whole Abba revival began to career along on a scale to equal that of their glory-glory years.

The climax of it all was *Abba Gold*. It dated back a couple of years to the eve of the nineties when Stig Anderson sold Polar Music. It wasn't an easy decision, but Stig felt he had no alternative. The various deals he'd set up around the world for Abba in different individual territories had caused all manner of headaches with the demise of Abba and the constant round of compilations and reissues. Where Stig had once been able to control everything connected with Abba anywhere, any time, it was suddenly all nightmarishly unmanageable.

Worse than that, Stig had fallen out with the members of Abba in the wake of the Swedish inland revenue's investigations into their tax affairs (which were settled out of court). He copped most of the blame for the financial disasters that had crippled the Abba business enterprise. Benny, Bjorn and Agnetha could only watch in horror as their share values collapsed and went down 70 per cent in a matter of months. In the end they lost a couple of million each as they landed in the puddle at the end of the rainbow. The investigations into the business collapse – and the mistakes which pushed them deeper into the mire as they were trying to salvage the situation – focused unsavoury attention on all their financial dealings and drove a sizeable wedge between Stig and the others.

It wasn't too long before the Swedish inland revenue were on the scent of a major scalp, with Bjorn and Agnetha identified as plum targets. The tax authorities went through their accounts with a fine-tooth comb and duly unearthed some irregularities in the financial whirl following the crash and the desperate movement of stocks and shares the company had conducted to keep them afloat. The tax people concluded that Bjorn and Agnetha had failed to declare profits from this dealing in the mid-eighties and should be charged with tax evasion. Between £600,000 and a million were mentioned as outstanding amounts owed by each on their 1985 accounts alone . . . with a clear indication that this was merely a drop in the ocean compared with what they were expecting to unearth as they investigated accounts from earlier years. Having already lost a couple of million on the share collapse in the first place, Bjorn and Agnetha weren't best pleased. They didn't quite know how or why but they somehow felt they'd been made to be the fall guys.

Stig Anderson was furious. His own reputation was being smeared by implication and his relationship with the others was beginning to fall apart as a result. He was particularly enraged that the tax authorities' investigations and suspicions had been leaked to the press, and he threatened – not for the first time – to become a martyred exile living in Britain, where he fondly imagined he'd be better appreciated. Bjorn and Agnetha were yet to be charged, but already newspaper headlines were suggesting they could go to prison and a major scandal was brewing. 'It's a threat to civil liberties and a breach of personal integrity,' he ranted. And so it was. In the event, the matter was cleared up out of court without too much blood spilt on either side. But mud sticks and the affair proved the final indignity in the slow deterioration of the relationship between Abba and their long-time mentor/friend/lyricist and manager, Stig Anderson.

Because Agnetha, Benny and Bjorn's lawyers discovered discrepancies of their own in the monetary tangle. They found themselves being accused of tax evasion on earnings they had never received. Lawyers traced the confusion back to the early eighties when they alleged they were promised that Polar would triple their royalties. The lawyers concluded there was only one thing to be done – Benny, Bjorn and Agnetha had to train their guns on Stig.

So the unthinkable duly happened and Abba made moves to sue Polar for estimated loss of earnings of £16 million, dating back to unpaid royalties on an agreement they claimed was made in '83. It was a messy, undignified conclusion to what had always been one of the great manager–artist partnerships in pop. Abba had always prided themselves that they had been the ones to beat the system, maintaining complete control over their careers and their money. Polar, in turn, had always boasted of the family atmosphere which had prevailed and which bound creativity and business inextricably together. Abba, after all, had attended monthly board meetings to maintain their influence and control over any decisions made on their behalf. Stig had been a father figure to them all, especially Bjorn, and nobody anticipated that they could ever fall out. Least of all over money.

In the end Abba and Polar were able to settle their differences privately without the indignity of having their dirty laundry displayed in court for all the world to see. But Stig was still mortified to find himself on the receiving end of legal action from Bjorn, Benny and Agnetha. He'd scarcely come to terms with the band's demise in the first place, nursing a strong conviction that once they'd got a few solo projects out of their system they'd be back to

ABBA

assume their Stig-given role as monarchs of the world. In the meantime he ran Polar as an ongoing outlet for Abba and its allied marketing concerns, which cantered merrily along despite the continued absence of its central characters. No change there. The Beatles industry just kept gathering speed the longer they stayed apart and, during Lennon's lifetime, the price of a reunion rocketed all the time. And the Presley, Monroe and James Dean industries continued to explode the more distance there came between the myth and reality and as succeeding generations fell in love with the romantic imagery and a manufactured legend that they were somehow martyrs to youthful rebellion against an establishment that didn't understand. Abba weren't in the same league – not yet anyway – but the marketing possibilities of their absence and the fact that the money on the table to coax their return was rising all the time weren't lost on Stig. He was quick to jump on anybody snagging Abba territory. Harry Enfield used a snatch of 'Money, Money, Money' on his 'Loadsamoney' record and rapidly found himself on the receiving end of a writ. Even self-styled noise terrorists the KLF – who later turned Tammy Wynette into a rap star – had an injunction slapped on them when they sampled 'Dancing Queen' in 1988. The KLF even flew to Stockholm to plead their case, but Stig refused to see them. They were ordered to destroy all copies of the tapes featuring Abba. Stig was doing nothing to discourage the notion that Abba weren't asleep, just resting their eyes.

It was an attitude that didn't endear Stig to the group any more than the financial mess confronting them. The further they moved in time from Abba, the less inclined they were to put the rusty wheels in motion again and they felt their futures as artists and as people were served no favours by the continued speculation of a reunion. Once the *Opus 10* project had failed to ignite their interest then that effectively sealed in their own minds the fact that it was over, once and for all.

Frida, the most positive about the idea of an Abba reunion, had flown the nest completely, pursuing new passions in fresh fields. She'd got over the split with Benny with surprising resourcefulness, after making her solo album *Something's Going On*. The first single from it, 'I Know There's Something Going On' – a Top Twenty record in the States – was, despite being written by Russ Ballard, as autobiographical as it comes, with a video leaving no doubt about what was in her mind as a man makes his choice between two women and Frida's character is left alone pondering the iniquities of the world. *Something's Going On* was, said Frida, 'a *woman's* album', and we waited – vainly – to see her striding out brandishing whips and attitude. It didn't quite happen that way, but it was still a significant step into independence for Frida. In America they'd be in therapy for years prattling on about space and personal growth; Frida just made a solo album and came out a changed woman. 'What I have experienced as a single woman has made me much stronger,' she said. 'I am far more self-assured and confident. Now I'm enjoying making my own decisions. I really am independent . . . it is difficult, but it's also a wonderful feeling.'

She had no hang-ups about Benny after that – a compartment of her life to be locked away and brought out to be admired on special occasions. She'd matured beyond belief from the awkward, introspective, suspicious character who'd been projected into the public domain with such unease all those years ago. She turned up to lend moral support to Bjorn and Benny's big night at the premiere of *Chess* looking serene and radiant.

She even sailed through the relative failure of *Something's Going On* and her subsequent solo album, *Shine*, to make any sort of dent beyond hard and fast Abba supporters. On *Shine* she again used a hot producer, Steve Lillywhite, and another ambitious cross-section of songs written by the likes of Chris Rea, Simon Climie, Kirsty MacColl and Stuart Adamson, with Bjorn and Benny also pitching in with one track, 'Slowly'. A good album, too, but to most neutrals Frida remained The Other One and the earth didn't move.

At this time – around '86 – she was ready for the projected *Opus 10* Abba comeback which Bjorn and Benny had been desultorily working on, but when that faltered she wasn't about to hang around any longer. Conditioned to disappointment, she acknowledged that solo stardom maybe didn't wait. She'd already given her tacit support to *Abbacadabra*, a musical based on Abba's songs presented at London's Lyric Theatre, starring the ubiquitous Elaine Paige and B. A. Robertson. Frida had even sung on a couple of tracks on the soundtrack album, including a duet with Robertson, 'Time', which became a minor hit at the end of '83.

Then Frida settled into her new independence with the relaxed satisfaction that only personal peace and self-assurance can bring. She moved to Freiburg in Switzerland and on 26 August 1992 she married architect Ruzzo Reuss – also a German prince – in Horsholm, Denmark. At ease with the past but more interested in the future, she found that the strains and stresses of Abba were easily replaced by saner pursuits like ski-ing, opera and golf . . . and concern for the environment.

Becoming a grandmother – her son Hans Fredericks-son became a musician and record producer – mellowed her even more and triggered a concern for the world which has effectively become her prime obsession since Abba. She is now a devout vegetarian and, since 1990, deeply involved in the Natural Step, a high-profile environmental group dedicated to promoting green issues. She's chairperson of Artists for the Environment, the performance wing of the Natural Step.

'I am trying to live a clean life both when it comes to my soul and how I get rid of my junk,' she told the *Daily Express*. 'I am now fully engaged on my work for the environment. I have become a safer and cleaner person-ality. During my time with Abba everything was so hectic I didn't have time to develop this way of life. Now I do.'

Since 1987 when she released a couple of Swedish-language singles with Swedish group Ratata, virtually all her celebrity status has been channelled into green issues. She was instrumental in putting together 'Artister For Miljo', a big open-air gala concert held at Borggarden, Stockholm, in the summer of '92 in grounds belonging to the royal family. The king and queen of Sweden, now good friends with Frida, attended the concert, which presented a mixture of classical, opera, jazz and pop music, prominently featuring Frida herself singing Julian Len-non's green anthem 'Saltwater', as well as an ecstatically received duet of 'What A Wonderful World' with a Swedish pop heroine from a later era, Marie Frederikkson from Roxette. The track was subsequently released as a single and Frida found herself back in the charts.

She felt no temptation, however, to resume her career. She no longer craves adulation and – a contented multi-millionairess – has no fiscal or spiritual need to sing. She now spends her time between her homes in Switzerland, Sweden and Majorca, mixing in the highest circles, a regular sight at VIP functions, and a woman of great serenity and dignity. She fleetingly gave her blessing to the *Abba Gold* celebrations, turning up with Bjorn and Benny for one award ceremony, but scarcely gives a thought to those days now. Then was another age, and she was a different person. She doesn't recognize herself from those days now. And watching her glide around Europe pricking public consciences in regal style as she generates support to save the world, few others do either.

Frida and Agnetha have barely spoken for ten years. There wasn't a great deal of communication between them at the best of times, and instead of helping her blossom, the split seems to have driven Agnetha ever more inward. Murderous letters, kidnap threats, marriage break-up, the unbearable pressures of press attention, career dissatisfaction . . . all conspired to drive Agnetha into a reclusive existence.

She had several lovers after Bjorn . . . and hundreds of proposals of marriage from complete strangers. For a while she found some comfort from Hakan Lonnback, the psychiatrist she called in when the marriage with Bjorn was careering into icebergs. The media also took great delight in relating details of her on-off affair with Lars Eriksson, himself a media-friendly personality and a famous Swedish ice hockey star. She also had relationships with fashion designer Dick Haakonsson and lived for a while with Thorbjorn Brander, a police sergeant assigned to protect her after the kidnap threats. These relationships all ended in tears.

On 15 December 1990 Agnetha did take the plunge again, marrying a divorced surgeon, Thomas Sonnenfeld, in such secrecy that even the Swedish press, famous for their campaigns of 'Agnetha-watching', were taken by surprise. It was a small triumph for Agnetha and a ceremony that couldn't have contrasted more with the razzmatazz of her first wedding. The marriage, though, fared no better. Two years later Agnetha was getting divorced again, retreating further into herself, living in seclusion at her mansion on the island of Ekero, near Stockholm, keeping herself remote from any public attention.

'I really don't miss all the fame and success of Abba,' she said at one point. 'We worked so hard for such a long time. We travelled the world, but in almost every place we visited it was work, work, work and we didn't have the chance to see anything. I've been to many places but I've no idea what they were about because we were working all the time.'

In the mid-eighties she got her wish to devote herself fully to family life, bringing up her children Linda and Christian on a farm full of horses, and living a healthy life sailing, ski-ing and playing tennis. Any remaining career ambitions were confined to acting. She remembered with fondness her brief role as Mary Magdalene in *Jesus Christ Superstar* and felt a pull towards theatre and cinema. In 1983 she took the first step down that (yellow brick) road, playing a Casanova's wife in a Swedish comedy called *Raskenstam*, directed by Gunnar Helstrom. She'd talk animatedly of her admiration for Meryl Streep, Jill Clayburgh and Jessica Lange and in her more whimsical moments she joked about her hatred of the continual intrusions into her private life and presented herself as a modern-day Greta Garbo. It was a joke that has come to bear more than a passing irony in the light of the kidnap

threats and her mounting obsession with privacy. She
received good notices for her role in *Raskenstam* and
there were other offers, other discussions about new
roles. She did perform the theme song for one movie, *P
& B*, but her movie career unaccountably came to
nothing as she tentatively moved instead back to music.

In 1983 she was back in the Polar studio recording her
first post-Abba solo album, *Wrap Your Arms Around Me*,
with the semi-legendary Mike Chapman, one half of the
Chinnichap songwriting/production team, who'd
offered the only serious consistent pop rivalry to
Ulvaeus/Andersson with their production line hits for
Sweet, Mud, Suzi Quatro, Smokie and, latterly, Blondie.
Engineered by Micke Tretow, it included a couple of
songs by Tomas Ledin and another couple by Russ
Ballard (fresh from contributing to Frida's album) and,
with this kind of back-up and the world's persistent
adoration of all things Agnetha, *Wrap Your Arms Around
Me* looked a surefire winner. Maybe it was just too poppy
and she would have been more fondly embraced if she'd
continued to be the tragic torch-singing beauty we'd
witnessed in those criminally neglected death throes of
Abba. Agnetha was seen to be playing games again when
we wanted real blood. She could have been Dusty
Springfield or Debbie Harry, but she came out as Lulu.
Agnetha probably never did know quite what she wanted,
but whatever it was she blew it with *Wrap Your Arms
Around Me*. A terrific pop album, but we're talking
wrong time, wrong place here.

There were two more solo albums from Agnetha
before she was through. *Eyes Of A Woman* came out in
the spring of '85, produced by Eric Stewart of 10cc, with
material by Stewart, Jeff Lynne (of ELO), Justin

Hayward of the Moody Blues, John Wetton and Geoff Downes of Asia, and a couple of her own songs. She was a good girl, travelled across Europe (boats and trains, not planes) doing the promotional circuit, and didn't grimace too much when they kept asking her about the next Abba tour and how wonderful it must be to have the sexiest bottom in the entire western world. Old habits die hard and Agnetha mouthed the stock answers about the break-up of her marriage to Bjorn like . . . a marionette. But it didn't change a thing. *Eyes Of A Woman* promoted old images of Agnetha as unimpeachable sex goddess when she felt tired and worn and would have done a whole lot better had she looked and sounded it. *Eyes Of A Woman* was clever and agreeable, but distressingly soulless; and while there were pockets of Europe which clasped it to their bosom in frantic displays of joy, notably in Sweden itself, it was largely considered an irredeemable flop.

For someone bred on a diet of barely remitting runaway success since her mid-teens, this was quite a bit of pride to swallow for the prickly Agnetha. She was constantly demeaning the value of commercial gain, and she was perfectly honest in her protestations of humility and plain living. But her delicate ego had been shot to pieces in the break-up of her marriage and the succession of departing lovers, and artistic failure did her no favours at all.

She had just one more crack at an international solo career – going to Los Angeles in 1987 to record *I Stand Alone*, produced by Pete Cetera of Chicago. But her heart for the battle seemed to have gone entirely. The album was a huge hit in Sweden, but did little elsewhere. She went through the motions of promotion, but the one single from the album to make any sort of impact appeared alarmingly anticipatory. It was called 'The Last Time'.

Sandwiched between were various recordings for the home market. In 1980 she'd recorded an album of children's songs with her daughter Linda, and in 1987 she did the same with her son Christian. A few other Swedish-language records appeared for the Scandinavian market and some of us live in hope that this gorgeous, gorgeous woman – as isolated, defeated and drained of enthusiasm as she might be – will shock us all and reappear to share the real emotions of her extraordinary life. Put *that* all into music and it would be something else . . .

Bjorn Ulvaeus opted out too. For a while. Having finally got *Chess* into production, Bjorn fulfilled a long-standing dream of living in England. He bought a £400,000 house in 16 acres in the Oxfordshire country-side around Henley-on-Thames with Lena, something of an expert in English literature, and their two daughters, Emma and Anna. Having felt that he'd blown his first attempt at family life, Bjorn was intent on making the most of it second time around. He took a step back from musical involvement, using instead his technical wizardry to set himself up as a computer consultant for small businesses. He became the model family man; together, good-humoured, sensible, classical music fan, fabulous wife, groovy kids, sci-fi book buff and fitness fanatic. He would jog daily and even took part in the odd marathon – he once completed the Stockholm Marathon in a creditable time of three hours twenty minutes. He made regular trips home to see Agnetha and their children, now teenagers, and eventually the pull became too over-whelming to resist any further and in 1990 the family sold up in England and moved back to Sweden, to the splendour of a house in an exclusive part of Stockholm once owned by the royal family. And, inevitably, he started working again with Benny Andersson.

Benny continued to feed his addiction to the studio during this time, constantly composing, and even releasing a couple of solo albums of primarily Swedish folk music, *Klinga Mina Klocka* (*Ring My Bell*) and *November '89*, both hits in Scandinavia. Most curiously he developed an interest in ornithology which resulted in him putting together a bizarre album of bird song collections. He also flirted with the role of Svengali, forming his own company, Mono Music, and taking a couple of Swedish groups under his wing. He produced and contributed the large bulk of the material for *Fiolen Min*, an album by the band Orsa Spelman; and produced and co-wrote material with the Ainsbusk Singers, a four-woman theatrical team combining music, comedy and drama. They took a couple of his songs, 'Lassie' and 'Alska Mej' ('Love Me'), into the Swedish charts. One member of that group, Josefin Nilsson, has been groomed for further international success by both Benny and Bjorn, who've not only written and produced material for her solo career, but also given her public support in television and radio interviews. His godlike status in Swedish musical history has been confirmed by the constant invitations to contribute music for almost every prestigious cultural event that comes to Sweden. He wrote the music for the official fanfare at the European football championship held in Sweden in 1992. And with Bjorn, he wrote a song ('Up To The Fight', sung by Tommy Koberg) for the Swedish team in the equestrian world championships in Stockholm.

And whenever Benny dipped out of the public eye, his son Peter (from his relationship with Christina Gronvall) kept the family fame going. During the eighties Peter became a pop star in his own right with the groups The Sound Of Music, Peter's Pop Squad and One More Time, and he even made his old man a grandfather when his wife Nanne Nordquist gave birth to a son, Charlie, in September 1990.

Out of the studio Benny remained . . . *Benny*. Relaxed and easygoing, but paradoxically passionately protective of his private life, deeply suspicious of any press attention and uneasy with the high-profile legacy of marriage to his TV star wife Mona. Although he'd initiated the split with Frida, it seemed at times as if she had adapted to the divorce a whole lot better than Benny.

He got into horses in a big way, setting up his own Rancho riding stables outside Svedala, breeding and buying a string of high class racehorses. Two of them, Rickenbacker and Burns, even competed in the Swedish Derby.

Since Bjorn's return to Stockholm, the old partnership has been back in gear working on a new musical based on one of Sweden's greatest literary works, *Utvandrarna* (*Immigrants*). A series of books by Vilhelm Moberg, *Immigrants* is a staple part of Swedish schoolwork, a classic telling the story of Swedish settlers in America in the 1850s. Putting it together has proved a long, slow haul – the original book is over 2,000 pages long and there have been times when Benny and Bjorn felt like abandoning the whole thing. It has made *Chess* seem like a doddle. They enlisted the help of a dramatist, and honed the story down to tell the tale of just one Swedish family's struggle for survival after emigrating to Minnesota. They continue to battle on with it and if they ever get it on stage they will regard it as the greatest achievement of their careers.

Given the dissipation of his flock, Stig Anderson ultimately resigned himself to the fact that Abba weren't coming back. The money squabbles and the introduction of opposition lawyers hurt him deeply and, now in his sixties, he saw no point in pursuing the struggle any longer. Heavy of heart, he decided to relinquish the precious Abba back catalogue.

It still wasn't straightforward. Some licensing deals in certain territories still had time to run, but the bulk of the world was taken care of when Polar packed up a decade of classic Abba music and sold it to Polygram. Nobody has ever put a figure on how much changed hands, but you can safely assume it wasn't a couple of ham sandwiches and a stick of chewing gum. Polygram parted with a mighty fistful of dollars for the privilege.

The deal was finalized on New Year's Eve, 1989, and Polygram probably considered it a bit of a risk. Abba's rehabilitation was already in progress, but there was no indication of the retrospective mania just around the corner. There had, after all, been numerous compilations with different ingredients in various formats, and only *The First Ten Years* album – put out while Abba still looked to be a vibrant force – dominated the charts to any degree.

Polygram's marketing department did a brilliant job, beautifully packaging the *Abba Gold* collection as a piece of classic pop history, and giving the group an air of class it'd always appeared to lack in its lifetime amid the explosions of tack. Polygram's presentation was not of a seventies period piece to be viewed with a nostalgic laugh and a giggle, but a great timeless work by one of the supreme acts of our lifetime. Which is precisely what they were. Only repeated misrepresentation prevented people seeing it before.

But Polygram were lucky too. They had no way of knowing that Erasure were to prelude the release of *Abba Gold* with a Number One EP of Abba covers. Or that Bjorn Again would bring the house down at the Reading Festival. Or that the biggest band in the world, U2, would appear at the biggest stages on the planet performing 'Dancing Queen', while expressing their undying devotion to Abba's music.

Luck and coincidence all contrived to make Polygram's investment the shrewdest business move of the year. But then, luck and coincidence have always been a major part of pop music. Pop is about nothing if not those who have the courage to back their instincts being in the right place at the right time.

So *Abba Gold* sold over seven million copies. Just like that. Without exciting too much interest or support from the four individuals concerned, all of whom were anxious in different ways and for contrasting reasons to have as little to do with the recycled Abba phenomenon as possible. Bjorn Ulvaeus did briefly emerge on the parapet for a couple of desultory interviews once the album had become a hit and he was satisfied that he wouldn't be seen to be an arm of Polygram's promotional campaign. Abba was great, but it was over and there was no going back. This was the message loud and clear both from Bjorn, who was speaking, and the other three, who weren't.

Further success for Polygram with *More Abba Gold*, talk of boxed sets and a further upsurge of tribute groups just keeps the post-Abba Abba market as phenomenal as it was first time round. And all the time the question keeps arising . . . *could* they? Is there any *conceivable possibility*? Would they *ever*? One promoter is said to have put £10 million on the table to finance an Abba reunion.

But *would* they? Oil crises and share crashes taken into account, none of them needs the money. They are all rich enough to live their lives several times over in absolute comfort without making any significant dent in their individual fortunes.

And there's the pressure of expectation. After all *this*, the world would demand so much from Abba second time round that the traumas created by such intense anticipation would surely scupper any possibility of recreating that magic. There's an old boxing adage that they never come back and it's pretty much true of pop bands as well. Why take the risk and tarnish the memory?

Most doubtful of all, would you ever get Agnetha back into a studio again? Would you ever get Agnetha back into a studio with *Frida* again?!? There have been parallels before, of course. Ritchie Blackmore and Ian Gillan were practically *killing* each other in Deep Purple and spent several years publicly wishing the plague to claim the other and swearing they'd never share a stage together again if it was the last place left standing on earth. What happens in 1993? Deep Purple go back on the road with Ritchie Blackmore and Ian Gillan in the line-up. They still didn't talk, but by the third gig they were back to trying to kill each other.

It's almost inconceivable that Frida and Agnetha could ever get it on to bury the past and attempt to go through it all again. Almost, but not *quite*.

Anybody who can go out on stage wearing a flared Napoleon pant suit is capable of *anything* . . .

DISCOGRAPHY

ABBA

SINGLES

People Need Love/Merry-Go-Round (En Karusell)	1972
He Is Your Brother/Santa Rosa	1972
Love Isn't Easy/I Am Just A Girl	1973
Ring Ring (Bara Du Slog En Signal)/Ah Vilka Tider	1973
Ring Ring (*English*)/Merry-Go-Round	1973
Waterloo/Honey Honey (*both sung in Swedish*)	1974
Waterloo (*English*)/Watch Out	1974
Honey Honey/King Kong Song	1974
So Long/I've Been Waiting For You	1974
I Do, I Do, I Do, I Do, I Do/Rock Me	1975
SOS/Man In The Middle	1975
Mamma Mia/Intermezzo No. 1	1975
Fernando/Hey, Hey, Helen	1976
Dancing Queen/That's Me	1976
Money, Money, Money/Crazy World	1976
Knowing Me, Knowing You/Happy Hawaii	1977
The Name Of The Game/Wonder (Departure)	1977
Take A Chance On Me/I'm A Marionette	1977
Eagle/Thank You For The Music	1977
Summernight City/Medley	1978
Chiquitita/Lovelight	1979
Voulez-Vous/Does Your Mother Know (twelve-inch)	1979

Does Your Mother Know/Kisses of Fire	1979
Voulez-Vous/Angeleyes	1979
Gimme! Gimme! Gimme! (A Man After Midnight)/ The King Has Lost His Crown	1979
I Have A Dream/Take A Chance On Me (*live*)	1979
The Winner Takes It All/Elaine	1980
Super Trouper/The Piper	1980
Lay All Your Love On Me/On And On And On (twelve-inch)	1981
One Of Us/Should I Laugh Or Cry	1981
Head Over Heels/The Visitors	1982
The Day Before You Came/Cassandra	1982
Under Attack/You Owe Me One	1982
Dancing Queen/Lay All Your Love On Me	1992
Voulez-Vous/Summernight City	1992
Thank You For The Music/Happy New Year	1992

ALBUMS

Ring Ring	1973
Waterloo	1974
Abba	1975
Greatest Hits	1975
Arrival	1976
The Album	1977
Voulez-Vous	1979
Greatest Hits Vol. 2	1979
Gracias Por La Musica	1980
Super Trouper	1980
The Visitors	1981
The Singles – The First Ten Years	1982
Live	1986
Gold	1992

More Abba Gold   1993

BENNY & BJORN

SINGLES

She's My Kind Of Girl/Inga Theme	1970
Lycka/Hej Gamla Man!	1970
Det Kan Ingen Doktor Hjalpa/Pa Brollop	1971
Tank Om Jorden Vore Ung/Traskofolket	1971
En Karusell/Att Finnas Till	1972

ALBUMS

Lycka	1970
Chess (*with Tim Rice*)	1982
Chess Original Broadway Cast Recording	1988

BJORN ULVAEUS

SINGLES

Raring/Vill Du Ha En Van	1968
Froken Fredriksson/Var Egen Sang	1968
Saknar Du Nagot Min Kara/Gomt Ar Inte Glomt	1969
Partaj-Aj-Aj-Aj/Kvinnan I Mitt Liv	1969

BENNY ANDERSSON

SINGLE

| Klinga Mina Klocker/Langsammazurkan | 1987 |

ALBUMS

| Klinga Mina Klocker | 1987 |
| November '89 | 1989 |

THE HEP STARS

SINGLES

A Tribute To Buddy Holly/Bird Song	1964
If You Need Me/Summertime Blues	1964
Donna/Farmer John	1965
Cadillac/Mashed Potatoes	1965
Bald Headed Woman/Lonesome Town	1965
No Response/Rented Tuxedo	1965
So Mystifying/Young & Beautiful	1965
Should I/I'll Never Quite Get Over You	1965
Sunny Girl/Hawaii	1966
Wedding/When My Blue Moon Turns To Gold Again	1966
I Natt Jag Dromde/Jag Vet	1966
Consolation/Don't	1966
Malaika/It's So Nice To Be Back	1967
Christmas On My Mind/Jingle Bells	1967
Mot Okant Land/Nagonting Har Hant	1967
She Will Love You/Like You Used To Do	1967
It's Been A Long Long Time/Musty Dusty	1968

Det Finns En Stad/Sagan Om Lilla Sofi	1968
Let It Be Me/Groovy Summertime	1968
I Sagans Land/Tanda Pa Varann	1968
Holiday For Clowns/A Flower In My Garden	1968
Speleman/Precis Som Alla Andra	1969
Speedy Gonzales/Ar Det Inte Karlek, Sag	1969

ALBUMS

We And Our Cadillac	1965
Hep Stars On Stage	1965
The Hep Stars	1966
Jul Med Hep Stars	1967
Songs We Sang	1968
It's Been A Long Long Time	1968
Hep Stars Pa Svenska	1969
How It All Started	1970
Hep Stars, 1964–1969!	1983
Basta (CD only)	1990

THE HOOTENANNY SINGERS

SINGLES

Jag Vantar Vid Min Milla/Ann-Margret	1964
Darlin'/Bonnie Ship The Diamond	1964
Den Gyliene Fregatt/Dar Skall Jag Bo	1965
Britta/Den Skona Helen	1965
Solola/Bjorkens Visa	1965
Den Skona Helen/Bjorkens Visa	1965
No Time/Time To Move Along	1966
Marianne/Vid En Bivag Bor Den Blonda Beatrice	1966

Baby, Those Are The Rules/Through Darkness Light	1966
En Sang En Gang For Lange Sen/Det Ar Skant	
Att Vara Hemma Igen	1967
Blomman/En Man Och En Kvinna	1967
En Gang Ar Igen Gang/Du Eller Ingen	1967
Mrs O'Grady/The Fugitive	1967
Borjan Till Slutet/Adjo Farval	1967
Sa Lange Du Alskar Ar Du Ung/Vilken Lycka	
Att Halla Halla Dej I Hand	1968
Marten Gas/Du Ska Bara Tro Pa Halften	1968
Maltidssang/Till Fader Berg Rorande Fiolen	1968
Elenore/Fafangans Marknad	1968
Den Som Lever Far Se/Sa Lange Jag Lever	1969
Om Jag Kunde Skriva En Visa/Casanova	1969
Vinden Sjunger Samma Sang/Hem Till De Mina	1969
Ring Ring, Har Ar Svensktoppsjuryn/Lev Som Du Lar	1970
I Folj Sa Gick Jag Med Herrarna I Hagen/Alvsborgsvisan	1970
Rose Marie/Elin Och Herremannen	1970
En Visa Vill Jag Sjunga Som Handlar Om Min Lilla	
Van/ Spelmansvisa	1970
Aldrig Mer/Lilla Vackra Anna	1971
Hjartats Saga/Jungman Jansson	1971
Tess Lordan/Rosen Och Fjarlien	1971
Tiden/Ida & Frida & Anne-Marie	1972
Dar Bjorkana Susa/Calle Schewens Vals	1972
Om Aftonen/Till Min Syster	1973
Brittisk Ballad/Ingrid Dardels Polska	1974
Sjosala Vals/Vals I Valparaiso	1975
Linnea/Fritiof Anderssons Paradmarsch	1975

EPs

Jag Vantar Vid Min Milla/Ann-Margret/Ingen Enda Host/Ave Maria No Morro	1964
En Mor/Korsbar Utan Karnor/Gabrielle/I Lunden Grona	1964
Lincolnvisan/Hem Igen/Godnattsaga/This Is Your Land	1964
Britta/Solola/Eh Hattespeleman/Telegrafisten Anton Hanssons Vals	1965
Bjorkens Visa/En Festig Dag/Vildandens Klagan/Finns Det Liv Sa Finns Det Hopp	1965
Vid Roines Strand/Marianne/En Man Och En Kvinna/ Vid En Bivag Till En Bivag Bor Den Blonda Beatrice	1966
Blomman/En Sang En Gang For Langesen/Det Ar Skont Att Vara Hemma Igen/Tank Dej De' Att Du Och Jag Var Me'	1967
Marten Gas/Borjan Till Slutet/Marie Christina/ Adjo Farval	1967

ALBUMS

Hootenanny Singers	1964
Hootenanny Singers (2nd Album)	1964
Hootenanny Singers Sjunger Evert Taube	1965
International	1965
Many Faces/Manga Ansikten	1966
Civila	1967
Basta	1967
5 Ar	1968
Bellman Pa Vart Satt	1968
De Baste Med Hootenanny Singers & Bjorn Ulvaeus	1969

Pa Tre Man Hand	1969
Skillingtryck	1970
Vara Vackraste Visor	1971
Vara Vackraste Visor Vol. 2	1972
Dan Andersson Pa Vart Satt	1973
Evert Taube Pa Vart Satt	1974

AGNETHA FALTSKOG

SINGLES

Folj Med Mig/Jag Var Sa Kar	1967
Slutet Gott, Allting Gott/Utan Dej Mitt Liv Gar Vidare	1968
En Sommar Med Dej/Forsonade	1968
Den Jag Vantat Pa/Allting Har Förändrat Sig	1968
Sjung Denna Sang/Nagonting Hander Med Mej (*duet with Jorgen Edman*)	1969
Snövit Och De Sju Dvargarna/Min Farbor Jonathan	1969
Fram For Svenska Sommaren/En Gang Fanns Bara Vi Två	1969
Tag Min Hand Lat Oss Bli Vanner/Hjärtat Kronprins	1969
Zigenarvan/Som En Vind Kom Du Till Mej	1969
Skal Kara Van/Det Handlar Om Karlek	1969
Om Tarar Vore Guld/Litet Solskensbam	1970
Som Ett Eko/Ta Det Bara Med Ro	1970
En Sang Och En Sanga/Jag Skall Gora Allt	1970
Kongens Vakt Parad/Jag Vill Att Du Skall Bli Lycklig	1971
Manga Ganger An/Han Lamnar Mig For Att Dommer Till Dig	1971
Nya Ord/Drom Ar Drom Och Saga Saga	1971
Vart Ska Min Karlek Fora/Nu Skall Du Bli Stilla	1972

Tio Mil Kvar Till Korpilombolo/Sa Glad Som Dina Ogon	1972
Vi Har Hunnit Fram Till Refrangen/En Sang Om Sorg Och Gladje	1973
Golliwog/Here For Your Love	1974
Dom Har Glomt/Gulleplutt	1975
SOS/Visa I Attonde Manaden	1975
Nar Du Tar Mig I Din Famn/Jag Var Sa Kar	1979
Never Again/Just For The Fun (*with Tomas Ledin*)	1982
The Heat Is On/Man	1983
Wrap Your Arms Around Me/Take Good Care Of Your Children	1983
Can't Shake Loose/To Love	1983
It's So Nice To Be Rich/P & B	1983
I Won't Let You Go/You're There	1985
One Way Love/Turn The World Around	1985
The Way You Are/Fly Like The Eagle (*duet with Ola Hakansson*)	1986
Karusellvisan/Liten & Trott (*with son Christian*)	1987
Pa Sondag/Min Namn Av Blom (*with son Christian*)	1987
The Last Time/Are You Gonna Throw It All Away	1988
Let It Shine/Maybe It Was Magic	1988

GERMAN SINGLES

Robinson Crusoe/Sonny Boy	1968
Senor Gonzales/Mein Schönster Tag	1968
Concerto D'Amore/Wie Der Wind	1969
Wer Schreibt Heut' Noch Liebesbriefe?/Das Fest Der Pompadour	1969
Fragezeichen Mag Ich Nicht/Wie Der Nächste Autobus	1969
Ein Kleiner Mann In Einer Flasche/Ich Suchte Liebe Bei Dir	1970

Geh' Mitt Gott/Tausend Wunder	1972
Komm Doch Zu Mir/Ich Denk' An Dich	1972

ALBUMS

Agnetha Fältskog	1968
Agnetha Fältskog Vol. 2	1969
Som Jag Ar	1970
När En Vacker Blir En Sang	1971
Basta	1973
Agnetha	1974
Elva Kvinnor I Ett Hus	1975
Tio Ar Med Agnetha	1979
Nu Tandas Tusen Juleljus (*with daughter Linda*)	1980
Wrap Your Arms Around Me	1983
Eyes Of A Woman	1985
Sjung Denna Sang	1986
Kom Folj Med I Var Karusell (*with son Christian*)	1987
I Stand Alone	1987

ANNI-FRID LYNGSTAD

SINGLES

En Ledit Dag/Peter Kom Tillbaka	1967
Din/Du Ar Sa Underbart Rar	1967
Simsalabim/Vi Mots Igen	1968
Mycket Kar/Nar Dyu Blir Min	1968
Harlig Ar Var Jord/Rakna De Lyckliga Stunderna Blott	1969
Sa Sund Du Masta Ga/Forsok Och Sov Pa Saken	1969
Peter Pan/Du Betonar Karlek Lite Fel	1969
Dar Du Gar Lamnar Karleken Spar/Du Var Framling Har Igar	1970

En Liten Sang Om Karlek/Tre Kvart Fran Nu	1971
En Kvall En Sommarn/Vi Vet Allt Men Nastan Inget *(duet with Lars Berghagen)*	1971
Min Egen Stad/En Gang Ar Ingen Gang	1971
Kom Och Sjung En Sang/Vi Ar Alla Bara I Borjan	1972
Vad Gor Jag Med Min Karlek/Allting Ska Bli Bra	1972
Man Vill Ju Leva Lite Dessemellan/Ska Man Skratta Eller Grata	1972
Fernando/Ett Liv I Solen	1975
I Know There's Something Going On/Threnody	1982
To Turn The Stone/I've Got Something	1983
Here We'll Stay/Strangers	1983
Belle/C'est Fini *(duet with Daniel Balavoine, France only)*	1983
Time/I Am The Seeker *(duet with B. A. Robertson, UK only)*	1983
Shine/That's Tough	1984
Come To Me/Slowly	1984
Sa Lange Vi Har Varann/Du Finns Hos Mig *(with Ratata)*	1987
Om Du Var Har/As Long As I Have You *(with Ratata)*	1987
Anglamark/Saltwater *(Artister For Miljo)*	1992

ALBUMS

Frida	1971
Min Egen Stad	1972
Frida Ensam	1976
Something's Going On	1982
Shine	1984
Pa Egen Hand *(CD only)*	1991

INDEX

All Pan Books are available at your local bookshop or newsagent, or can be ordered direct from the publisher. Indicate the number of copies required and fill in the form below.

Send to: Macmillan General Books C.S.
            Book Service By Post
            PO Box 29, Douglas I-O-M
            IM99 1BQ

or phone: 01624 675137, quoting title, author and credit card number.

or fax: 01624 670923, quoting title, author, and credit card number.

or Internet: http://www.bookpost.co.uk

Please enclose a remittance* to the value of the cover price plus 75 pence per book for post and packing. Overseas customers please allow £1.00 per copy for post and packing.

*Payment may be made in sterling by UK personal cheque, Eurocheque, postal order, sterling draft or international money order, made payable to Book Service By Post.

Alternatively by Access/Visa/MasterCard

Card No.

Expiry Date

Signature _____

Applicable only in the UK and BFPO addresses.

While every effort is made to keep prices low, it is sometimes necessary to increase prices at short notice. Pan Books reserve the right to show on covers and charge new retail prices which may differ from those advertised in the text or elsewhere.

NAME AND ADDRESS IN BLOCK CAPITAL LETTERS PLEASE

Name _____

Address _____

_____

_____

_____

8/95

Please allow 28 days for delivery.
Please tick box if you do not wish to receive any additional information. ☐